A PRESIDENTIAL CIVIL SERVICE

Public Administration: Criticism & Creativity

A Presidential Civil Service

FDR'S LIAISON OFFICE FOR PERSONNEL MANAGEMENT

MORDECAI LEE

The University of Alabama Press
Tuscaloosa

The University of Alabama Press
Tuscaloosa, Alabama 35487-0380
uapress.ua.edu

Hardcover edition published 2016.
Paperback edition published 2021.
eBook edition published 2016.

Typeface: Garamond and Scala Sans

Cover image: The seal of the US Civil Service Commission

Cover design: Michele Myatt Quinn

Paperback ISBN: 978-0-8173-6023-8

A previous edition of this book has been cataloged by the Library of Congress.
ISBN: 978-0-8173-1899-4 (cloth)
E-ISBN: 978-0-8173-8945-1

For my grandson, Ethan Jr., born in 2014 while I was writing this book. Like all proud grandparents, my wish for him is a good life. And, kibitzing a bit, my further hope is that his life will also include civic-mindedness, service to others, love of country, and a contribution to the betterment of society.

Contents

Preface

Merit and management are two quintessential American ideals. Reflecting the former, in an egalitarian and classless society, people should be able to rise and succeed based on their skills, training, and work experiences; not the luck of the genetic lottery, money, or favoritism. The SAT exam for college admissions seeks (however imperfectly) to embody this American principle. So does a general ban in employment law of any mandatory retirement age. Instead, individuals should be able to stay in their jobs, regardless of age, just as long as they can fulfill their duties. Similarly, a central tenet of the good government reformers of the Progressive era was that achieving a merit system in the public sector rested on having independent and politically neutral civil service commissions.

In a parallel American universe, management became the object of near-unanimous support. Modern organizations should be run by professional managers, not by founders, owners, stockholders, or do-good activists. The emergence of the professional management class to run large for-profit corporations represented that economic and social revolution. Nowadays, nearly every American university has a school of business administration, intent on credentialing the next generation of ambitious managers with MBA degrees. Indicating the importance of management to the world of business, some leading universities, including Yale, MIT, and Northwestern, have opted to have a school of management rather than of business administration. The importance of management has seeped deeply into nearly all aspects of modern American society: degrees in nonprofit *management* (sometimes a sub-genus of the MBA), departments of emergency *management* at all levels of government, pain *management*, even life *management*.

The problem is that merit and management are quite antithetical. It is desirable that all organizations function on the basis of merit. But try to imagine a for-profit corporation vesting all management powers in its CEO except human resources. The latter would be run by HR professionals autonomous from the CEO and not subject to the need to be pulling in the same direction nor with the same goals as the corporation at large. Imagine CEO Alan Mulally trying to save the Ford Motor Company from bankruptcy during the Great Recession, while the company's vice president for human capital did not report to him; in fact reported to nobody. Yet that is precisely what good government reformers advocated for government during the Progressive era. Autonomous and politically independent civil service commissions would have full powers over all aspects of personnel management. This would guarantee that the workforce of all executive branch agencies would be apolitical, staffed by permanent experts who would be recruited, compensated, promoted, and fired based on merit alone. Political patronage, no-show jobs, and incompetents would be driven out of government employment.

Merit and management lived side-by-side in government in a kind of undeclared truce during the early decades of the twentieth century. But, within a few years, some leaders in the effort to professionalize American public administration began pointing out the contradiction. These activists gradually coalesced around the idea that the management imperatives in government should trump the merit system as embodied in an independent civil service commission. Instead, the chief elected executive officer (president, governor, mayor) should have personnel powers in tandem with budgetary and planning capabilities. A patronage system could still be kept from tainting government employment without the need for an all-powerful and autonomous civil service commission. Rather, there should be a personnel management agency directly responsible to the chief executive, along with a counterpart, and by now common, budgeting agency.

The issue was joined in the late 1930s. In 1937, the President's Committee on Administrative Management (commonly called the Brownlow Committee for its chair, Louis Brownlow) recommended to FDR that as part of a comprehensive reorganization of the federal executive branch the US Civil Service Commission (CSC) be abolished and replaced by a presidential personnel director and by a department called the Civil Service Administration. The committee also recommended creating a small independent board to protect those aspects of the traditional merit system that did not conflict with the president's need to manage the federal workforce.

A battle royal ensued. From 1937 to 1939, Congress debated the Brownlow Committee's tradition-shattering proposals. Finally, in 1939, Congress agreed to delegate some reorganization powers to the president—though subject to a legislative veto option. Just to be sure, the new law explicitly prohibited FDR from touching the CSC in any reorganization plan he submitted.

Typically, FDR tried nonetheless to find a way toward his goal. Using his newfound reorganization powers, when he invented the Executive Office of the President (EOP) in September 1939, he included as one of its original five agencies a new entity called the Liaison Office for Personnel Management (LOPM). FDR blithely explained that the office would not conflict with the congressional prohibition on reorganizing the CSC because the new office would merely liaise. What could be more innocent than improved administrative communication and voluntary coordination? Yet, in reality, FDR was hoping that the small new agency might become a de facto presidential personnel agency, or at least a seed from which a de jure one could emerge if Congress were to be convinced later to undo the prohibition on reorganizing the CSC. That did not happen during FDR's presidency. Still, the historical record of what LOPM did from 1939 to 1945 provides performance data to examine how the concept of a quasi-presidential personnel management agency played out. Did it work?

In terms of formal organization and power, FDR was about forty years ahead of his time. In 1978, Congress enacted a civil service reform bill proposed by President Carter. The new law abolished the CSC and replaced it with the Office of Personnel Management (OPM), along with a small Merit Systems Protection Board. Even then, reform was not done. After that, calls for civil service reform were alive and well into the twenty-first century. For example, in 2014, the Partnership for Public Service released a report on reforms needed to give the federal government an improved personnel system. It included recommendations for organizational and structural changes, including the need to revitalize the Merit Systems Protection Board (Partnership 2014). But there was no suggestion to revert back to a CSC.

This book recounts and examines the political conflict between the ideals of merit and management during FDR's presidency, including the origins of the idea of executive-oriented personnel management, the fight over the Brownlow Committee's recommendation, and the subsequent activities of the president's Liaison Office for Personnel Management.

Two paths led me to this story, one political, the other academic. Regarding the former, in 1977, when I was a freshman member of the Wisconsin Legislature's State Assembly, the Speaker asked me to be the floor manager for a civil service reform bill. Here was merit at work, I tried to convince myself. As the only member who had a PhD in public administration, surely the Speaker had selected me for this responsibility because I was the most qualified. Actually not. As it turned out, no member with greater seniority wanted the job. Civil service reform was just so *borrrrrrring*, eye-glazingly detailed, and with no political sex appeal. Neither the news media nor constituents were interested in such inside-baseball legislative scut work. Politically, it was a thankless assignment. Yet I had a marvelous time prepping for the debate; explaining and defending the bill during its consideration on the floor of the Assembly; and deciding which amendments to accept and which to fight. Notwithstanding my lack of experience, it passed. Again, I wanted to interpret the positive result based on my merits as well as the merits of the idea. But as I gradually was learning, when a bill came out of committee and reached the floor, the default attitude of the members was "is there any reason *not* to pass it?" Oddly, at least to me, the onus was on the opponents, not the proponents. I was merely in the right place at the right time.

One of the issues in the bill (emanating from a gubernatorial study commission that had wrapped up just as I started my freshman term) was to abolish the state's independent civil service–type commission and replace it with a Cabinet-level personnel department that would be more responsive to the governor. The secretary of the new department would be nominated by the governor and require confirmation by the state senate. Another element of the bill was to declassify some senior administrative positions because they were policy-level positions. While some components of the bill faced sporadic and tepid attacks for politicizing the civil service system, those criticisms caught little traction politically or publicly. Personally, I had no reservations advocating for these reforms because they had been first promoted by FDR's Brownlow Committee in 1937. As a doctoral candidate in the early 1970s, reading the report on the need for presidential administrative management was *de rigueur*. My professors practically revered the public administrative theories embedded in the committee's report, especially the importance of an elected chief executive having all the managerial powers necessary to run the executive branch. The Brownlow Committee had identified three vital components necessary to accomplish that: budgeting, planning, and personnel. I was delighted to be able to apply at least something I had learned in graduate school to my work as a lawmaker. So much for the claim that academe was wholly disconnected from the real world.

The enactment of that new Wisconsin law gave me something of a minor national reputation as a legislative expert on the cutting-edge of state-level civil service reform. The National Conference of State Legislatures asked me to make presentations on the new Wisconsin law to legislative committees in Louisiana, Maine, and Washington State. In 1978, I was also invited to speak on personnel management reform at a national conference in Washington, DC, sponsored by the Council for Applied Social Research and the American Society for Public Administration (Lee 1979).

The other path to this study, the academic one, began two decades later, when I joined the professoriate. Left over from grad school, I was still interested in FDR's 1939 action to implement part of the Brownlow Committee report by creating the Executive Office of the President (EOP). It was an epochal moment in the evolution of the modern managerial presidency. Nowadays, given the size of the White House staff and the multiplicity of EOP agencies, it is hard to imagine the contemporary presidency without such major undergirding. Roosevelt deserved—

depending on one's ideological orientation—the credit or the blame for that infrastructure. When he first established the EOP, he placed five agencies within it: the White House Office (mostly consisting of six administrative assistants authorized by Congress when it adopted small parts of the Brownlow report), the Bureau of the Budget (previously in the Treasury Department), the National Resources Planning Board (previously the National Resources Committee), the Office of Government Reports (previously the National Emergency Council), and the Liaison Office for Personnel Management (previously nothing). (In 1940, Roosevelt activated a sixth EOP agency, the Office for Emergency Management [Lee 2012a, 28].)

Scholars had shown great interest in the first two units of EOP's original five units, with substantial historical literature published on White House staffing and on BOB (renamed by President Nixon in 1970 as the Office of Management and Budget [OMB]). There had been less, but some, writing on the National Resources Planning Board, which Congress defunded in 1943 (Clawson 1981). As a newly minted professor, I noticed there had been little to no writing about the fourth EOP unit, the Office of Government Reports. That eventually led to my first book, a biography of that agency (Lee 2005a). Inevitably, I continued to be curious about the fifth of the original EOP entities, the Liaison Office for Personnel Management, if only because it had been largely ignored by academic researchers. This represented a gap in the literature on EOP and its history. But a sterile exercise in filling an empty space on the EOP bookshelf was not enough of a rationale for such an inquiry. I wondered if there was adequate justification to try to fill that gap or perhaps not.

In part, the absence of a literature on LOPM was understandable because it decidedly was not what Brownlow and FDR had in mind originally. At the end of the subsequent three-year legislative battle over enacting the Brownlow Committee's many recommendations, Congress flatly prohibited the president from using his newly delegated reorganization powers to touch the CSC *at all*. So, there seemed to be little FDR could do to promote the idea of presidential personnel management. Creating LOPM was therefore generally viewed by scholars as a kind of political fig leaf, with the president creating a token entity that was supposedly the implementation the Brownlow recommendation, but really could not be. Also, LOPM was very small, consisting of about half a dozen staffers, including secretaries. It was headed by William H. McReynolds, who simultaneously served as one of the six new administrative assistants to the president authorized in the 1939 reorganization law. Famously, these new staffers were to have a Brownlowian "passion for anonymity." The consensus of government historians seemed to be that LOPM was a nearly fake and miniscule agency and was surely not deserving of scholarly attention.

Yet I was still curious about LOPM, not merely as an abstract imperative to fill out the literature on the original five EOP agencies, but more on the idea behind it and its subsequent work. I wondered if LOPM had actually accomplished anything, especially along the lines of what Brownlow and FDR had asserted regarding the need for a presidential personnel agency. Was LOPM in any way a successful culmination of the political war between the ideals of merit and management? Or was it truly a symbolic agency, doing little and accomplishing less?

Another parallel academic trail also led me to this subject. I was curious about McReynolds, LOPM's head. I had first run across him in my study of the US Bureau of Efficiency, where he had been its assistant chief until Congress disbanded the bureau in 1933 (Lee 2006). A few years later, he again popped up when I was studying a wholly different subject: the PR of the pre-WWII arms production buildup. In 1940, FDR had named McReynolds as the White House liaison officer and secretary of his newly invented National Defense Advisory Commission, a job which McReynolds held in addition to continuing as head of LOPM and presidential administrative assistant (Lee 2012a). These widely disparate assignments made me more curious about McReynolds's public service career, especially about his White House work. Again, there was little to no academic literature on his public administration career.

Hence this volume, partly deriving from my long-ago role in the Wisconsin legislature advocating for reforming the state's civil service system into a management-oriented structure and partly reflecting my academic curiosity about this largely unknown agency and its director.

A note on the referencing style used here. Generally, the parenthetical citation style of author-date is the most concise for references to published material. On the other hand, citations of archival and journalistic sources (especially when the latter are non-bylined) are briefest when referenced in chapter notes. I've used both citation styles in this book, depending on the category of the source. This dual referencing style is pragmatic, but a bit unorthodox. However, the 16th edition of the *Chicago Manual of Style* recognized the parenthetical referencing style as equally acceptable as its more traditional note-based style. Regarding documentation of sources, section 14.70 of the *Chicago* style guide called for flexibility and permitted defensible variations from its own guidelines, as long as the work did so consistently. Hence, to avoid the prolixity and cumbersomeness that would arise from using only one of the two referencing styles, both are used in this book. My thanks to the staff of the University of Alabama Press for being willing to permit me to use this dual-referencing style.

My grateful acknowledgement to the many archivists and librarians who helped me. The major source of documents came from the Roosevelt Presidential Library (Hyde Park, NY). While I was there, its staffers, led by Bob Clark, were uniformly patient and helpful notwithstanding what must have felt to them like a thousand questions and requests from me. Brownlow's diary (for 1933–36) at the University of Chicago archives was also helpful. From afar, my queries were diligently answered by staffers at the Truman Library (Independence, MO), Eisenhower Library (Abilene, KS), Johnson Library (Austin, TX), US Senate Historian's Office, Small Special Collections Library of the University of Virginia (Charlottesville), Special Collections Research Center at Syracuse University (NY), and the Brookings Institution (Washington, DC). My appreciation to all.

As usual, the interlibrary loan staff at my home institution's Golda Meir Library performed what looked like miracles to me, fulfilling almost all my requests, including for some obscure and unusual catalog items, sometimes held by only one library in the world. Through persistence and persuasion, they were often able to obtain scans or even loans of materials that usually did not circulate. My thanks to all of these never-say-die professionals. Finally, a thank-you that has been a perennial in my books. Andrea Zweifel, a staffer at my home institution, had proofed all my previous books. By the time this one was ready for her, she had received a much-deserved promotion and was no longer in my unit. I was greatly relieved when she said she would be glad to keep her streak going by proofing this one as well. As with her previous efforts, she has again saved me from so many embarrassing goofs.

As always, all mistakes in the book are mine alone. Lots of people tried to show me the error of my ways. So I cheerfully accept the blame for any remaining flubs or errors.

Abbreviations

AP: Associated Press
BOB: Bureau of the Budget (an agency in the Executive Office of the President)
CPA: Council of Personnel Administration (initially an independent entity, later part of the US Civil Service Commission)
CR: *Congressional Record*
CSC: Depending on the context either the US Civil Service Commission or a generic term for such entities at any level of government
CSM: *Christian Science Monitor* (daily afternoon newspaper published in Boston)
CT: *Chicago Tribune*
EOP: Executive Office of the President
FDR: Franklin Delano Roosevelt
FDRL: Franklin D. Roosevelt Presidential Library, Hyde Park, NY
GAO: General Accounting Office
HR: Human Resources
ICMA: International City Managers' Association
LOPM: Liaison Office for Personnel Management (an agency in the Executive Office of the President)
McRP: William McReynolds Papers, Roosevelt Presidential Library
NCSRL: National Civil Service Reform League (later the National Civil Service League)
NYHT: *New York Herald Tribune*
NYT: *New York Times*
OPM: Office of Personnel Management
PACH: Public Administration Clearing House
PCAM: President's Committee on Administrative Management (also known as the Brownlow Committee)

WP: *Washington Post*
WWI: World War I
WWII: World War II

A PRESIDENTIAL CIVIL SERVICE

William H. McReynolds. Courtesy of Franklin Roosevelt Presidential Library.

Introduction

If there ever was a single idea that united the disparate clusters of good government reformers in the Progressive era (roughly 1890–1920), it was the imperative to establish a merit-based workforce throughout the public sector. Civil service reform was a rallying cry that, astonishingly from a contemporary perspective, mobilized large portions of the population. According to Morris, "thousands, even millions, lined up behind the banner, and they were as evangelical (and as strenuously resisted) as any crusaders in history" (Morris 2010, 405).

This was largely a reaction to the corruption of the spoils system in politics, with government jobs given out based on party loyalty and with little regard to qualifications and work record. Along with patronage came no-show jobs, padded public payrolls, favoritism, nepotism, and all manner of overt waste of the taxpayer's funds. With the growth of the educated middle-class in an increasingly industrial and urban country, citizens rallied around the principle of merit. Merit in government captured the zeitgeist of the times. Public servants should be recruited, hired, evaluated, promoted, compensated, and discharged based exclusively on the merits of their skills and performance. This would be the one best way and the most efficient method for experts to operate government agencies.

This principle of merit encompassed almost all elements of the broad spectrum of Progressive-era reformers. Contemporary historians have rightly dismissed the term "Progressive Movement" as a chimera. There was neither a single unitary movement nor a monolithic Progressive ideology. Rather, Progressives consisted of activists from almost all locations on the political spectrum. These "goo-goos" sought a wide variety of often conflicting good government reforms. Some from left-of-center sought more democracy, such as direct election of US senators, open primaries, recalls of elected officials, initiative and referendum, expansion of the franchise, and recall of judicial decisions (Lee 2013a). Others, on the conservative side, wanted to insulate executive branch agencies from elected officials who may be pandering to the populace of allegedly increasingly ignorant voters.[1] The impact of election results needed to be hemmed in, so that no matter who won, there would be no significant effect on the public service. Some of their suggestions included the short ballot, nonpartisan elections, part-time legislative bodies, and an appointed judiciary (Lee 2011). Coming from these nearly opposing political philosophies, conservatives and liberals alike viewed the need for a merit-based civil service as a central tenet of their reform agendas. Hence the broad popularity of civil service reform.

The near-universal support by reformers of all stripes for establishing the merit system at all levels of American government was a fixed point in reform policy agendas during most of the Progressive era. Then, beginning in the mid-1910s and greatly gaining momentum in the 1920s and 1930s, a small group of public administration specialists began rethinking this orthodoxy. Was the merit system as overseen by an independent bipartisan civil service commission the be all and end all of good government? Was insulating the government's workforce from political direction by elected officials truly a reflection of modern democracy? This new generation of reformers suggested the need for effective *management* of executive branch agencies by the elected CEO, whether he (as they all were in those days) be president, governor, or mayor. Perhaps civil servants had gotten too insulated from popular will and election results? Shouldn't a president be given the management tools to try to accomplish the policy goals he was elected on? This group began pushing for a new iteration of civil service reform, that of personnel management. Sure, merit principles should continue to be protected from the spoils system, but not at the expense of undermining the essence of democracy, namely that elections had policy consequences. In their view, a unitary executive needed to be strengthened. They were little concerned about any co-equal role of elected legislatures in overseeing and co-managing administrative agencies.

The argument about merit vs. management raged for nearly half a century. Kaufman identified the competing camps in public administration as those placing neutral competence as the supreme value vs. those emphasizing executive leadership (Kaufman 1956).[2] Using slightly different terminology, Beaumont looked back over this twentieth-century binary choice as "protectionism vs. better management" (Beaumont 1974, 426).[3]

For the first few decades of the controversy, merit prevailed. Then, as the federal government became increasingly cumbersome in its operations and effectiveness, the tide turned. Management as the central principle of government HR systems finally triumphed in 1978, when Congress passed a civil service reform law pushed by President Carter. It abolished the US Civil Service Commission (CSC) and replaced it (largely) with the Office of Personnel Management (OPM).

This book is the biography of an idea. It investigates the emergence of the initial advocates of management over merit, which climaxed during the presidency of Franklin Roosevelt. The fight over the power to direct the personnel of executive branch agencies played out, of course, in the context of political ideology and partisan politics. Republicans and conservative southern Democrats opposed expanding FDR's ability to pursue the goals of the New Deal by blocking any increased power to steer the bureaucracy in the direction he preferred. Conversely, liberals wanted FDR to have more power to be able to accomplish his agenda. Yet it would be an oversimplification to reduce the fight of merit vs. management exclusively to mere partisanship. This would drain the substance and content from policy arguments, as too often occurs when the media nowadays covers controversies on Capitol Hill by focusing on winners and losers or frames election coverage with an obsessive orientation to the horse-race aspects of the campaign.

While politics certainly played a part in the conflict over civil service reform, this was also a battle of ideas, specifically a battle focusing on the question of which idea—merit or management—was the prerequisite for good government? What good government is can be in the eye of the beholder, but the two camps generally agreed in principle about the benefits of a merit-based civil service. Rather, the issue they argued over was the degree of autonomy that a civil service system should have *vis-à-vis* the elected chief executive. They were debating the importance of the chief executive's management of administrative agencies. Which approach led to better government?

This controversy presents an interesting historical chapter about a battle of principles and how each side tried to prevail. If ideas matter in the American political system, then how did this issue arise, how did it play out, who won, and why? Furthermore, the fight of merit vs. management also presents a case study of the implementation of an idea notwithstanding ostensibly successful opposition. President Roosevelt was flatly prohibited by law from using his new reorganization powers, granted him by Congress in 1939, to affect the US Civil Service Commission (CSC). Nonetheless, he established a small agency in the new Executive Office of the President (EOP) to move towards his goal of presidential management of federal personnel. Given the statutory limitations this agency operated under, what did the president's Liaison Office for Personnel Management (LOPM) actually do and what did it accomplish, if anything? Was it a token fig leaf for a president to make the political claim that he got what he wanted or was it a covert, but relatively successful, implementation of the supremacy of management over merit?

Review of the Literature

The proposal for a presidential personnel management agency to replace the CSC was one of the recommendations contained in the report of FDR's Brownlow Committee (formally the President's Committee on Administrative Management [PCAM]) which was released in January 1937. The committee's work and the subsequent political battle in Congress to implement its many recommendations have routinely and justifiably received attention in the literature, including that on the Roosevelt presidency (Katznelson 2013; Kennedy 2005), federal administrative history (Bertelli and Lynn 2006; Rosenbloom 2000), reorganization (Moe 2003; Seidman 1998), modernizing of the federal government (Kettl 2009; Light 2008; Stanton and Ginsberg 2004), presidential-legislative relations (Fisher 1998), American political development (Skowronek 1982, 288), and the managerial presidency (Gailmard and Patty 2013; Pfiffner 2011; 1999; Hess 2002). In the context of this larger battle over FDR's reorganization plan and executive power, this general literature understandably pays little to no attention to the specific proposal for a presidential personnel agency and its implementation.

As would be expected, the more specialized literatures in public administration and its subfield of public personnel management note the Brownlow proposal for central presidential personnel management, but tend to pass over it lightly and focus much more on the issues of expanding the proportion of federal employees in the civil service system and the general theme of centralized presidential executive management (Stillman 1998; Ingraham 1995; Loverd and Pavlak 1995; Ingraham and Rosenbloom 1992; Mosher 1982). Similarly, the two in-depth historical studies of the Brownlow Committee include a discussion of its recommendation for, and the political fight over, a central presidential personnel agency (Karl 1979; Polenberg 1966). But they pay almost no attention to the concrete record of FDR's subsequent Liaison Office for Personnel Management.

When scholars *have* paid attention to LOPM, what have they said? Their observations have largely been quite derogatory and negative. When President Eisenhower abolished LOPM in 1953 (delegating its role of personnel management advising to the CSC chair), Somers endorsed the decision. He wrote that LOPM was "not conspicuously successful" (Somers 1954, 135). His was an influential view, in part because four years earlier he had written a well-regarded and authoritative book on the importance and value of presidential staff units engaging in coordination and policy-oriented guidance (Somers 1969 [1950]). If Somers, who had praised the coordinating work of "assistant president" James Byrnes's Office of War Mobilization and Reconversion (OWMR), thought poorly of LOPM, then surely this was a reputable conclusion. Then, more than four decades later, Arnold echoed and reconfirmed Somers. As a leading scholar on the managerial presidency, Arnold's views can be seen as a near-definitive and equally influential statement of how the more recent literature viewed LOPM. He described it as merely "a ghost of the Brownlow Committee's original intention" because, in part, it was limited to "a one-person office lacking formal authority" (Arnold 1997, 416). He thought so little of its value that he did not even mention it in his comprehensive and widely-regarded history of reorganization and the managerial presidency (Arnold 1998).

Generally, textbooks reflect the conventional wisdom and literature-generated knowledge of what information is important to impart to those coming into the discipline. An examination of three current textbooks used in public personnel administration courses helps assess perceptions of the relative value of the 1930s duel between merit and management, specifically for a presidential personnel agency to replace an independent civil service commission. The longest running current textbook in personnel management is, at the time of writing, in its 7th edition. It noted the Brownlow Committee recommendation for a civil service administrator to replace the CSC and to be directly accountable to the president. However, it concluded that "these recommendations were not then enacted into law" (Naff, Riccucci, and Freyss 2014, 10). There was no mention of LOPM. In the 5th edition of Dresang's textbook, he quoted from the PCAM staff report on personnel management and noted that the committee recommendation for a presidential agency passed in the Senate, but was defeated in the House (Dresang 2009, 108). As a result, Dresang noted, FDR "did follow the spirit of the proposed reforms as much as possible," such as encouraging the CSC to shift to a more personnel management–oriented model (24). He made no mention of LOPM. The 5th edition of Hays, Kearney, and Coggburn (2009) notes the change in the dominant model of personnel administration in the 1930s from "guarding employees, applicants, and the public from the spoils system" to the beginning of an era that emphasized "cooperation with management" (Klingner 2009, 13). It does not mention LOPM.

Finally, retrospective writings in public administration journals on PCAM were equally skimpy on personnel management. For the fiftieth anniversary of PCAM's report, former staffer Fesler noted the recommendation to centralize personnel management along with budgeting and planning, but omitted any mention of LOPM, apparently not seeing it as an implementation of PCAM's suggestion (Fesler 1987). The approach of the seventieth anniversary of PCAM's report also prompted some discussion in journals of the recommendation for a central personnel agency and the committee's underlying staff report on personnel matters. But, again, no discussion of LOPM as part of its legacy (Stivers and Hummel 2007; Newbold and Terry 2006). The most extensive discussion of the run-up to the creation of LOPM and its record of activities is in Van Riper's history of the CSC, published more than fifty years ago. He gave it faint praise. LOPM was a "limited victory" for PCAM's principle of management over merit (Van Riper 1958, 337).

In summary, as a generalization, the Brownlow Committee has received its due attention in the historical and specialized literature, including—sometimes—its recommendation for a presidential personnel management agency to replace the CSC. However, FDR's subsequent effort to *implement* it by creating LOPM as a non-statutory agency has been of little interest to researchers and is largely absent in the published literature. It is a heretofore unreported chapter of American governmental history.

Rationale for the Book and Potential Audiences

Does this all deserve a book? As presented here, the subject includes the intellectual and policy origins of the concept of an executive-centric personnel agency to replace the CSC, the reorganization battle in Congress over such an agency, LOPM's creation, its subsequent record of performance, and the eventual creation in 1978 of the Office of Personnel Management to replace the CSC. In size, measured by staffing and budget, LOPM was a speck of an agency compared to the hefty bulk of most federal executive branch entities. At its height during WWII, it employed only about half a dozen people, including secretaries. Size isn't everything. I suggest four (overlapping) reasons justifying such a book: the battle of ideas over the best way to manage the governmental workforce, the fight for institutional primacy in the federal government, an unstudied chapter in the history of American public administration, and a political history study of lost alternatives.

First, LOPM was the end result of a fierce battle of ideas regarding how to manage governmental employment. Should a merit system be overseen by a civil service commission, an independent regulatory agency headed by three commissioners, representing both parties, who would be free to select the commission's president/chair? Or should oversight of human capital be viewed as one of the key tools of management and, therefore, given status comparable to the Bureau of the Budget? In that latter worldview, personnel management would be a presidential agency, headed by an individual who would serve at the pleasure of the president. HR policies would reflect the president's priorities and goals as part of his overall management of the executive branch. The two perspectives represented theories that were rooted deeply in American culture and values.

Merit was the longtime battle cry of the Progressive-era reformers and the middle class, seeking a political system without corruption and spoils. Civil servants should be free from any political taint, instead should be expert professionals who were hired, compensated, and promoted without partisan considerations. Civil service reform had been a mass movement leading up to its enactment at the federal level (for only a fraction of federal employees) in the 1883 Pendleton Act and widespread enactment in states and localities. Civil service commissions were viewed as the best protectors of the merit system.

Yet at the same time occurred the rise of the management class (Chandler

1999). Large corporations were no longer run by owners and boards of directors. Instead, the American solution was for a professionally trained class of managers who would make all important decisions regarding the operations of the corporation. The rise of management as an idea was a kind of endorsement of the new American political economy. Managers were the new heroes, a new class of supermen, the men who would make tough decisions based on the facts. All power would be vested in them and their decisions would affect all others in the hierarchy below them. Only managers could see the whole picture from their high perch and, therefore, only they could make strategic decisions. In this authoritarian pyramid, no questioning or criticism was permitted. Everybody had to pull in the direction indicated by the manager.

Given the dominance and idolatry of business in the American political economy, the common perspective has been that government needed more businesslike practices. Transposing business administration to public administration was presumed to be valid and preferred. Government needed to be made as efficient as business. In this context, giving the president the managerial powers to run the executive branch like a corporate CEO, including the powers of budgeting, personnel, and planning, was a no-brainer. How could anyone be against good management? After all, could one conceive of a situation in the business world where the CEO had no power over the HR director? That the HR director reported separately and directly to the board of directors? Or reported to no one? This would, of course, be unacceptable in a business context. Personnel policies needed to reflect the priorities set by the CEO for the overall successful functioning of the corporation. Why not the same principle for managing in the public sector?

Therein was the conundrum: what was the one best way for running the government? Merit and management both seemed to represent valid and accepted practices in America. In that context, this book traces, as has not before been presented in the literature, the battle of ideas between merit and management and the results of that battle. Who won and why?

A second rationale for this study is that the 1930s fight in Washington between merit and management was a key—if largely historically ignored—round in the conflict between Congress and presidents over separation of powers. Who was king of the hill? Was Congress or the president the alpha branch of the US Constitution? Much of twentieth-century American political history has been framed as the rise of the White House and the decline of Capitol Hill. Most of nineteenth-century history viewed presidents as somewhat glorified and passive clerks in the context of what Woodrow Wilson termed "congressional government." Federal agency managers, except those appointed by the president and serving at his pleasure, tended to look to Congress for guidance and power. Laws and appropriations were *legislative* prerogatives and such congressional enactments were where power came from. True, the president had a constitutional role in the endgame of the lawmaking and appropriations process, but even then the president's veto could be overturned by a congressional super-majority.

Then, largely beginning with Theodore Roosevelt, followed aggressive assertions of presidential power *vis-à-vis* Congress, especially based on the constitutional designation of the president as the exclusive holder of executive power and as the military commander-in-chief. One of the key battles between the legislative and executive branches during the Progressive era was over budgeting. Who *made* budgets? After all, deciding to spend a dollar on X and not on Y was the most tangible reflection of priority setting, of what was important to the federal government and what wasn't. Supporters of the status quo approved of what was called legislative budgeting. In that dynamic, agencies submitted their budget requests to Congress and responded to explicit or implicit congressional priority setting. The president had no role at the front end of the process. The Treasury Department would ministerially transmit to Congress the budget requests of federal agencies without any active role. It was merely a forwarding office.

Most of the goo-goo reformers of the Progressive era thought they had a better idea: *executive* budgeting. In their view, what Congress did was haphazard, decentralized, lacking in consistency of policy principles, and incapable of handling the financial decision-making necessary in an increasingly complex federal executive branch. Their solution was for the president (or governor or mayor) to put together a comprehensive and integrated budget proposal that reflected his priorities and goals. Sure, Congress had the final word, but the bulk of lesser (or less controversial politically) policy matters already embedded in the budget proposal would inevitably be acquiesced to by Congress. This would improve the quality of governmental operations and increase the efficiency of government. The president would oversee the executive branch as, apparently, the Founding Fathers really wanted. Only a minority of reform activists, such as William Allen, supported continuation of legislative budgeting, saying it was more democratic (Lee 2013b). After a long and bitter fight, Congress reluctantly gave the president budgeting primacy in 1921 (Kahn 1997).

The fight between FDR and Congress over primacy in personnel management was a synecdoche of this larger century-long political battle. Congress preferred the status quo of the CSC, including the commission's balanced partisan representation and independence from presidential control. Given those parameters, one had to look to Congress for any major changes in personnel management policy. FDR argued that for the president to manage the executive branch, he needed to have personnel powers commensurate with the budgetary powers Congress had given presidents in 1921. Good management required an integration of budgeting, personnel, and planning, he said. The three managerial tools were interrelated and all needed to be housed under the president and subject to his directives. To all involved in this fight, it was clear that the creation of a presidential personnel agency to replace the CSC would be another major victory of the executive in the conflict over primacy in the constitutional system. In the context of this struggle for power, there is a close parallel to the battle of ideas discussed above: Congress was defending merit and the president was for good management.

The third rationale for this study is as a contribution of the history of American public administration. In his 2013 Gaus lecture at the American Political Science Association, Durant called for increased attention to history as part of the study of government (Durant 2014), as did Raadschelders writing a few years before that (Raadschelders 2010). More complete knowledge of the past increases understanding of the status quo and of trends. It identifies the decisions and nondecisions that contributed to the present state of public affairs. A closer study of the 1930s fight of merit vs. management contributes to several historically oriented literatures. In public administration, the Brownlow Committee has been viewed as the orthodoxy of federal reorganization. This book fills out the story of one of the Committee's recommendations and the end result. As such, it is a study of management history highlighting the central conception of management as a value that was put forward as more important than the traditional merit-based government employment system. Within public administration and management studies, the subject touches on subfields including HR management, organizational design, and management theory.

Fourth, Zelizer has noted the increased attention by political historians and policy historians to "lost alternatives" (Zelizer 2012, 55). While historical winners are prominent in the narrative of events, he suggested that the study of the losers and of the alternatives they proposed adds nuance and texture to history. Sure, they lost, but what was it they were advocating for? Ideas, even losing ones, can contribute to historical understanding. In this case, it is the superficial judgment of history that merit, Congress, and political conservatives triumphed over management, President Roosevelt, and left-of-center Democrats. That would place the story recounted here in the category of an alternative that lost.

But ideas rarely die, hence the appeal of studying lost alternatives. In this case, the outcome was merely the false dawn of presidential personnel management. In the short term, one can assess not only the winners and losers of the political battle, but also if LOPM was anything more than a token entity to permit FDR to claim he won? Or at least to keep the idea alive to fight another day? Then, based on the unstudied historical record of its activities, was the resultant LOPM significant or not? If the former, then perhaps the conventional wisdom that FDR lost the fight needs to be corrected. Even if LOPM was not significant in its time, the existence of the entity kept the losing side's idea alive. Ultimately, four decades later, FDR and Brownlow were vindicated by history when, in 1978, Congress approved President Carter's proposal to abolish the CSC and replace it with the Office of Personnel Management, headed by a presidential appointee.

The potential audiences for this book flow from these four rationales for the relevance of the subject. The disciplines that would likely have an interest in the book are American history, political history, public administration, and political science. Other more specialized academic subfields that might also be interested in this study include American political development, federal history (as reflected in the work of the Society for History in the Federal Government), studies of FDR's presidency, management history, human resources and personnel management, organization theory, and public policy.

A brief explanation of the book's scope and structure. Inevitably an inquiry into the political battle of merit vs. management and the subsequent record of LOPM involves some discussion of specific HR policies in play at the time. However, this study is not intended to be a comprehensive history of HR and public personnel administration per se, nor a review of the scores of proposals over the years to reform HR policies in the federal government. Similarly, it is neither a history of the CSC nor an examination of the many congressional enactments during the FDR presidency (and after) tinkering with specific conditions of employment for selected members of the classified service. Those latter foci have already been well covered in the literature, albeit in some sources that are dated (e.g., Van Riper 1958; Kammerer 1951). Rather, the focus is on conflict over the larger theoretical and philosophical concept of merit vs. management as opposing principles in public administration and then the subsequent political fight over organizational control and accountability of federal HR management. That is followed by an examination of the role that LOPM actually played in personnel management, notwithstanding Congress banning the president from using his new reorganization powers to touch the CSC.

Regarding structure, interesting history is often the telling of a good story. The best stories unfold as they do in life, without knowing in advance what the next development will be, let alone the final outcome. Therefore, this book presents in chronological order the birth of the idea of executive-centered public personnel management to supersede autonomous civil service commissions, FDR's political fight to enact the idea, the functioning of the idea as he eventually implemented it, its demise, and finally, decades later, its rebirth. While perhaps these events are more happenstance than anything else, by nice coincidence this sequential approach fits the prototypical structure of a story: a beginning, middle, and end. In this case, there was a postscript to the end: another beginning.

1
Origins of the Idea of a Presidential Personnel Agency, 1913–1936

In the beginning, there was not much government in the US (though there was *some* [Mashaw 2012]). Consequently, there was less of a need for a comprehensive governmental employment system, let alone a professional personnel department in government agencies. In fact, the reason back then for the large number of local elected offices—such as county clerk, clerk of courts, register of deeds, sheriff, and treasurer—was because these were one-man departments. They had no staff. On the federal level, when Jefferson took office, the executive branch employed only 153 people at the seat of government (excluding field staff such as post office workers, customs collectors, and Indian agents). Thirty years later, the number of federal employees in Washington was still only about double that (Lee 2012b).

It was the large growth in the number of federal employees, especially after the Civil War, which led to excesses in the spoils system and gradually increasing public interest in civil service reform. But Congress and political machines in cities and states, ever hungry for patronage, were major roadblocks to any depoliticization of government employment. According to Morris, "It is difficult for Americans living in the first quarter of the twenty-first century to understand the emotions which Civil Service Reform aroused in the last quarter of the nineteenth" (Morris 2010, 404–05).

The Orthodoxy of an Independent and Apolitical Civil Service Commission

The assassination of President Garfield by a disappointed office seeker capped this popular movement. It was the seismic political event that enabled reformers to overcome such entrenched political obstacles. In 1883, Congress enacted the Pendleton Act, establishing the nonpartisan and independent Civil Service Commission (CSC) to oversee a merit-based employment system in the federal government. (Significantly, it only covered a minority of federal employees.) The popular movement for civil service reform also focused on state and local governments. The first state to enact a law creating a civil service system overseen by an independent commission was New York, due to the efforts of Democratic governor Grover Cleveland and Republican assemblyman Theodore Roosevelt (Lee 2012b). Later, Roosevelt was one of the three federal CSC commissioners who avidly investigated and exposed political violations of federal law protecting a nonpartisan and apolitical classified service (R. White 2003).[1]

But what, exactly, was meant by injecting a merit system into public sector employment? By the 1920s, the movement for civil service reform had coagulated into orthodoxy. Several central tenets defined a "true" merit-based employment system in government. The specific goal was the employment of expert professionals who would hold permanent appointments and not be subject to political oversight. Many elements of an approved civil service system focused on attaining complete control over the management of a merit-centered workforce. There should be apolitical control over the front, middle, and end stages of the employment cycle, including recruiting, testing, certifying, promoting, evaluating, rewarding, handling grievances, disciplining, and firing.

The most prominent element of this orthodoxy was the creation of a civil service commission. This entailed multi-member body consisting of an odd number of members, with appointees representing both political parties. Most importantly, it would function as an independent (quasi-regulatory) commission, not as a department in the executive branch. It would not be accountable to the elected chief executive in the way that the secretary of a Cabinet department served at the pleasure of the president. Instead, the ideal CSC really reported to no one and was largely outside the orbit of normal public administration. It stood alone, autonomous, nonpartisan, and apolitical as the guardian and implementer of the merit system.

For example, the 1915 version of the reform movement's model civil service law stated that a civil service commission "should not be controlled by or responsible to any political officer" (National Assembly of Civil Service Commissions 1915, 5). It was to be an independent agency apart from the executive and legislative branches, essentially its own supervisor. In 1922, the Governmental Research Conference proposed some changes in the scope and operations of municipal CSCs, but emphasized the continuing principle of assuring that personnel administration would be "under professional rather than under political guidance" (Governmental Research Conference 1922, 60).

The first textbook in American public administration, published in 1926, described "a typical civil service law" as including guarantees of a CSC's political autonomy from the chief executive (L. White 1926, 231). The next year, in a summary of the state of American public administration, Willoughby noted that a principle of personnel matters "that has been almost universally adopted" included the dictate that a CSC "shall be deemed to be one standing outside of the administration and responsible primarily to the legislature or directly to the people" (Willoughby 1927, 355–56). (He disagreed with it.)

In 1931, a revised model law for cities continued to require that both political parties be represented on a three-person CSC (National Civil Service Reform League 1931a, 3). The counterpart model law for state governments required that two of the three appointees be selected from an eligibility list as a result of a civil service recruitment and examination process. These two commissioners would themselves be within the classified service with the usual civil service protections. Roberts described such an independent structure as the "*instrument* of reform," in other words, not merely one of several component parts of a civil service reform program, but rather the central element of it (Roberts 1996a, 16, emphasis added).

The strong preference for a multi-person independent civil service commission continued to be held as an article of faith by civil service reformers for a long time. In 1939, the National Civil Service Reform League and National Municipal League jointly issued a new model state civil service law. They acknowledged that "a few" governments now preferred a civil service structure headed by a sole administrator. But, "there is a marked tendency" for multi-member commissions with the commissioners reflecting a nonpartisan commitment to creating, maintaining, and protecting a merit system (National Civil Service Reform League and National Municipal League 1939, 8–9). A decade and a half after that, their 1953 model law only slightly revised that characterization, stating there was still "a marked tendency" for multi-member commissions, though admitting there were "many" examples of personnel departments headed by a single administrator. Nonetheless, their 1953 model law continued to prefer the traditional approach of a multi-member CSC (National Civil Service League and National Municipal League 1953, 6–7).

Questioning the Orthodoxy, 1913–1932

Civil service reform and the larger movement for good government had triggered, in turn, the gradual emergence of public administration. Somewhat akin to business administration, public administration would be several things simultaneously: a profession of practitioners, a social science–based research subject, a training program for future practitioners, and an academic discipline. The significance of this emerging field was perhaps in its different orientation from what had preceded and birthed it. Civil service reform was largely focused on a negative goal, namely of reducing government corruption, especially by abolishing patronage jobs. CSCs would be the bulwark against dirty politics, standing at the ramparts and defending good government from the hordes of nefarious politicians trying to get their grubby hands on jobs for their cronies. To the good government progressives, this was a clear cut issue of good and bad, right and wrong, that had active support from large numbers of the citizenry.

On the other hand, public administration encompassed the perspective of management and was a field of interest largely to only a few insiders, the self-selected professionals with specialized expertise. What was needed to improve the quality of government management? Given that public administration emerged after the peak of the Progressive era good-government and reform movements, the new field built on a premise growing out of its origins in a merit system now ensconced nearly universally in the American public sector. The battle for clean government had largely been won or was in the midst of being reached. A politically neutral and competent workforce was in place or coming into place through a classified system with extant CSCs as the guardians of this merit-based personnel system. Given that the merit system was here to stay, what next? Or, at least, what were the consequences of this new normal?

These early public administrationists began wondering if all the elements of a merit system were congruent with the smooth and efficient management of government. In particular, if presidents, governors, and mayors were the heads of the executive branches of their respective governmental units, could they function as executives were supposed to? Could they pursue and implement the businesslike functioning of the public sector? Perhaps the good government folks had gone too far and succeeded too much in removing executive oversight and direction over the classified service?

An early and tentative manifestation of this new thinking was raised in 1913 by President Taft's Commission on Economy and Efficiency. Largely a failure in actual results approved by Congress, it nonetheless debuted the voice of the new public administration profession. The commission was chaired by Frederick Cleveland, the co-founder of the trailblazing New York Bureau of Municipal Research, the "mother" organization of the field that had subsequently birthed several entities, including a training program for professionals and similar organizations in other cities. Member Frank Goodnow, a professor at Columbia, had written in 1900 a seminal book for the field, titled *Politics and Administration* (Goodnow 1967). As a result, some called him the "Father of Public Administration." The third major member of the commission was W. F. Willoughby, who was beginning to emerge as a major figure in the field (Lee 2011).

By early 1913, President Taft was a lame duck, having been defeated by Democrat Woodrow Wilson (with the assistance of former president Theodore Roosevelt, who ran as a third-party candidate after Taft beat him for the Republican nomination). Taft was metaphorically clearing off his desk, making one last effort to advocate congressional approval of the commission's reform and reorganization recommendations or, at least, to get into the official record his and its ideas. On January 10, Cleveland testified at a hearing of the House Appropriations Committee. The committee was most interested in the commission's recommendation for a presidential Bureau of Administrative Control. The rationale for such an organization grew out of the increasing calls by reformers for an executive budget, with a president preparing and submitting to Congress a unified annual budget proposal. (It was eventually adopted in 1921.) Besides a budgeting agency, the proposed bureau would encompass the key central managerial responsibilities for a president vested constitutionally with directing the executive branch. One entity within that administrative bureau would be a central Bureau of Personnel.

This subject did not come up in Cleveland's oral testimony or in his answers to questions, only in a memo he subsequently submitted at the request of the committee's chair. The reference to a central Bureau of Personnel was opaquely described (common to Cleveland's writing style) and quite unclear in some key details. It was buried in a section on the management practices of other countries, especially Great Britain. Cleveland wrote that, based on the UK's precedent, "the executive head should be provided with an independent organization for exercising control both over the subject of the efficiency of the personnel and over the character of the results obtained in the several departments" (US House 1913, 48).

A month later, and with only a few weeks left in his term, Taft sent a message to Congress containing a budget plan for the next fiscal year as a way of demonstrating tangibly what an executive budget would look like. An appendix summarized the changes in laws that Congress would have to approve to permit an executive budget and related central responsibilities of the president. The list of proposed statutory changes included an "amendment of the civil-service law so as to broaden its functions and give to the Executive a bureau of personnel" (US Senate 1913, 117).

These two descriptions of a central presidential personnel agency were clear as mud, perhaps deliberately so. Both said that the goal was a central *personnel* agency, a broader management function than that of the current CSC as guardian of the merit system. Both described the bureau as under "the executive," presumably meaning the president, but avoided saying so explicitly, let alone clarifying the accountability relationship between the personnel agency and the White House. Also, confusingly, the proposed central personnel agency was described as "an independent organization." This could have meant the traditional characterization of an autonomous CSC, but the ambiguity could have also have meant that the agency would simply not be affiliated with any Cabinet departments, hence having the generic standing of an independent agency within the executive branch. If the latter, then the new agency would be much more subject to the president's direction, more like the managerial role of a Panama Canal Commission and less like the independent regulatory and quasi-judicial role of the Interstate Commerce Commission. This 1913 idea for—apparently—a presidential personnel management agency was offered so tentatively, so opaquely, and so late politically that it was almost universally unnoticed and quickly sank out of sight.

It was nearly ten years later when other public administration leaders began promoting it anew. William Mosher suggested the need to update the agenda of civil service reform (Mosher 1921). As a member of the National Institute of Public Administration (the successor to Cleveland's Bureau of Municipal Research), Mosher suggested that the time had come for a new phase in the reform movement. The original goals of civil service reform, in his view, had been "prohibitive" in nature, and then "regulatory." Both were negative in orientation, trying to end or prevent bad things. Now was the time for a successor paradigm, that of a "constructive" approach to the broad gamut of public personnel management. Mosher called for a central personnel agency that would "become a part of rather than apart from the rest of the administration." Furthermore, there was a need for the professionalization in the staffing of such an agency, so that it could focus on employing trained experts in all manner of personnel administration, rather than clerks following rules. This was quite a radical departure from the civil service reform orthodoxy. Even so, Mosher was careful not to discuss the relationship of his central personnel agency with the chief executive, whether a president, governor, or mayor. However, his cautious description of the new agency being part of "*the* administration," rather than, say, "the executive branch" appears to be a deliberate reference to a president's administration, rather than to public administration generically.

The next year, Lewis Mayers of the Institute for Government Research (later the Brookings Institution, which was headed by Willoughby of the Taft Commission) suggested something similar (Mayers 1922, chap. 15). He proposed spinning off the regulatory and quasi-judicial role of the CSC into a small separate body that would hear appeals on personnel matters. The rest of the CSC would become a "central personnel administration" agency, with an affirmative role in promoting good personnel management throughout the federal executive branch. He was vague on the organization of the non-judicial agency, at one point seeming to suggest it be headed by a single commissioner (at least for all recruitment responsibilities). Mayers was apparently trying to straddle two distinct approaches, wanting a management-oriented central personnel agency while at the same time wanting it to be nonpolitical.

Paralleling these theoretical proposals was the emergence in Maryland of a single civil service commissioner, rather than a multiple-member commission (Telford 1923). This was very controversial with traditionalists because the membership could not be balanced between the two parties and because decisions would not require the agreement of at least two people. Furthermore, a one-person commission looked a lot like a department head, blurring the distinction between an independent commission and a state agency head reporting to the governor.

These challenges to the traditional platform of civil service reformers came to a head in 1923. A special committee of the National Municipal League (which included Mosher) submitted a controversial report with recommendations for a revised reform plan. Among many recommendations, it suggested a major break with the traditional reform agenda of an independent CSC protecting the merit system. In its place, the committee sought a central personnel agency that would focus on all aspects of personnel management, not just those associated with protecting a classified workforce. "After some forty years of experimentation with the civil service commission," the report declared, "the time has clearly come for laying more and more emphasis on positive functions. . . . The civil service commission should be transferred from the sentry box at the entrance gate of the building to an office adjacent to the executive and chief administrator" (National Municipal League 1923, 451). If that wasn't clear enough, the committee said it "contemplates a personnel agency that would be part and parcel of the administration and of equal rank and authority with the other centralized agencies like the budget division and the central purchasing department" (463).

In a seeming bid to attract the support of traditionalists, the committee suggested a major change in the method of appointment of the sole civil service commissioner. The previous template had the members of the multi-member body nominated by the chief executive for a specific term and with the requirement of political balance on the commission. Instead, the committee suggested that the sole commissioner would attain office by a strict civil service appointment process, including constituting a special board to recruit and evaluate candidates, a competitive examination, and a list of top three eligibles. The list would be submitted to "the executive official or body," who would select one. Once appointed, he would serve for an indefinite term and could only be removed from office for cause. Hence, the civil service would be headed by a member of the classified service, from a list of finalists selected by civil service professionals, and with a lifetime appointment. This would, in the logic of the committee, guarantee the continuation of an independent and apolitical direction of the civil service system, one of the major tenets of the reform movement.

There was lots of opposition. One member resigned rather than sign the committee report, another stayed on, but issued a kind of dissenting opinion (442). Most criticisms came from longtime activists in the civil service reform movement. Robert Moses said it was "wholly unworkable" (Moses 1923, 477).[2] Clinton Woodruff opposed shifting from a multiple-member commission to a single commissioner. He felt the former was at the heart of the reform movement's goals of creating and nurturing a merit system (Woodruff 1923). William Foulke said the claim that the fight against the spoils system had been won was false, that there were still many politicians and machines trying to prevent a merit system or force it to contract (Foulke 1923).

In large part, the traditional dogmas of the Progressive era civil service reform movement stayed in place in the 1920s, with the alternate approach of a centralized executive agency for personnel management acknowledged, but not endorsed by the bulk of the traditional reformers. While the National Civil Service Reform League generally maintained its traditional support for an independent, multimember, and politically balanced CSC, a splinter group called the Better Government League endorsed a central personnel agency "with an administrative head responsible directly to the President."[3] Later the (slightly renamed) Civil Service Reform League tried to straddle the difference by presenting both approaches in the evolving versions of its model laws.

The new wave of public administration professionals tried to keep their idea alive, such as when Willoughby (former member of Taft's Commission) in 1927 enunciated the *Principles of Public Administration*. He went the farthest in this loose network of new reformers by explicitly tying a central personnel agency to the presidency, writing that the president should have the same powers over personnel management as he had in the area of budgeting and should have in all matters of management coordination, control, and responsibility (Willoughby 1927, 356–57). In a report written in 1928–29 (but not published until 1931), Feldman, a professor at Dartmouth's Amos Business School, strongly endorsed the principle of a central federal personnel agency, writing that would be "most desirable" (US House 1931, 255). However, he carefully avoided endorsing or opposing the many conflicting approaches surrounding the fate of the CSC. Some plans sought to expand the CSC's role to all personnel matters; others to abolish it and replace it with a new central agency for personnel management. Feldman appeared most intrigued by the scenario of subsuming the new agency into BOB, comparable to the chief coordinator office that had existed in BOB in the 1920s, the head of which was a de facto "Federal business manager" (248–49). Why not a counterpart federal personnel manager?[4] Trying to be a fair-minded and accurate academic researcher summarizing developments while still promoting the agenda of the new reformers, Leonard White dryly noted that "the proper organization of the personnel agency is still the subject of discussion and experimentation" (L. White 1929, 430).

Congress did not seriously consider any major structural or organizational changes to the CSC. At the time, most of its attention was on classification process for all federal positions and the bifurcation of the responsibilities between the feuding CSC and Bureau of Efficiency, with the new Personnel Classification Board and Bureau of the Budget trying to mediate the argument (Lee 2006, 94). The only notable presidential attention in the 1920s to federal personnel administration occurred in 1921, when President Harding created a Federal Personnel Board as a way to professionalize HR throughout the executive branch and to promote personnel policies that the CSC did not have jurisdiction over (Gaus 1922, 773). But the board was stillborn, never meeting once between 1921 and 1924 (Filer 1924, 226).

President Hoover Tries to Reform Personnel Management

Herbert Hoover came to the presidency with the reputation of an engineer and manager who was interested in improving public management through reorganization and reform (Lee 2006, 101). Regarding HR, in 1931 he issued Executive Order 5612 reviving Harding's dormant personnel board with a revised title of Council of Personnel Administration. The executive order appointed the chair of the CSC as the automatic chair of the new council. This was a modest way to use presidential power to integrate and coordinate the control-based legal powers of the CSC with the more positive perspective of personnel management.

Hoover charged the council with the mission of promoting "a more effective and economical system of employment and personnel management." Here was an acknowledgement that personnel management was a broader topic than the CSC's somewhat circumscribed statutory mission and that coordination of an improved HR system was a factor in enhancing the overall management of the executive branch. But, as is apparent from the wording of the purpose of the new council, while *effectiveness* may have been a laudatory management improvement goal, it was *economical* management that was of political and budgetary interest. Hoover's secular and long-standing interest in restructuring the federal executive branch and improving its management became inextricably linked during the Great Depression with the dominant political and congressional mood to deal with the economic collapse by cutting spending, including reducing the size of the federal workforce.

About a year after his executive order creating the Council of Personnel Administration, Hoover sent a message to Congress calling for a comprehensive reorganization of the federal government. As part of it, he fully embraced the emerging thinking about merit systems, largely seeking to implement what the new public administration experts had been advocating. Hoover proposed creating an agency called the Personnel Administration that would encompass all extant federal HR-related agencies. It would be "a service agency" to the entire executive branch, helping accomplish a modern personnel management system, in contrast to the prohibiting and limiting role of the CSC (US House 1932a, 3). The new agency would be headed by a personnel administrator. The CSC would continue to exist in a very diminished capacity, as a regulatory and quasi-judicial body. To assure close coordination between the reduced CSC and the Personnel Administration, Hoover suggested that the personnel administrator would also automatically be the chair of the downgraded CSC.

Congressman John Cochran (D-MO), as chair of the Committee on Expenditures in the Executive Departments,[5] introduced H.R. 8389 largely as an implementation of Hoover's recommendations for personnel reorganization. (The bill changed the name of the agency from Hoover's Personnel Administration to Civil Service Administration.) The main addition to Hoover's original proposal was clarifying how the administrator would be appointed. He would be nominated by the president and subject to Senate confirmation (US House 1932b, 1). There would be no fixed term of service, permitting the president to fire the incumbent at any time. Also, there were no qualifications for that office, meaning that the nominee would not have to have previous personnel management experience. As a presidential appointee requiring Senate confirmation, this office would clearly be a senior one, comparable to departmental secretaries and ambassadors. (In comparison, the head of the Bureau of the Budget was not subject to Senate confirmation at the time.)

Hoover's proposal and the bill to implement it were radical departures from the prevailing orthodoxy. In one fell swoop all federal personnel matters would come under one roof, be within the executive branch rather than independent of it, be headed by a sole director, and be part of a president's administration. Without saying it, this would create a presidential personnel management agency, the HR counterpart to the Bureau of the Budget. (At the time, BOB was formally part of the Treasury Department, but under the president's direct control.)

The public hearing on the bill largely overlooked the revolutionary aspect of the proposal. Instead, it focused on smaller-bore issues: economy (how much money would be saved?), agency turf issues, opposition from existing agencies to being swallowed by the expanded CSC, and if the model of the sole administrator of the Veterans Administration was an organizational design that was transferable to the proposed Personnel Administration (US House 1932b).[6]

Indicating the power of that personnel orthodoxy, the chair of the CSC had to state carefully that his "personal" opinion was in favor of the bill and that the commission had not "formally" taken a position on it, and one of the other two commissioners submitted a statement of his opposition (US Congress 1932b, 4–5,

71). Eventually, a much watered down version of the bill (mostly transferring the duties of the Personnel Classification Board to the CSC) was included in the omnibus Economy Act of 1932, which Hoover signed in mid-1932 (Lee 2006, 126, 131). The status quo of an independent CSC had been retained.

Later in 1932, Professor John Pfiffner assessed the trends in personnel administration. He summarized the conventional wisdom, namely that "many friends of the civil service movement will shudder at the thought of placing all personnel matters directly under the mayor, governor, or city manager." (And, impliedly, a president.) Lightly hinting at his preference (without violating the academic template of disinterested expert neutrality), he concluded his article by giving the last word to rebutting the traditionalists' fears of political control of personnel by the chief executive: "It is thought that more adequate [budgetary] support will result from connection with the chief executive's budget agency," rather than a legacy independent commission (Pfiffner 1932, 332). The convoluted construction permitted him to avoid saying *who* thought that, but it was an implied endorsement of the "new movement" challenging the old reform orthodoxy, especially noting the benefits of a closer link between budgeting and HR.

After he was defeated for reelection, Hoover made one last stab at comprehensive reorganization. Significantly, in his proposal to Congress in late 1932, he backed off from his controversial personnel reform ideas. His plan did not include his earlier proposal for a personnel administrator and Personnel Administration and did not call for any significant changes in federal personnel management or the legal scope of the CSC (US House 1932c, 6). Perhaps this was a belated recognition of the power of the status quo of the civil service reform movement's orthodoxy. A demonstration of that political reality was that even Hoover's minor remaining proposal relating to personnel management, that of merging the Employees' Compensation Commission into the CSC, triggered congressional opposition (US House 1932d, 3).[7]

Hoover's retreat on radical reorganization of the federal HR system into a personnel administrator and Personnel Administration was not a one-off post-election grasp for *any* modicum of reorganization, no matter how minor. That his thinking had permanently changed was confirmed when the former president spoke to a civic commission on civil service reform in 1934 (see next subchapter). He endorsed professionalizing federal HR by *expanding* the scope of the CSC to encompass all aspects of personnel management. Hoover declined to support other options raised as tentative questions by members of the commission, such as bringing the CSC into the management of a presidential administration or replacing the commission with an administrator (Commission of Inquiry 1935a, 475–76).

During FDR's First Term: The Commission of Inquiry on Public Service Personnel, 1933–1935

Like so many in his patrician class, Franklin Roosevelt, as a budding politician from upstate New York, was a supporter of the good government movement, including civil service reform. In 1907, at age twenty-five, he joined the New York Civil Service Reform Association (L. White 1945, 139). Later, in the 1920s, he publicly proposed that the presidential platforms of both parties endorse civil service reform and then served on a task force of the National Civil Service Reform League (NCSRL).[8] He also agreed to serve as a member of the technical advisory group of personnel experts organized by the nonprofit Bureau of Public Personnel Administration, an early effort to professionalize HR management in government.[9]

Indicating his lack of dogmatism (for which he later became famous), as early as 1920, FDR expressed some dissatisfaction with the current federal personnel system. In a speech to the 1920 Democratic presidential convention, he said that the consequences of the current civil service was that "the most efficient employees leave the service when they are becoming most valuable," while the "less useful" stayed for life (National Municipal League 1923, 444–45n5).

FDR's mixed views on the civil service system were partly indicated by the legislation he submitted to Congress during 1933 to create an alphabet soup of emergency agencies to deal with the economy. Routinely, he asked that the workforce of those agencies be exempted from the classified service. Routinely, the Democratic Congress elected with him in 1932 acquiesced. Minority Republicans (and some Democratic conservatives) reflexively denounced this approach as a revival of the spoils system and a full-employment bureau for New Deal political supporters and Democratic Party campaign workers. Largely agreeing with the Republicans, two leading academic experts in public administration were opposed to the exemptions. John Gaus and Leonard White criticized FDR's stance, concluding that "the political scientist and the publicist have failed to make the country aware of the large body of professional civil servants" who could handle such assignments (L. White 1934, 450).[10] (The reference to "publicist" was probably to civil service reform advocates who relied on publicity to mobilize public opinion in support of civil service and other good government policies.)

As discussed earlier in this chapter, the emergence of an alternative to the civil service reform orthodoxy was largely representative of the rise of the new academic discipline of public administration and, in parallel, of non-academics who sought to professionalize the practice of the profession. Those activists, including Louis Brownlow, Charles E. Merriam, and Luther Gulick, gradually coalesced into the Social Science Research Council (SSRC) and then, a few years later, its sub-group, the Committee on Public Administration. Almost exclusively underwritten by Rockefeller philanthropic funds, these entities and activists wanted to pursue so-called scientific studies of public administration and to discover scientific principles of the field. The Rockefeller family was interested in supporting good government, just as long as it was not controversial or involved in politics. The activists and funders both wanted to create a value-free, nonpartisan, neutral, and technocratic body of knowledge that would improve the implementation of public policy without any involvement in politics and policy adoption (Lee 2014; Roberts 1994).

The election of FDR—and the jolt it caused with the major expansion of public administration at the federal level—provided an opening for a more ambitious agenda by these academics and professionalizers, and the Rockefellers. In November 1933, Robert Crane, the SSRC executive director, wrote the president to inform him that the council was considering funding two blue-ribbon research commissions, one on public service personnel. It would be a broad-based investigation of government staffing and the effectiveness of the then-current merit system. This would cover all personnel issues, including recruitment, training, selection, performance assessment (also called efficiency ratings), classification of positions, promotion, firings, appeals, and pensions. The structure and management of CSCs and alternatives to CSCs were within the scope of the commission's inquiry, but not leading or explicit issues.

Crane asked for FDR's reaction to the two SSRC initiatives and—hopefully—White House expressions of support. Given that the personnel study would likely entail surveys of federal agencies, the president's blessing would smooth the way for agency cooperation. Roosevelt replied that he approved of the study, in particular because the subject was of "major significance in the life and welfare of the American people" (Commission 1935b, vi).[11] (Given how controversial the Rockefellers still were, Crane's inquiry indicated indirectly the potential political sensitivities regarding SSRC's source of funding. For example, a sub-headline in the *Los Angeles Times* coverage of the creation of the commission was "Research to be Financed by Rockefeller Trust."[12] The concern about the link to the Rockefellers was later part of FDR's finely tuned political decision-making when he insisted that the Brownlow Committee would be an official White House study and pointedly excluded Rockefeller funding from tainting the eventual report.)

With FDR's semi-blessing, in December 1933 the SSRC formally created a Commission of Inquiry on Public Service Personnel and allocated $57,500 for its expenses.[13] It was shaped and designed to look like a major independent blue ribbon citizens' panel. Following the template that reformers evolved during the Progressive era, the goal was to develop credibility through its membership and operations, maximize publicity, represent the public interest, and benefit from qualified nonpartisan experts, both from within the US and in Western Europe. Its chair was a senior academic (L. D. Coffman, president of the University of Minnesota) and members included representatives of the private sector (Ralph Budd, president of the Chicago, Burlington & Quincy Railroad; Arthur L. Day, Vice President of Corning Glass Works), a senior political scientist (Merriam), and a former practitioner (Brownlow). Gulick was staff director, and he hired four experts to assist the commission by gathering and submitting "relevant facts" (Commission 1935b, vii). The commission also requested detailed reports by experts on different aspects of public personnel, eventually publishing those reports as twelve monographs.

During 1934, the commission held hearings in ten American cities, as well as in London (at the American Embassy), with invited testifiers from the public sector, business, and academe. It subsequently published a 721-page transcript of its hearings (Commission 1935a).[14] The mainstream media, as one of the traditional supporters of civil service reform, duly reported on the work of the commission, giving it additional stature and credibility. In particular, hometown hearings triggered local coverage.[15] But other news pegs, such as the announcement creating the commission and the release of the final report, also prompted coverage.[16]

The idea of shifting government personnel administration from an independent civil service commission to a manager who would report directly to the chief elected executive (whether president, governor, or mayor) was a secondary, but relatively constant, theme of the study commission's work. The concept was raised in the staff paperwork to the commissioners and by commissioners during the public hearings.[17] William Beyer's research monograph for the commission on municipal CSCs categorized the traditional orthodoxy as the "early" model that had prevailed for the preceding thirty years. He suggested that they had largely accomplished the original goal of the civil service reform movement, namely of replacing the spoils system with merit employment. Now, he softly concluded, the "best arrangement probably is to have a personnel director immediately responsible to the chief executive," mirroring the new consensus on budgeting and purchasing directors (Beyer 1935, 100).[18]

Testifying in support of the reform orthodoxy at the hearing in New York City, Eliot Kaplan of the Civil Service Reform Association nonetheless conceded that he would like to see CSCs "give more attention to aiding the administration." But when Brownlow asked point blank about the model of a "single personnel administrator," Kaplan replied that such a model might work in the absence of a CSC, but establishing and maintaining a CSC was preferable (Commission 1935b, 204, 206). On the other hand, at the Chicago hearing, Clarence Ridley of the International City Managers' Association (ICMA) stated that a corollary of the city manager approach was "that the chief administrator should have control over personnel matters" (230).

After the end of the hearings and the submission of all the research monographs, staff member Lucius Wilmerding Jr. prepared a summary, along with his own recommendations for desirable personnel reforms. Among them he proposed "centralizing control of administration in a single body subordinate to the chief executive." This would include the now-traditional budget bureau and "a division of personnel with duties of controlling the civil service in all matters except those which concern merely the day-to-day management of the departments." Rather than abolishing the CSC, he suggested it be retained, but with the sole duty of conducting examinations during the open competition stage of recruitment. All other general personnel matters would be vested in "the central personnel bureau" (Wilmerding 1935, 272–74).

The commission's formal report and recommendations were released in January 1935. Brownlow later reminisced that the larger themes of the report emerged from the conversations the commission members had "in our long train trips across the country" for the hearings. One theme was "the need for better organization for personnel administration and less about the spoils system and even less about the civil service system as a means of fighting it" (Brownlow 1958, 296–97).

Specifically, the final report called for superseding the traditional orthodoxy of independent CSCs, which had a negative and policing orientation about employment issues and tended to focus on tight regulation and controls. This paradigm was understandable and necessary to fight the spoils system and to create a civil service of experts who were separated from politics. Now, the needs were very different. Modern government required development of a *career* service system. The commission's recommendation in the area of CSC and organizational structure built on that theme. Each unit of government needed to have "an agency for personnel administration, to render constructive personnel service instead of devoting its entire attention to the policing of appointments, as has been all too common under civil service. The personnel agency must have adequate powers, staff, and appropriations to maintain and develop the career service system and render personnel service to the operating departments and their responsible officers" (Commission 1935b, 4). The recommendation was carefully worded. It did not explicitly state the obverse and inevitable corollary to its preferred outcome: the near abolition of CSCs. This probably would have looked like too large a break from the past, instead of the evolution and improvement that the commission was seeking to represent.

Later in the report a few details were added. Each public personnel agency would be headed by an appointed director who would be "thoroughly qualified"

(31). It was unclear who would make the appointment and what "thoroughly" meant in terms of qualifications. It apparently had a meaning different from that required of the staff of the personnel agency, the latter needing to have "technical" skills and expertise. There would still be a vestigial CSC or board, largely for more formal roles such as promulgating rules and hearing legal appeals.

For this aspect of the reforms the commission was recommending, its most controversial aspect was left unstated until the sixth-to-last page of the 84-page report. The new personnel agencies as the successors to the old CSCs "will have to establish themselves *as part of administration*, not as an outside interference" (78, emphasis added). This would be crucial for a successful pivot from the old civil service system to "modern personnel administration" (79).

The report in general was praised in all the right places. The *New York Times* editorialized it was "a counsel of perfection."[19] The *Christian Science Monitor* (*CSM*) editorial stated that it was "excellent."[20] Charles Beard, *éminence grise* of the academy, reviewed it in the *American Political Science Review*. He characterized the report as "one of the landmarks in the history of American thought about government." He particularly liked that it "swept away a whole flock of slogans, clichés, and escape-formulas employed by superficial thinkers" (Beard 1935).[21]

In the *New York Herald Tribune*, Ordway Tead, a prominent management theorist, specifically endorsed the CSC reorganization recommendations in the report. He wrote that the commission "wisely insisted" on this major reformulation of personnel management from a negative approach to a positive one. These changes "do not involve alterations of fundament law so much as they do a new attitude on the part of civil service commissioners and of administrators and new proceedings in managerial operation."[22]

However, a reviewer with a more traditional civil service reform background who was active in the National Municipal League would only describe the report as "helpful and provocative" and stated that it would "provide the basis for a valuable discussion" (Woodruff 1935, 205). It was a hint that the reforms proposed by the commission, including shifting from the focus on merit to that of management, would not be easy to implement. The orthodoxy was alive and well, with deep roots and vitality. This symbolic shot across the bow foreshadowed a battle royal that was about to unfold.

Planning Behind Closed Doors for FDR's Second Term: The President's Committee on Administrative Management, 1936

It is not necessary to recount the full history of the President's Committee on Administrative Management (a.k.a. the Brownlow Committee) as it has been well presented in the literature (Newbold and Terry 2006; Roberts 1996b; 1995; Karl

1979; Polenberg 1976). A few details of that larger battle are relevant to the focus on the idea of a presidential personnel agency.

First, as alluded to earlier, FDR flatly rejected having Rockefeller funding to underwrite the study. He felt the link "would have a bad effect on the Hill."[23] This meant that there was no formal link between the official federal PCAM and the Rockefeller-funded Commission of Inquiry on Public Service Personnel or the SSRC, which had sponsored it. Nothing from the commission's report would obligate or automatically transfer over to PCAM.[24] While the ostensible purpose was to avoid the tainting that would be insinuated by using Rockefeller funding, what FDR cared about even more was that PCAM would be wholly under his political and editorial control.[25]

Second, reforming the federal personnel system was high on FDR's initial and self-generated agenda for the committee's attention. During his first meeting with Merriam and several federal staffers in February 1936 about the idea of a presidential reorganization initiative, Roosevelt immediately volunteered that he wanted to be sure PCAM's report would not include any recommendations on some important topics that he already knew he was against, such as creating formal assistant presidents or a formal Executive Committee of the Cabinet. This naturally led to a discussion of what topics were okay. Brownlow quoted the president telling the PCAM members about his dissatisfaction with the structure of the CSC and how it impeded his own personnel management duties: "The way it works, the President is handicapped in trying to find out what the commission wants. If they come into this office and I ask them a question, all three of them have to go out in the corridor or some other place, hold a caucus, and come back and answer me.... Sometimes weeks later they may give me some sort of answer. I would like to deal with one man alone" (Brownlow 1958, 421).[26]

FDR was far from the first senior federal official to articulate the perspective that public administration was more effective in an agency directed by one person compared to that of a multi-member governing commission. In 1781, Alexander Hamilton wrote "that an administration by single men [as opposed to committees] was essential to the proper management of the affairs of this country" (quoted in McCraw 2012, 62).

By the end of the February 1936 meeting, FDR approved a short list of four topics for PCAM to bring recommendations on, one of which was "Civil Service arrangements."[27] Merriam described the subject the president raised a bit more specifically, as "the problem of the organization of the Civil Service (particularly the Commission)."[28]

Third, as a result of the president's guidance, PCAM's work relating to the CSC reorganization largely reversed the standard sequential logic model of methodical and empirical social science research. This typically began with an open-minded collection of data, followed by internal staff studies summarizing the thrust of the data, and then concluding with a final report based on the facts. For CSC reorganization, the basics of the final report came first, then came finalization of the staff study to undergird it, and data collection was largely was not done at all. This was not empirical and value-free social science. Instead, it was normative (and somewhat partisan and ideological) reorganization masked to look like the former.

In many respects, the Brownlow Committee's personnel agenda was simply act two of the preceding Commission of Inquiry. Regarding the idea to shift from a merit system protected by an independent CSC to a management-oriented personnel agency, Brownlow, Merriam, and Gulick were ready to pick up exactly where they had left off in 1935. As a result of these factors, PCAM's confidential work during 1936 showed only minor evolution in the basic idea of replacing CSCs with executive-centered personnel management agencies.

FDR publicly announced the creation of the committee on March 22, 1936. PCAM's work on this subject then began with a Merriam memo to Brownlow and Gulick in advance of their first official meeting on April 11. Merriam listed a dozen possible subject areas for the group (excluding, of course, subjects FDR had already vetoed). The second of twelve was: "Should we reconsider the position of the Civil Service Commission as a personnel agency in relation to the Executive?"[29] It was approved, and PCAM quickly hired Floyd W. Reeves as the staffer to write the personnel report. Reeves had recently left the TVA and was on an extended leave from his faculty position at the University of Chicago (Niehoff 1991).[30]

Brownlow met with FDR on April 28 and May 6.[31] The president approved the working agenda the committee members had developed, along with the input of the committee's newly hired staff director, Joseph Harris (who previously had worked for the SSRC Committee on Public Administration).

By late April, a five-page outline of the personnel agenda, initially drafted by Reeves and edited by Harris, was circulated to the committee members and staff in advance of meetings on May 9–10. It went to the heart of the matter quickly, starting with the conclusion that "the need for more effective personnel management and for a staff agency charged with this responsibility is apparent." The CSC was not, heretofore, functioning as a policymaking or policy-development body for the breadth of federal personnel management issues nor for executive branch–wide matters. In fact, its work was "somewhat routine in nature," mostly dealing with examinations for applicants for vacant classified positions. Therefore, the central question for the staff and committee emanated from the Commission of Inquiry on Public Service Personnel: "Is a civil service commission an essential element in a sound system of personnel administration in the federal government, or should all aspects of personnel administration be made a part of administrative management?"[32]

All details and questions flowed from the premise that there should be a central personnel agency. But should it be a free-standing presidential agency or a unit within a larger central presidential management agency, combining personnel with budgeting, purchasing, and accounting? For the central personnel entity, how much should it be staffed by permanent civil servants? In particular, should the positions with major responsibility in the agency be civil service or at-will appointments? If the latter, appointed by whom? The president? The head of the central administrative management agency? Finally, should the CSC be retained in some vestigial manner, perhaps as monitor and official guardian of a nonpartisan and apolitical career service? Or perhaps to exercise quasi-judicial functions, such as hearing appeals?

After feedback and suggestions during the May 9–10 meetings of the committee members and staff, Reeves was asked to submit a "rough draft" of the key parts of his report in *three weeks*. This hurry-up schedule demonstrated that PCAM was not a study committee engaging in data collection, but rather a recommending body that did not need to wait for empirical results or in-depth research. Reeves began his draft with the doctrine that "personnel administration is an integral part of general administration, and cannot be segregated from management and separately discharged without disadvantage both to the administration of the personnel function and to general administration."[33]

By now, it was a settled issue that Reeves and PCAM would recommend a central personnel agency that would be within the president's office. Reeves's late May draft began fleshing out the details. The agency would have the mission to initiate, recommend, review, and decide all important matters of personnel policy. Implementation would be left to the personnel offices in executive branch departments and independent agencies. The new presidential agency would be headed by a single administrator, if only because the board structure of the CSC demonstrated lack of accountability, supervision, decision-making, and efficiency. The new central personnel agency should be of equal rank and standing with the central fiscal control agency (i.e., BOB or its successor) and any other central management-related agencies. All the central management agencies would report to the same assistant to the president.[34]

The senior officials of the central personnel agency would be "appointed in *accordance* with the civil service rules and regulations" (emphasis added), a phrasing that implied a process different from appointment *through* the civil service process. Also, specifically about the head of the new agency, Reeves's draft suggested that the *initial* head of the agency be appointed "by a specially appointed civil service board of examiners," but was vague about subsequent agency heads.[35]

The CSC would be retained, but with a much more limited role, "relieving it of much distracting detail."[36]

PCAM staff director Harris was relatively satisfied with the initial draft. In early July, he circulated a mimeographed version of it to all PCAM staff members for feedback and suggestions. One relatively new idea added during this process was that the head of the central personnel agency would either automatically be the chair of the CSC or the secretary to the commission, thus tying whatever would remain of the CSC more closely to the central agency and under its control. Then, in August, Harris planned to circulate the revised version to "30 or more other persons" specializing in personnel matters and who were in sync with the direction PCAM expected to take.[37] However, by now, Reeves was receding into the background, giving up control of his draft report. Revisions were being done by Paul T. David (also from the TVA)[38] and John F. Miller (from Gulick's IPA),[39] who were described as "assisting" Reeves.[40]

By late October, the recommendations for the central personnel agency had been further refined by the committee members, Harris, and senior staffer Herbert Emmerich. The head of the agency would have the title Civil Service Commissioner and all the substantive powers of the CSC would be transferred to him. He would be a nonpolitical personnel professional, appointed by the president from a list of three highest scoring candidates selected through a competitive civil service examination process. The old CSC would now be called the Civil Service Board, have seven members, and be an advisory council to monitor and promote the principles of a merit system.[41]

On November 14, just weeks after he was reelected, FDR met with Brownlow and Gulick. They updated him on how the report was gelling and sought feedback on what he liked so far and didn't. Based on Gulick's summary of the meeting, FDR approved the premise of the personnel plan, namely that personnel management, along with planning and budgeting, were the basic working tools of a manager and therefore should operate close to and under the president's direction. FDR characterized the CSC as "hopeless" (Brownlow 1958, 382). He gave "instant and unqualified approval" for the idea to make the CSC an advisory board while shifting all its substantive powers to a single central personnel officer (L. White 1945, 141). According to Gulick, the president also enigmatically added that the reorganization of the CSC "may help us elsewhere, too" (quoted in Brownlow 1958, 382).[42]

With the president's approval and feedback, the committee went into high gear to prepare the penultimate version of its report and be ready to submit a final draft to the president in mid-December. On December 10, Emmerich and G. Lyle Belsley submitted a further revision of Reeves's original draft.[43] In it they renamed the central personnel agency as the Civil Service Administration and the title of its head as the Administrator of Civil Service. They retained the appointment process for the initial agency head through a special board of examiners and clarified that this process would apply to all subsequent ones, as well. However, they clarified the qualifications of the position, moving it from a technocratic CSC-type staff professional to someone who would be "highly competent, should possess a broad knowledge of personnel administration, and should be a trained executive." Their other important revision was that the administrator would "hold office at the discretion of the president." This was not a civil service–style position with removal only for cause, did not have a set term, and was a political appointee serving at the pleasure of the president.[44]

Meetings with the president and revisions to the draft now came fast and furious. Brownlow (and sometimes other PCAM members) went to the White House to go over the evolving draft with the president on December 18, 20, and 23 and January 4 and 6. For the coupling of the proposals to expand significantly the proportion of federal employees who would be under the merit system with the modernization of federal personnel management, FDR wrote on one draft: "I think that is grand, I have Oks all down the line."[45]

Minor changes in the personnel section, mostly in tone and style, were now frequent. In terms of substance, the new civil service administrator was now expected to be "a qualified and experienced executive," rather than a "trained" one. In an effort to conform to customs of senior appointments and reduce potential criticism, the administrator was now to be nominated by the president to the Senate and would require the Senate's confirmation.[46] When reviewing the last draft of the report, FDR asked to change one of the enumerated responsibilities of the new advisory Civil Service Board. He deleted its role in the appointment of special boards and panels for difficult and new problems and replaced it with a much blander role of advising the president on matters "which cannot be handled satisfactorily through established channels."[47]

It was now time to go public.

2
The Political Battle over Creating a Presidential Personnel Agency, 1937–1939

Unveiling the Idea, January 1937

The Brownlow Committee report was formally submitted to the president on January 8, 1937, with FDR briefing congressional leaders on the 10th (before it was released publicly), holding a press conference on it on the 11th, and sending it to Congress and the CSC on the 12th. It was a political bombshell all around, including the civil service recommendations. Of the five major committee recommendations, the second and third related to HR:

> 2. The managerial agencies of the Government, particularly those dealing with the budget, efficiency research, personnel, and planning, should be greatly strengthened and developed as arms of the Chief Executive.
> 3. The merit system should be extended upward, outward, and downward to cover all non-policy-determining posts, and the civil service system should be reorganized and opportunities established for a career system attractive to the best talent of the Nation. (PCAM 1937, 4)

The contents of the report fleshed out these recommendations. Taking on the orthodoxy, it stated: "After more than 50 years of experience with civil service in Federal, State, and local governments, there is overwhelming evidence to show that the original theory of merely protecting appointments from political influence through a legalistic system of civil-service administration is inadequate to serve democratic government under modern conditions. There is still need for protection, but the urgent new need today is for the development of a real career service through positive, constructive, modern personnel administration" (PCAM 1937, 7).

The report spared little from its critique of the current CSC, including that "the board form of organization is unsuited to the work of a central personnel agency." It was "slow, cumbersome, wasteful, and ineffective" tending to "a negative, protective, and legalistic role." Its members were appointed on a partisan basis and its mission contained "a fundamental flaw," namely of administering the civil service system while simultaneously being expected to "appraise and criticize its own administration." By shifting to a single civil service administrator, personnel management would have "a degree of unity, energy, and responsibility impossible to obtain in an administrative agency headed by a full-time board of several members." The process of selecting the administrator through a special examining board would assure a competitive and nonpartisan basis for selecting an HR professional with full technical qualifications and experience. This process would demonstrate that "the merit principle would be extended to the very top of the Civil Service Administration." The president would have to choose from the three candidates certified by the special board and Senate confirmation would be required. While the person would serve at the pleasure of the president, successors could only be named through the same process. The committee report argued that "personnel management is an essential element of executive management. To set it apart or to organize it in a manner unsuited to serve the needs of the Chief Executive and the executive establishments is to render it impotent and ineffective" (PCAM 1937, 9–11).

This criticism of the CSC was based on the view that its autonomy was a significant obstacle to making personnel management more responsive to the president's management duties. But, contradictorily, in a separate part of the report the committee tried to tamp down potential claims of the politicization of civil service by arguing that its recommendation to create a presidential personnel agency was not all that different from the status quo. After all, it said, the CSC was currently directly responsible to the president, its members were appointed by the president, and—despite having indefinite terms—served at his pleasure.[1] Therefore, shifting to an individual civil service administrator would not be all that much of a change.

(The Reeves report and the other staff studies were not released at that point. Ostensibly in honor of the second anniversary of the Commission of Inquiry in January 1937, Gulick edited an issue of the *Annals* on government personnel issues. It included an article by Reeves which essentially summarized his PCAM staff study, although carefully not attributing the contents to the committee [Reeves 1937].)

The president did not try to downplay or hide the section of the report relating to personnel management. At the White House briefing for Democratic congressional leaders, he said that the CSC "is the weakest agency in the government." He needed the basic management powers to lead the executive branch, specifically with new presidential managerial agencies for fiscal, personnel, and planning matters. Regarding personnel, he said "the President needs a single administrator to operate the civil service system. He should be part of my establishment" (Emmerich 1971, 208).

At his press conference, FDR said that 80 percent of the population believed in the principles of a nonpolitical merit-based career system for government and asserted that the committee recommendations would uphold and enhance those principles. The new Civil Service Board would be a public guardian of those principles, while the new administrator would appropriately shift the broader managerial responsibility for personnel (along with planning and budgeting) to "an adjunct of the President's own office" (Roosevelt 1972, 9: 57). The press had only one question on that point, regarding the civil service administrator's term of office. Brownlow, who attended at the president's request, jumped in, clarifying that if a president fired the incumbent, the president could choose someone else from the list of three from which the incumbent had been chosen, rather than requiring a new examination process (Roosevelt 1972, 9: 93–94).

In his message the next day to Congress, as a kind of cover letter to the report itself, the president noted that the committee report criticized many current aspects of federal operations, including his own; "nor does the Committee spare the inadequacy of the civil-service system." In his own summary of the five recommendations, he slightly reworded the third on personnel administration, evidently to be more explicit about the suggested change and to preempt some likely criticisms. He said PCAM sought to "reorganize the civil-service system as *a part of management* under a single, *responsible* administrator, and create a citizen board to serve as the *watch dog of the merit system*" (US Senate 1937a, 3, emphasis added).

That same day, FDR sent a copy of the report to the CSC, with the mild apology: "I had hoped for an opportunity to talk with you before sending the Reorganization Report and Message up to Congress, particularly with reference to the part that affects the present status of the Civil Service setup." Probably trying to prevent the CSC from going public in opposition, he said that he wanted "to talk to with you about it just as soon as possible," implying that the commission should feel bound to withhold public reaction until such a meeting took place.[2]

Initial Reactions, 1937

Indicating the centrality and importance of the personnel section of the reorganization plan, it was specifically criticized on Capitol Hill in the first wave of reactions to the president's message the day it was received (and the day after FDR's press briefing). According to the *Washington Post*, "objections were raised to transferring administration of the merit system from a bipartisan commission to a single administrator, who would be directly under the President."[3] The conservative *Chicago Tribune* said that Congressman Bertrand Snell (R-NY), the House Minority Leader, "assailed the abolition of the Civil Service Commission."[4]

Within a few days, the *New York Herald Tribune* editorialized in favor of the Brownlow personnel recommendations, *except* its CSC reorganization. The paper characterized the plan for a single civil service administrator as "at once autocratic and cumbersome," declaring that it "would crush the whole system under the charge of politics." The editorial complained that the Brownlow recommendation was "a misguided faith in academic theory. The bi-partisan system has worked. It ought to be retained."[5]

There were countervailing positive voices as well. For example, after a vote by its national board of directors, the League of Women Voters endorsed the plan because it would be "the beginning in earnestness to enlist, train and reward public servants skilled in managing our common concerns."[6] Professor Leonard White, a former Republican CSC member (appointed by FDR), now back at the University of Chicago, also endorsed the Brownlow plan, even though it did not reflect his vision of where "the center of gravity" of personnel management now held by the CSC should be relocated. He preferred to create a new executive staff attached to the Council of Personnel Administration, which was made up of the personnel directors of all executive branch departments and agencies.[7] Even though moving the CSC's powers to a presidential personnel agency was not White's ideal reform, he nonetheless endorsed the Brownlow recommendation.[8] White also elliptically endorsed the PCAM reform in an article in a British academic journal (White 1937, 553).

A pair of former CSC presidents expressed opposing views. Republican William Deming denounced the plan, saying that the CSC operated well as a multimember body, was efficient, was so busy that one person could not handle the workload, and that quasi-judicial responsibilities required a body that was autonomous and independent. Furthermore, he argued that "the standing of the merit system would be lowered by the proposal of the President."[9] On the other hand, Thomas Campbell, also a Republican appointee and now governor of Arizona, endorsed the Brownlow plan. He said the single administrator would "result in better and more effective personnel administration" because "commissions are clearly not suited to the performance of administrative duties . . . commissions carry on their work by compromise and indecision. This is an inefficient method of operation and usually results in needless confusion."[10]

The same happened with the leaders of the two major organizations of federal employees (but not labor unions, which were prohibited at the time). Luther Steward, president of the National Federation of Federal Employees, endorsed "without qualification" the Brownlow personnel recommendations.[11] His counterpart, Charles Stengle, head of the American Federation of Government Employees, said the plan "is destined to bring about regimentation of thinking on civil service policy" because it "would make the administrator the creature of the President, or vice versa."[12]

A national civic education radio broadcast presented a balanced program of speakers on both sides of the civil service controversy. Thurman Stoner, a lawyer active in the Democratic Party in Buffalo (NY), opposed the expansion of the merit system and especially the plan "to centralize control in the hands of a political appointee of the president himself."[13] Mrs. Eugene Meyer, a civic activist from Washington, DC (and wife of the owner of the *Washington Post*), supported it. Reacting to Stoner's and other public criticisms, Meyer said "such fears seem to me unnecessary." After all, she argued, the administrator would be monitored by the new Civil Service Board and would have to be highly qualified to be one of the three finalists recommended to the president by the special examining panel. It would be "impossible" for a political hack to make it to the list of finalists. The qualifications were so stringent that she hoped the position might appeal to personnel managers from the corporate world, not just those from the public sector. Meyer did, however, demur regarding the appointee serving at the president's pleasure. She suggested that the position should be in the classified service and the appointee only be dismissible for cause. Nonetheless, in all, she thought the advantages of a single administrator "are very great" and outweighed the status quo.[14]

CSC president Harry Mitchell finally got to see the president on January 28.[15] Speaking for the other Democratic commissioner, Mrs. Lucille Foster McMillin, as well as himself, he expressed strong disapproval of the plan, but committed to FDR not to openly and proactively lobby against it. In his memoir, Mitchell said he asked FDR what he should say if he (Mitchell) were asked his views, especially at a congressional hearing? Mitchell claimed that FDR replied, "Say whatever you think is right. You don't have to agree with my views unless you agree with them" (Mitchell 1985, 212).

In the diplomatic language of their post-meeting exchange of letters, Mitchell wrote "there is no thought that we would do anything to retard the program, but that we may feel free to answer questions asked by Members of Congress or others who have to do with the framing of appropriate legislation."[16] Mitchell then proceeded with a full-throated defense of the status quo by listing in the four-page letter all the "objections" he and Commissioner McMillin had. He used the traditional arguments for the orthodoxy, including the bipartisan nature of the commission members, the load of work, the benefits of a three-person decision-making body, and the quasi-judicial nature of some of the CSC's work.[17]

The president asked Brownlow to help draft a reply.[18] After conferring with Gulick and Merriam, Brownlow recommended avoiding specific point-by-point rebuttal and instead focusing the response on the generic argument that "administration is made more efficient" when conducted by a single head of an agency than a multiple-member board, and attached a draft reply.[19] FDR accepted part of the draft and dictated revised language in other parts.[20] The signed letter to Mitchell made more than a generic argument about the administrative inefficiencies of boards. FDR also stated that "Personnel administration must become an administrative arm of the executive just as is budget administration. It seems to me that this can be done better under the individual head system rather than under a board director just in the same way that a Budget Director always works out better than a Budget Commission."

To soften his refusal to budge, FDR asked Mitchell to "render indispensable assistance" during the process of "perfecting" the Brownlow plan, implying that some of Mitchell's concerns could possibly be resolved as long as they conformed to the principle of a single administrator of civil service. The president concluded with a veiled and mild threat of "knowing that I may count on you in this" request for cooperation.[21]

Congressional Consideration, 1937

The initial hearings on the Brownlow plan were conducted by the Joint Committee on Government Organization, consisting of the House and Senate Select Committees on reorganization. They took place from February through April (US Congress 1937). The initial presentations were by PCAM's three members, but largely dominated by Brownlow. Questions and comments by senators and congressmen ranged from skeptical to critical, sometimes focusing on large issues, sometimes small. However, the longer the proposal was pending on Capitol Hill, the greater the objections and concerns from outside stakeholders who would be negatively affected if it were to pass.

In the case of the CSC proposals, one stated concern came from an unanticipated direction. PCAM had been careful to circumscribe the process and qualifications for the civil service administrator. This was intended as reassurance that the appointee could not be someone who primarily had a political and partisan background. Instead, the examination process would end up with a list of three most qualified personnel experts recommended by a special examining board. During the hearings, several (majority party) members asked Brownlow why he was precluding the most qualified men, implicitly from the business sector, who would be reluctant while at the peak of their careers to participate in a competition for a job. If offered a position, they would likely accept it, but would not agree to be an applicant and candidate for it. In other words, why was the process so restrictive?

Brownlow had been expecting criticism from traditional civil service reformers against the PCAM plan, not from the other direction, of reducing the limitations on who the president could appoint. Brownlow smoothly replied that he did not expect the special examining board to conduct itself like the routine civil service processes for masses of positions. Rather, it could use measures of judgment that could be more selective than traditional factors and encompass broader concepts of "examination" markers, such as a person's writings, reputation, and accomplishments. He added that the examining board could invite individuals to apply and could assure them of discretion in their consideration (US Congress 1937, 105–06). Behind the scenes, several position papers were quickly drafted to address these concerns and tried to defend the original PCAM proposal from this unexpected criticism and to flesh out in more detail how the special examination process could include semi-recruitment of these "best men."[22]

Another interesting detail came out when Brownlow was questioned about why PCAM recommended that the president be given *six* administrative assistants (with "a passion for anonymity")? Why that number? Brownlow replied by listing six major areas under the president's executive responsibilities. One would be "a liaison officer" for personnel matters (US Congress 1937, 5). It was a foreshadowing of precisely what role William McReynolds would have: he would be one of the six administrative assistants to the president and his duties would include being the liaison officer for personnel management (chap. 3).

The audaciousness and sweep of the entire plan gradually accrued opposition. The Congress of 1937 was very different from those of FDR's first term. It would no longer pass comprehensive bills without exacting investigation and deliberate consideration. A reporter neatly captured the growing opposition to the civil service portion of the bill, stating that it "makes the civil service a sort of appanage of the White House."[23] Gulick hit back, saying in an article published in April 1937 that the PCAM personnel plan had been "criticized, particularly by individuals who have in the past made no contributions to the advance of civil service," but that it had "received the enthusiastic endorsement of those who have participated during the past five years in the renaissance of the movement for better government personnel" (Gulick 1937, 301).

By spring, it was clear that an omnibus bill encompassing all the subjects of PCAM's report and the president's message would not be passed, quickly or otherwise. It was sticky politically, gathering increasing opposition and criticism the longer it was pending. It didn't help that another reorganization bill was pending at the time. FDR called it court reorganization, but it was dubbed court packing by his opponents. The two bills gave the term reorganization something of a negative political meaning, largely trumping the earlier good-government usage.

The Democratic leadership in both houses had largely given up on pushing the Brownlow reorganization plan through as it was, and they considered it dead. FDR refused to accept that congressional verdict. He pressed the leadership to keep pushing for it. As a way to try to deflect the criticism of a single bill containing so many proposals, in May, congressional leaders reintroduced the package as four separate bills, one of which dealt with the CSC reorganization and a few other matters.[24] Reflecting the early and unexpected criticism of the limitations on the examination process for the civil service administrator, the bill deleted them, giving the president a free hand to nominate whomever he wished. The person had to have technical qualifications, but that was a relatively relaxed criterion compared to what the examination panel could have used. This loosening up of the front end of the process, however, was somewhat tightened at the back end, namely the issue of release. Instead of serving at the president's pleasure, the civil service administrator would be appointed to a fifteen-year term and could only be fired for cause (defined as inefficiency or neglect of duty). This change in the status of the incumbent similarly reflected an effort to be responsive to early criticism, in this case that PCAM was trying to politicize HR.[25]

To give some renewed momentum to the repackaging (and slight revision) of the CSC reform plan, PCAM released the Reeves study in late May, ostensibly proving the rightness of the president's personnel management plan because a nonpartisan expert in the field supported the changes.[26] The authorship of Reeves's report on personnel was now attributed to Reeves and Paul T. David. However, the published version reflected the further revisions made to the original Reeves draft by Miller, Emmerich, and Belsley, as discussed in the preceding chapter (PCAM 1937, 55–133).

Things were looking a bit better. Congressman John Cochran (D-MO), chair of the House Select Committee on Government Organization, attacked the Republicans for criticizing the proposal for a single head of civil service. He said that the Republicans had supported a similar reorganization plan submitted in previous years by Republican presidents.[27] A news story noted the opposition to the "creation of a single civil service administrator, but the President is expected to have his way."[28]

Best of all, the Brookings Institution avoided contradicting the PCAM recommendations relating to personnel management in its own report to congress on HR, released in June 1937. In 1936, in parallel to the president's reorganization initiative, the Senate (specifically, a committee chaired by conservative Senator Harry Byrd [D-VA]) hired Brookings to research and report on federal operations. Theoretically, PCAM and Brookings had separate missions and would not overlap and, therefore, would never be in a situation of disagreeing on the same topic. Behind the scenes, during early 1937, this was not the case regarding the role of the General Accounting Office (GAO).[29] There was fierce disagreement between the two entities, which raised the basic question if public administration was truly a value-free and nonpartisan field (Roberts 1995). PCAM breathed a sigh of relief when the Brookings report on the CSC in June omitted any comment on the PCAM reorganization plan "because that problem lies directly and fully in the field of the President's Committee on Administrative Management" (US Senate 1937b, 516).[30] So, even Byrd could not base his opposition on Brookings. That meant his was ideological and political opposition, not that of professional and scientific public administration.

The Senate Select Committee held a new round of reorganization hearings in August, this time limited to the bill that covered civil service and a few other PCAM issues (US Senate 1937c). The hearings indicated how positions had hardened on CSC reorganization, the sharper characterizations of it, and the inevitable rhetorical exaggerations that both sides engaged in.

Merriam and Gulick testified early in the series of sessions. (Brownlow was ill and homebound for about two months.) Their theme was that the PCAM recommendations were neither a bolt out of the blue nor hatched in the out-of-touch academy; rather, they largely reflected an accumulation of proposals for reform that had been made publicly in the past, including some of President Hoover's ideas and those of the Commission of Inquiry. These were not radical out-of-left-field or pie-in-the-sky ideas, but were instead ideas that had been in the public realm for years.

Many of the testifiers were already on the record as supporting or opposing the PCAM personnel recommendations. A newer voice of support came from the National Civil Service Reform League. The league had originally been the promoter of the orthodoxy of an independent and autonomous CSC, later straddling the opposing solutions of an independent multi-member board and a one-person board in closer relationship with the chief executive. Now it moved closer to the new reformers who had been pressing to overturn *in toto* the paradigm of the old reformers. The league's executive secretary, Eliot Kaplan, endorsed shifting the managerial work of the CSC to a single administrator. However, he asked to reinstate the PCAM's suggested civil service–type examination and appointment process for the new administrator. Kaplan also distinguished between ongoing administration of the civil service system and the adoption of new policies and regulations. For the latter role, he suggested creating a new three-person council to do that, but more closely allied with the president and the civil service administrator (US Senate 1937c, 144–45).[31]

New voices against the CSC reorganization included the conservative National Association of Manufacturers (136) and the Veterans of Foreign Wars (162). The latter said that the check-and-balance system of the three-member CSC was desirable. Senator Fred Brown (D-NH) challenged that claim. What did they think of the operation and leadership of the federal Veterans Administration, given that it was headed by a single administrator? Did the group think the VA should also be headed by a three-person commission? This was a relatively new line of argumentation for the supporters of FDR and PCAM: why was personnel management to be exempted from the general principle of clear and unitary agency leadership? The spokesman for the Veterans of Foreign Wars replied by claiming that the VA had no policymaking role, that it was merely implementing laws passed by Congress, while the personnel area required some degree of policymaking and regulation-adoption.

CSC president Mitchell also testified, submitting a long statement (largely similar to his letter to the president in February), but claiming that the concerns being raised were merely "to point out apparent inconsistencies in the bill in order that if desired the committee may arrange for clarification" (271). But when pressed for his position, he strongly opposed the reorganization to a single administrator because "it will eventually have the effect of making the Commission more political" (273). Committee chair James Byrnes (D-SC), an ally of FDR, challenged that assertion. Wasn't it true that the membership of the CSC always had a majority of its members representing the majority party? Yes, said Mitchell (who was appointed by FDR as a Democratic member of the commission). Wasn't it true that the two Democrats on the commission could enact any policy they preferred, even if opposed by the minority Republican commissioner? Yes, said Mitchell. Then how would it be different if a Democratic president appointed a Democratic civil service administrator, was the implicit question that Byrnes left unstated. Finally, Byrnes asked why Mitchell assumed that the decisions of a single administrator "would not be patriotic," while those of the current two Democratic commissioners were. Mitchell, thoroughly flustered, retreated by saying his observations were merely hearsay (274).[32]

Responding to FDR's strong insistence, the leadership of both houses arranged for the civil service bill to be reported out of committee in the late summer of 1937, so that the bill could be quickly taken up for floor debates while Congress was in session. The Senate committee report came out on August 17, recommending the bill without any amendments. As an indication of how toxic politically the term "reorganization" had become, due to the simultaneous legislative battles over court reorganization and executive branch reorganization, the title of the committee's report was "Government Organization," not government *re*organization (US Senate 1937d). (The court packing bill had been defeated in the Senate just a few weeks earlier, on July 22).

Regarding the CSC portion of the bill, the committee report largely echoed PCAM's arguments. "Old type" CSCs had a control approach to personnel management, motivated primarily to prevent the spoils system of employment. This was "a negative, passive, protective role, little concerned with the problems of building up a vigorous, able personnel administration. This type of civil-service administration is unsuited in this modern day to meet the needs of an age of administration" (9). What was needed was "a single, technically qualified administrator" (3). The committee's report went to some lengths to defend the president's and PCAM's approach. It noted that President Hoover had made a similar suggestion in 1932, that Wisconsin and Maryland had one-person state CSCs, and that "the trend" was in that direction. Then it made a somewhat novel argument. If one accepted the premise that personnel and budgeting were central management tools for a chief executive, then should the head of the Bureau of the Budget be replaced by a three-person commission? "No one" would recommend that. Such a structure "is equally unsuited to civil-service administration" (11). (A few months later, at the turn of the year, Byrd filed a very negative minority report. See the next subchapter.)

On August 18, the day after the Senate committee report, the House Select Committee on Government Organization also reported out a narrower bill, limited to personnel matters. In contents, it was slightly different from the Senate committee's bill, but largely followed the same basic approach. A major difference was that the House bill retained the Civil Service Board as an advisory and watchdog body, while the Senate bill made no mention of it. A minor difference was that the civil service administrator would serve an indefinite appointment, which apparently—though this was left unstated—meant he would serve at the pleasure of the president. Like the Senate bill, the committee report asserted that the reform it was proposing would "follow in the main the principles embodied" in recent state personnel reorganization laws passed in ten states in 1937. Those principles included "the close relationship of personnel administration to general administration, and not . . . the negative aspects of civil-service administration as in the past" (US House 1937, 3). The major problem of the status quo was that "it is difficult if not impossible for the President to exercise effectively the direction and leadership in bringing about more effective personnel management" (2).

Accompanying the majority report was a minority report from the two Republican congressmen on the select committee. In a one-paragraph statement, they fiercely opposed the bill because it "will destroy the last hope of any nonpartisan protection for the civil-service employee" and because the advisory board "would absolutely be unable to function satisfactorily." The creation of a Civil Service Administration headed by an administrator in lieu of the CSC "is designed to accomplish political control over the selection and retention of our Government employees" (US House 1937, Part 2).

But then nothing happened. There were still a few days left in the 1st session of the 75th Congress, which did not adjourn until August 21, the end of the week after the two bills had come out of committee. In mid-October, the lack of action prompted FDR to use his constitutional power to call Congress back into a special (2nd) session. On the evening after signing the proclamation for the special session, he held a Fireside Chat on the radio to explain to the public his reasons. One was reorganization. Of the inaction on reorganization he said, "I recognize that democratic processes are necessarily and rightly slower than dictatorial processes. But I refuse to believe that democratic processes need be dangerously slow" (Roosevelt 1969, 1937: 434–35). In a message to Congress on the first day of the special session, he restated the need for reorganization, including "a personnel agency . . . through which the Chief Executive may coordinate the executive functions." The benefits of reorganizing the civil service system would include "a statutory modernized machinery for the permanent enforcement of merit principles in appointment, promotion, and personnel management throughout the government service" (Roosevelt 1969, 1937: 498).

Even then, and for the rest of 1937, neither house took up the bills that had been reported out and recommended by the majorities of Senate and House committees in August. The special session, from November 15 to December 21, was a bust regarding reorganization. In part this reflected the larger political scene. The political blowout over the court packing bill along with the Brownlow reorganization bills had severely damaged FDR's political standing. In November 1936, he had won reelection by a landslide. Now, in the fall of 1937, less than a year later, he was at a nadir of political influence. No longer was this a Congress that passed practically everything he had recommended during his first term. Now, he still had the support of the leadership, but not all of the rank-and-file members. They would no longer take on faith bills that the president recommended. They were much more leery of following him. The leadership may have been pushing for floor consideration of the CSC bills from the Senate and House select committees, but could no longer count on passage. Rather than risk another major loss for the president after the court packing failure, the leadership had little maneuvering room and less optimism about dominating the results. So neither bill was sent to the floor for a debate and vote. For the moment, CSC reorganization (along with the other PCAM topics) was stalemated on Capitol Hill.

Two days before Congress was to convene in the special session, former president Hoover weighed in. He wanted to rally the opposition and countervail any perceptions of political momentum in favor of the personnel reorganization.

PCAM and the congressional committee reports had claimed throughout 1937 that their version of reorganizing the CSC was similar to what the Republican president had suggested in 1932. Speaking at the dedication of the new Maxwell Building of Syracuse University's School of Citizenship and Public Affairs, Hoover saw no validity to any kind of similarity between his principles of civil service administration and FDR's. Hoover said of the proposal for a one-person civil service manager that "no matter what the words of that bill may purport to mean, it is clear that the plan is to destroy the progress we have made and substitute personal political control." The current CSC approach needed no reforms, as it "has for fifty years given fine service and held high standards of training and freedom from politics in public service."[33] Hoover, sometimes called "the Great Engineer" for his professional work before entering public service, had credibility on this issue. Having addressed the topic of federal reorganization repeatedly since serving as President Coolidge's secretary of commerce, he was viewed as a management expert and student of government organization. Hoover's views gave further impetus to the opponents of CSC reorganization. But Hoover's newly stated opposition could still be discounted as motivated at least in part by partisan and ideological reasons, rather than being that of a truly nonpartisan and neutral public administration *expert*.

Trying to put the best possible interpretation on how the idea had been treated on Capitol Hill in 1937, PCAM staff director Harris wrote that the concept of a civil service administrator "has called out some criticism, but, in general, friends of civil service are in favor of the change" (Harris 1937, 868). Not really.

The Brookings Report by Lewis Meriam, December 1937

The terms of the debate changed on December 1. That day, the Brookings Institution released a 62-page pamphlet titled *Personnel Administration in the Federal Government: An Examination of Some Pending Proposals* that was a flat-out attack on the PCAM-inspired idea for civil service reform (Meriam 1937).

Its author was Lewis Meriam, one of Brookings's staff researchers. Meriam had the same kind of credentials that Brownlow and Gulick had. He was Harvard graduate, held a law degree, and started his career as a researcher in the US Bureau of Census and the Children's Bureau, at which time he had published several policy studies. He had been on the permanent full-time staff of the Institute for Government Research (a predecessor of Brookings) since 1916. One of his major activities in the 1920s had been heading a study of federal Indian affairs and administration that had been commissioned by the secretary of interior and funded by the Rockefellers (Meriam 1928). Just a year before the CSC pamphlet was published, in 1936, Meriam was awarded a PhD from Brookings itself.[34] In other words, he, too, was a public administration expert.[35] Harris, who disdained Meriam for his overt and covert opposition to PCAM's report, nonetheless acknowledged that Meriam "at that time was greatly admired for his knowledge of how national government works" (Harris 1983, 150).

Not only that, but Meriam was viewed especially as a *personnel* expert within the larger field of public administration.[36] For example, Harry Mitchell, president of the CSC beginning in May 1933, recalled the awkward structure he found when he arrived, of a presidentially named CSC secretary (a statutory designation assigned to the president to make) and a separate CSC-appointed chief examiner. To untangle the inevitable disharmonies that arose between the two office holders, the CSC turned to Meriam for advice. Mitchell described Meriam as a man "who had considerable knowledge of Civil Service matters" (Mitchell 1985, 205). Meriam's report recommended that the commission have "a single executive officer responsible for the administration of all the activities of the Commission" (206).[37] The problem was that FDR could use his statutory powers to appoint a CSC secretary whenever he wanted to, without approval of the commissioners and without coordination with the designated chief examiner. According to Mitchell, the commissioners met with FDR (early in his first term) to talk it over. He agreed not to appoint a secretary, permitting the chief examiner to serve as the commission's chief administrative officer, too (207).

Meriam circulated in the same small professional networks of the PCAM members and staff. For example, he occasionally spent summers teaching at the University of Chicago, including a course on personnel administration. When there, he routinely interacted with Brownlow, White, and Merriam professionally and socially. Meriam also had occasional contact with Guy Moffett, the Rockefeller philanthropies' funding officer for public administration. In 1934, Meriam helped organize the public hearings of the Commission of Inquiry (chap. 1) in Washington and was the resident manager of Brownlow's Public Administration Clearing House (PACH) small branch office there for several years. In general, Brownlow thought well of him in 1933–34, placing Meriam partially on his payroll and sometimes conferring with Meriam on various research projects.[38]

Just months before releasing his critique of PCAM's CSC recommendations, Meriam spent the summer of 1937 at the University of Chicago. One of his courses that summer was called "Personnel Administration in Public Welfare." Given that Brookings approved his civil service reorganization pamphlet for publication in November 1937, Meriam likely had been drafting it (or at least thinking about it) in Chicago that summer, while at the same time socializing with his soon-to-be all-out adversaries.[39]

Meriam was not a one-dimensional conservative. For example, in early 1937, when Brookings was finalizing its general report to Senator Byrd as the counterweight to PCAM's report, Meriam expressed frustration in-house that Byrd et al. viewed economy and efficiency in government in too simplistic a way. The subject was more textured than that, he said, and while government was not perfect, not *everything* it did was wrong and wasteful.[40]

Meriam's personnel report came out a few months after the sharp disagreements between Brookings and PCAM on reorganizing GAO broke out into open warfare in spring 1937 (Roberts 1995). In that context, Meriam's critique can be seen partly as Brookings hitting PCAM back where it hurt. The introduction to the personnel report, authored by Fred W. Powell, head of Brookings's Institute for Government Research, hinted at this in a somewhat defensive tone. He said that the pending bills on civil service reform "deserve *critical* examination" because of the importance of the topic. Given this situation, "the Brookings Institution has therefore *asked*" Meriam to prepare the report (Merriam 1937, v, emphases added). This implied that Meriam was not the report's prime mover and had passively accepted an assignment originating with senior management. Further buttressing the ostensible credibility of its contents, Powell stated the report had been vetted not only through Brookings's "customary staff committee," but also by three other of its staff researchers. This special treatment suggested that Brookings was preemptively trying to reinforce the credibility of the results from expected criticism by PCAM and the supporters of the president.

Meriam's 1937 criticisms of PCAM's HR recommendations were not a bolt out of the blue. In 1931, Feldman's report to Congress (chap. 1) quoted from a Meriam position statement supporting more centralized personnel management, but opposing elimination of the CSC. Meriam argued back then that his scenario was merely a kind of go-slow reform approach compared to those calling for wholesale reorganization, including abolishing the CSC. Instead, Meriam wrote, let a new central personnel agency establish itself and create a record over several years before deciding irrevocably if the CSC should be abolished and its responsibilities transferred *in toto* to that new agency (US House 1931, 258–59).[41]

Meriam was nothing if not consistent. In 1934, he testified before the Commission of Inquiry as an expert from Brookings. (This was separate from his role in helping organize the Washington hearing.) Gulick asked him if "the government as a whole needs a personnel officer?" Meriam replied, "We have a centralized personnel system in the Civil Service Commission. This should be the central personnel office." Gulick tried again: didn't the structure of the CSC "thwart good administration?" Answer: no, "the Commission doesn't thwart good administration," rather such legislatively enacted policies as veterans preference and geographical apportionment of employment (by states) impeded good and efficient personnel management in the federal government. Brownlow tried a different tack. Wasn't there a danger with the current structure of the commission that it could become too cooperative with departments and agencies? No, said Meriam (Commission 1935a, 109). (By the end of that year, Brownlow had pushed Meriam entirely off his PACH payroll.[42])

The 1937 Brookings report was a fierce attack on PCAM's proposals for reorganizing personnel management and the underlying rationales for those recommended changes.[43] Meriam found nothing beneficial in abolishing the three-person CSC and replacing it with a civil service administrator who would serve in the president's office and a seven-person Civil Service Board that would be wholly advisory. The three-person CSC worked well, Meriam said. If it had problems, that was largely due to inadequate funding by Congress or antipathy by a president. Also, the tone and language of the report were more personal and pointed than the abstract and impersonal academic style of detachment and moderation.

One of Meriam's recurring lines of attack was the misapplication of the city manager model of public administration reform to the federal government. A city manager was wholly accountable to a city council, and hence had only one political boss. To assign all personnel responsibilities to the city manager and his personnel director made sense. But not so in the federal government. The president was not the federal equivalent of a city manager. Rather, administrative agencies were responsible to two political bodies, the president and Congress. Therefore, it was impossible to argue—short of amending the Constitution—that a president should have the same control over personnel management as a city manager (18, 28). The CSC was a form of administration that could be accountable both to the legislative and executive branches, he said.

Meriam attacked head-on PCAM's claim (dating back to the Commission of Inquiry) that there was a need to support and develop a "career service" rather than a civil service. He sneered at that term as a mere "slogan" (35) that, if it were a serious proposal, should be fully debated by Congress and "not be slipped over by the use in a statute of such an ill-defined term" (37).

Meriam listed many reasons for the benefits of a three-person CSC: a debate between commissioners could lead to better decisions; could prevent hasty and ill-thought out "enthusiasms" (49); and there was a formal record underlying each decision. Another benefit was that this more formal and open process gave federal managers and officials "protection against a possibly arbitrary, high-handed, single administrator" (48). Finally, a multi-member commission created the possibility of what nowadays is called diversity, not only the tradition of a bipartisan commission, but also of representation of both genders, of different religions, and so on. PCAM's one-man civil service administrator would be the opposite of the benefits Meriam identified.

Meriam also attacked the generic PCAM critique of the inefficiencies of commissions vs. the smooth managerial work of a single administrator. He described the proponents of the PCAM dogma as "themselves believers in a large measure of one-man power and authority. Some of us would use the term 'autocratic power'" (49). He said this was exactly what happened recently in Australia, when the one-person head of the civil service "wrecked" the Australian civil service (50).

In general, Meriam praised the orthodoxy of the civil service reform movement. It was "detached, apart, unreachable" in terms of presidential pressures, especially highly political appeals and cases (52). He then contrasted the same scenario with a civil service administrator. Showing his personal engagement, in the only exclamation mark used in the report, Meriam stated: "Imagine a personnel administrator under such circumstances telling the President of the United States that the case is grossly improper!" (52–53). Having the federal government's personnel manager directly under the president would inevitably politicize personnel management because "the closer an officer is to the President, the more he will be guided by the President's wishes" (29).

Regarding the proposal for a fixed fifteen-year term for the administrator, Meriam sarcastically said "intentionally or unintentionally, that provision is what is technically known as a 'joker'" (53). If a president could only fire the administrator for inefficiency or neglect of duty, then in reality the president could deem anything as inefficiency or neglect of duty and fire him. The president would be "prosecutor, judge, and jury." Any abuses by a president could only be remedied by impeaching the president, which, of course, was beyond the realm of political reality. So, in actuality, a president could fire an administrator with impunity and for any claimed reason. This was a de facto at-pleasure appointment.

As for the proposed seven-member Civil Service Board, which would be largely advisory and serve as a watchdog of a merit-based civil service, Meriam "questioned" the value of the idea (54). The only concrete duty of the new board would be to create an examination panel to prepare three names for the president as qualified to be the civil service administrator. Meriam judged that this process may well impinge on a president's constitutional right to appoint his administrative officers. Regarding its watchdog role, Meriam noted that an unpaid board of lay citizens who would meet four times a year in Washington would not have the wherewithal to judge events in the civil service or proactively inject themselves in controversies. Instead, they would largely be dependent on the administrator for facts and agenda items and would be otherwise cut off from the routine networks of communication in Washington. Meriam lauded the advantages of a full-time board meeting daily in the capital. For example, a benefit for the three current commissioners was to "mix in the administrative and governmental life at Washington and in the field, to attend congressional hearings, to go to lunches and dinners, formal and informal, where government people talk shop" (56).

Meriam summed up his opposition to the CSC reform bills then pending in Congress with forceful assertions:

- "there is a salutary principle that the burden of proof rests upon those who propose a change; they must prove first that the existing situation is unsatisfactory or bad, and second, that the remedy they propose would give better results."
- "the facts seem to be that no public personnel agency in this country has done better work or recruited an abler, more efficient staff."
- "Federal agencies under the Civil Service Act of 1883 have attained a prestige certainly as great as that of the best state [civil] services and far above that of most municipal and state [civil] services."
- "The contention here made is that the Commission was wise in staying out of the operating field and not attempting to mix control, management, and promotion. Such a mixture would lead only to hopeless confusion and inefficiency." (58–59)

Meriam concluded his report by characterizing his criticisms as "attacks [on] proposed remedies" (59) and stating that he had the counterpart obligation to propose positive alternatives to the fatally flawed PCAM plans. He listed seven relatively modest ideas for tinkering with the status quo of the laws governing the CSC's role and its operations. His last suggestion, phrased in a way that was directly aimed at Congress, was to "let the president have on his staff a person of his own selection as his assistant in the managerial and promotional aspects of personnel administration *but do not* give this assistant any power to give orders to operating officers and more particularly do not give him any power or control whatsoever over the Civil Service Commission" (61–62, emphasis added). Meriam described the duties of such a presidential assistant as a "liaison." (In the retrospect of history, Meriam won. Formally this was exactly what the president eventually did and what Congress permitted. Informally, it was the opposite.)

The final paragraph of Meriam's report was a call to arms for the status quo: "Believers in concentration of power in the executive will say that these recommendations savor of the old system of checks and balances. The American Constitution is based on checks and balances; and so long as the fundamental law is thus designed, the administrative structure should be in harmony with it and not contradictory to it" (62).

Meriam's report had the effect of redefining the scope of the conflict over the CSC. It caused the splash he hoped for, including a front-page story in the *Washington Post*.[44] Now, instead of a fight between supposedly old-fashioned civil service reformers and new-fashioned ones, this was repositioned as an ideological battle located on the left-to-right political spectrum. Suddenly, the ingrained opposition to changing the status quo and to FDR became the full-throated and justifiable position of Congress's conservative coalition. These southern Democrats and minority Republicans were electrified by the Brookings report. It gave them substantive credibility and legitimacy, even gravitas, in their arguments against CSC reorganization. Now they had their own "expert" opinion that they could pose in contrast to the PCAM administrative experts. No longer was the fight over implementing a PCAM bill a situation of a unified voice of apolitical expert opinion pressing politicians to do the only right thing conceivable. Regarding civil service reform, PCAM had lost its monopoly on public administration wisdom (Roberts 1995; 1996).

In a political sense, Meriam's report was a shotgun blast aimed at reinvigorating the orthodoxy and central tenets of the civil service reform movement and rebutting the claims of the new reformers that the traditional approach was anachronistic. The Brookings pamphlet was the prime document that conservatives relied on in the coming debates. For example, sometimes excerpts of Meriam's report were inserted in the *Congressional Record* as the ultimate rationale for opposition to the PCAM report on CSC reorganization.[45]

Senate, 1938

What a difference a year made. In January 1937, the just-reelected Roosevelt released the PCAM study and his message to Congress for a sweeping reorganization of the federal government. It was a time of heady optimism, of being able to overcome the inherent weight of the status quo on Capitol Hill. Now, a year later, with none of the PCAM recommendations enacted, the year started with a blistering report by Senator Byrd, bolstered by the Brookings pamphlet of late 1937.

Byrd's minority report (to the select committee's report) attacking the CSC reorganization was largely based on Meriam's views. It had given him a new foundation and authority for the positions he had taken before its release. In Byrd's committee minority report, he repeated some of the arguments that Meriam had used, including the contention that a one-person administrator would preclude heterogeneity, such as of different genders, and that it would eliminate the independence that a quasi-judicial body needed to have. Byrd especially attacked the proposed civil service administrator because he would be beholden to the president "who is the head of a political party," suggesting the return of patronage and spoils (US Senate 1938, 4). Instead personnel matters should be handled by a bipartisan commission that was autonomous from the president. Byrd also attacked PCAM's effort to link the expansion of the classified service with the reorganization. They were separate concepts, he said. Adopting one did not necessitate adopting the other.

Yet Senator Byrnes had committed to FDR to keep pushing for Senate adoption. In late January, he introduced a revised version of the Senate bill (S. 3331), this time restoring the proposed advisory seven-member Civil Service Board to the bill. This was a modest attempt to co-opt at least one of the critiques that opponents were promoting.[46] Byrnes brought it to the floor on February 28, and the debate over the bill lasted (on and off) for more than a month.

During that time, outside opposing groups were much more vocal and active than supporters. The New York State Chamber of Commerce said the change was "endangering the merit system and the freedom of the civil service from partisan politics."[47] A conservative organization, the American Defense Society, which had mobilized against the court packing bill, now objected to the elimination of the bipartisan CSC and its replacement with someone who served at the pleasure of the president.[48] The sole Republican on the CSC, Samuel Ordway (who had succeeded Leonard White) said the bill was "a definite threat" to the very concept of a civil service system.[49] The National Grange (a farmers' organization) was "strongly opposed to the scrapping of the Civil Service Commission."[50] Even the NAACP opposed it, fearing the power of one man's control over personnel management (not that the CSC had been particularly aggressive or proactive on racial equality).[51] The American Federation of Labor said the proposal would give "autocratic, dictatorial authority" to the president and his civil service administrator.[52] Reaching the peak of hyperbole, the head of the United Civil Service Employes [*sic*] likened the proposal to pre-independence America when "the King of England gave control of the colonies to his friends."[53] For these groups, it was an article of faith that a merit system absolutely depended on an independent and bipartisan CSC.

One of the few public statements in support was from Paul David, the ostensible co-author of the PCAM staff paper. He said that if enacted, "the improvement in Government personnel during the next five years would make the preceding 50 years look like nothing."[54] Another came from a relatively new organization, the United Federal Workers of America, which in a back-handed and tepid endorsement stated that the shift from a three-person to a one-person governance of the civil service staff was "not of vital importance" and that it did not oppose the change.[55] Somewhat surprisingly, late in the congressional debate, the national Junior Chamber of Commerce endorsed the civil service portion of the bill.[56] This went against the near-monolithic opposition by business-oriented organizations.

In the news media, influential *New York Times* columnist Arthur Krock said the CSC plan "makes a poor substitute for the present system."[57] Franklyn Waltman, the *Post*'s congressional reporter and occasional columnist, said that if the plan were adopted, all government personnel would be "placed under the thumb" of the civil service administrator, a distinctly negative spin.[58] The *New York Herald Tribune* editorialized against it, saying it was "likely to prove highly undesirable in government, particularly in New Deal government."[59] In an editorial, the *Washington Star* objected that "control of hiring and firing would pass into the hands of one personnel director."[60] A Wheeling (WV) newspaper editorialized against the "ousting" of the bipartisan CSC as a "brazen affront to the Nation."[61]

One of the few media voices in favor of the civil service reorganization was nationally syndicated columnist Walter Lippmann. He meticulously and systematically examined the arguments of the opponents and then refuted each one. No, the bill did not really give the president any more power over civil service than before. No, the CSC did not have any quasi-legislative powers and, therefore, none would be transferred to the president. No, the CSC did not really have quasi-judicial powers to handle appeals, so that could not justify keeping the status quo. His conclusion: "So it does not seem to me that the objection to this part of the bill can be sustained, and that the opposition would do well to move on to more serious and more substantial issues."[62]

The administration still had a host of New Deal allies in the Senate who would normally give the benefit of the doubt to legislation the president recommended. But they weren't passionate about civil service reorganization. Their conservative opponents, on the hand, were. The Meriam report gave them new ammunition and credibility to use against the changes. The long Senate debate was fierce, though most of the passion and heat came from the opponents, with only a handful of the president's supporters joining Byrnes in speaking in favor of the civil service reorganization.

Most of the floor speeches covered familiar arguments, but it was nonetheless a "hot debate."[63] There were some relatively sharpened thrusts and parries on the issue of the organizational structure of personnel management. For example, under the original 1883 civil service law, the CSC was required to submit its proposed rules and regulations to the president. Only the president could promulgate them officially. Generally, when presidents approved these CSC submissions, they did so as executive orders (which explained the large number of executive orders relating to civil service matters for all presidents from Cleveland to FDR). Opponents made much of the delegation of rule promulgation to the civil service administrator without a presidential sign-off.[64] Given that the administrator would be appointed by the president and serve at his pleasure, this seemed like a distinction without a difference, with the exception that the *ancien régime* saw a president partly as clerk and opposed expansion of powers to the bureaucracy. Seeing no substantive difference, floor manager Byrnes yielded on the matter and accepted an amendment retaining the duty of promulgating civil service rules with the president.[65] Byrnes similarly yielded on stating the conditions under which a president could discharge the civil service administrator before the end of the fifteen-year term. Byrnes insisted that as the executive officer, a president had the generic power to remove him, and therefore no cause for release need ever be stated.[66]

Another attack was that the three-person commission had been a stable and long-standing organization. Shifting to a new governance of the classified service would "place the stability of the entire service in jeopardy." In particular, what if the president named the head of the Democratic National Committee as civil service administrator?[67] A related point was a classic defense of the status quo: "What is the matter with the present Civil Service Commission? What is the trouble with it? What is wrong about it?"[68]

There were three relatively new arguments in support of the bill. Floor manager Byrnes countered to the advocates for the current three-member commission by asking if the Tennessee Valley Authority was truly more efficient and well managed due to its commission form of governance? Wouldn't the TVA be more efficient managerially with a sole executive, compared to the current squabbles and conflicts on the board? This "diverse control" by a divided board was disrupting efficient management.[69] Senator George Norris (I-NE) tried to reverse the argument about the fifteen-year term of the administrator. Wasn't it true that current CSC members served without specific terms? Wasn't it true that a president could release any at will? In that case, wouldn't there be more stability in federal personnel management with an administrator serving a fixed term, though subject to removal, than a three-person commission who were also subject to presidential removal?[70] Finally, Robert La Follette Jr. (P-WI), tried to bring a reality check to the relatively abstract debate. (One reporter complimented the debate as "on a high level" compared to the regular standards of the time.[71]) Based on his own personal experiences with reform efforts in Wisconsin (by his father as governor and his successors), he asserted with some credibility that a one-person civil service manager would be "a great step forward in the extension and improvement of the merit system."[72]

The meta-narrative that the conservative coalition had hurled at FDR since the beginning of his presidency was that he wanted to be a dictator, comparable to Mussolini and even Hitler.[73] The PCAM reorganization bill in general, and the shift from a civil service commission to an administrator specifically, fit into that meta-narrative. Rather typical of the anti-Roosevelt rhetoric used by Republicans and conservative Democrats, Senator Arthur Vandenberg (R-MI) stated that the entire reorganization plan meant the country was "going farther down the road toward authoritarian, centralized, one-man government in the United

States." The civil service reorganization, would be "a Presidential civil-service dictatorship."[74] Joel Clark (D-MO) said it would be "an absolute dictatorship over the personnel in the whole United States Government" with the administrator having the power of a "czar" over all civil servants.[75]

The one-sidedness of the month-long debate (who wanted to be in favor of dictatorship?) was viewed as representative of the sense of the Senate. The main author of the amendment to retain the three-person CSC predicted the day before the vote that he had 50 votes (of 96). Whether that was accurate at that moment or not, "the margin vanished overnight following personal appeals by Administration spokesmen."[76] On March 15, the Senate voted down the amendment 38–50.[77] The pro-New Deal bloc of majority Democrats were standing by FDR. The *Post*'s reporter said it was a major win for the president, a "serious blow" to the conservative coalition, and a "personal victory" for Byrnes.[78] Another reporter characterized it as "the first big Administration victory on the reorganization bill and settles one of the three major issues."[79] The conservative *Chicago Tribune* blared in its headline that the vote "metes death to Civil Service board" and was a key loss over the "dictatorship bill." Its reporter said the opponents of the bill were "disheartened" by their defeat.[80]

In the run-up to the vote on the entire bill, opponents kept hammering away against the section of the bill that would replace the CSC with a civil service administrator.[81] But the vote on the amendment had been their high-water mark on the issue. After an "impassioned" final debate on the entirety of the bill, on March 28 the Senate approved it 48–42. It was a "sweeping victory" for reorganization, including reforming the organization of personnel management.[82]

The civil service structural reorganization had been one of the three most controversial points in the Senate debate on the bill. This helps convey the centrality of the debate over the question of who was in charge of personnel management. It most definitely was not the usual eye-glazing and boring debate over the finer details of civil service policy and regulation. To supporters and opponents, it was the ball game, the most important element of the future of personnel management in the federal government.

House, 1938

Now it was the House's turn.[83] FDR wanted to get ahead of the expected onslaught of conservative rhetoric in the upcoming House debate alleging that the bill would create a de facto dictatorship. He released a letter pointedly stating that he was "as much opposed to American Dictatorship" as anyone and that the "charges of dictatorship are made out of whole-cloth." He characterized many of the arguments against the bill as "silly nightmares" and stated that "the opposition has planted bogies under every bed" (Roosevelt 1969, 1938: 179–81). An indication of the seriousness and perceived urgency of the matter was that Roosevelt's press secretary released the statement at a post-midnight press conference. This was a somewhat last-minute effort to present the president's views, just after a House committee reported the bill to the floor for debate and before the debate began.[84]

That any president would feel compelled, due to the political situation, to deny he wanted to be a dictator seems peculiar in the hindsight of history. But the voices dominating the public debate were so strong and insistent on that point that FDR needed to address it head on. This seemingly odd public statement by a president helps convey the brutality of politics at the time, when over-the-top accusations took on the appearance of credibility by sheer repetition.

The version of the Senate bill that the House select committee reported to the floor slightly modified the Senate version by deleting the fixed fifteen-year term for the civil service administrator. Instead, the administrator would serve for an indefinite term. While not providing a specific explanation for this change, the committee majority report generally argued that the civil service should parallel the existing template of another presidential managerial agency, the Bureau of the Budget. After all, the budget director served an indefinite term at the pleasure of the president. Similarly, the leadership of the counterpart personnel agency should be the same. This would permit "the President to exercise effectively the direction and leadership in bringing about more effective personnel management" (US House 1938, 31).

Republicans on the committee filed a minority report opposing the bill. Regarding the CSC reorganization, they presented just about every objection to the plan that had been raised over the last year. It "destroys" the bipartisan CSC, replacing it with a "partisan" administrator; it would give the president "political control" over all federal employees, and current employees would no longer "feel safe"; and the seven-member board was "ridiculous" because it would be "without any power whatever" (US House 1938, 40).

In the meantime, New Deal Democrats suffered a major loss. The chairman of the House Civil Service Committee, Robert Ramspeck (D-GA), announced his opposition to the reform.[85] This gave significant credibility to the opposition because he was perceived as an expert on personnel matters. One reporter called Ramspeck a "valuable recruit" to the opposition.[86] Ramspeck elaborated on his opposition during the House floor debate. His substantive objection was that the bill would endanger the principle of a merit system and insert politicized decision-making. The head of the agency would no longer be a civil service administrator, but rather "a patronage administrator," even "a patronage dictator."[87]

However, based on some of Ramspeck's comments during the floor debate, there also seemed to be a personal and power issue contributing to his views. The CSC reorganization should have gone through his committee, not the select committee, he said. Adding insult to injury, the select committee had not afforded him any input into the bill, nor consulted him, until the very last stages of its work, giving that late consultation the appearance of tokenism.[88] One reporter later concluded that Ramspeck's position was influential because it "enlisted the support of other members of the House Civil Service Commission [*sic*, should be Committee] who were smarting under the affront of not having been consulted" in the drafting of the bill.[89]

The extensive House floor debate in late March and early April lasted nearly two weeks. It was even more pointed, partisan, and vitriolic than the Senate debate. Republicans and conservative Democrats repeatedly said that the CSC changes would "wreck" the merit system,[90] would be "the destruction" of half a century of the federal civil service system,[91] reflected FDR's "Napoleonic" approach to the presidency,[92] would recreate the classified system as "a football of politics,"[93] and were "a reversion to the political spoils system,"[94] while the new watchdog board would be "a mere gesture,"[95] and the plan was "a bold, open, and clear political raid on an established institution in our natural life."[96]

Fewer voices were heard in support of the CSC reform. Most came from the members of the select committee and from the Democratic leadership. The most imposing participant in the debate was the majority leader, Sam Rayburn (D-TX). He seldom spoke during floor debates. In this case, he said, he felt "very strongly and very earnestly" that he needed to point out the "propaganda" campaign against the bill that was supposedly inundating the members. These were not representative of public opinion; rather, they were manufactured by the interests that always opposed FDR's reforms. Rayburn especially wanted to call out the minority party's rhetoric, which, in quoting from such letters and telegrams, claimed that the public-at-large opposed the reorganization bill because "it might bring about revolution or it might bring about bloodshed." This tactic of claiming to speak for public opinion and using hyperbolic rhetoric against FDR—much like the campaign against his utility holding company bill—had failed in the past, Rayburn said, and deserved to be treated the same way now.[97]

It was a "raucous debate, punctuated by boos, laughter, and sarcastic comments" (Dunn 2010, 11). Press coverage conveyed the slugfest nature of the debate, comparable to the importance of the court packing bill. One headline indicated that neither side appeared to be dominant: "Merger Civil Service Plan Hard Fought by Both Sides."[98] Another story said that "the leadership of both sides was anxiously counting noses."[99]

When coverage highlighted one side or the other, it was, generally, favoring the opposition, depicting the Democrats on the defensive. One reporter noted that the galleries of the House were packed and that "spontaneous outbursts of applause" came in reaction to attacks on the bill.[100] When the president conferred with the House leadership, it was "to save his government reorganization bill from House defeat."[101] A reporter speculated that the administration might abandon the CSC portion of the bill to save the rest of it.[102] Trying to capture the flavor and atmosphere of the debate, the AP reported opponents "resumed their bombardment" of the bill and "successfully resisted all efforts to cut short the debate."[103] According to the *Post*, conservatives "switched their assault to other controversial sections of the bill—notably in provisions for a single Civil Service administrator."[104]

In the run-up to the final vote, the floor leaders of the bill used the routine parliamentary tactic of accepting some amendments to the bill in response to criticisms made during the debate—in the hopes of mollifying specific clusters of members, incorporating their concerns into the bill and, hopefully, drawing them into voting in favor of the bill. So, for example, during the debate some members claimed that the bill was a threat to veterans because it could be interpreted as impliedly repealing (or giving the administrator the power to repeal) the current policy of awarding veterans preference points when certifying finalists for a vacancy.[105] The amendment was wholly unnecessary, because the bill did not affect the statutory policy of veterans' preference. The amendment was redundant and merely symbolic. But if adopting it could gain support for the bill, then it was worthwhile doing.[106]

The showdown vote came on an amendment from Ramspeck that the bill's floor manager opposed. In it, the CSC would be retained as it was, and the civil service administrator would be its highest staffer, essentially the director general of CSC's staff.[107] While superficially retaining the idea of a civil service administrator, it wholly reversed the intent of the bill, by shifting the administrator to be supervised by the CSC rather than by the president. Both sides threw everything they could into the debate on the amendment, as it was more than a mere test vote on the CSC reorganization, it was the *entirety* of the personnel management portion of the bill. They made partisan, ideological, and political arguments for and against Rampseck's amendment. They quoted from what states were doing with their civil service systems, what experts supported, and what politically attentive outside groups said about the bill.

FDR won. The amendment was rejected 83–115.[108] This showed a relatively comfortable majority supporting the bill, although not a substantial one, especially with conservative Democrats voting with the Republicans. The supporters of the plan breathed a sigh of relief, figuring this was the high-water mark of the opposition.

But later that day, a motion to refer the bill back to committee emerged as the culmination of the opposition and its debate strategy of doubt-raising. After all, a motion to refer the bill back to the committee, they could argue, was not a substantive vote against the bill; merely a request for some modifications and improvements to reflect the issues which were raised in the floor debate. It was a seductive argument for some House Democrats who would be facing the voters in about six months in the mid-term elections. Understanding what was at stake, the vote occurred in "a dramatically hushed chamber" (Dunn 2010, 11). Despite all the efforts of the administration and the Democratic leadership, the vote to recommit to committee passed 204–196. When the results were announced, "a visceral roar of spiteful cheers" welled up from the opponents (12).

The political interpretation of the vote, contrary to the strict meaning of the motion in parliamentary procedure, was that the House had killed the bill. According to the *Post*, it was a "lethal blow" to reorganization in what was "the most dramatic legislative battle" since the court packing bill.[109] The head of one of the few federal employee organizations that supported the bill acknowledged that the civil service reorganization "became a political issue" and was "caught in the whirlpool of politics." He acknowledged that the idea for a civil service administrator in lieu of the CSC was dead.[110]

For the opponents of a one-person civil service administration, it was a major win, one that took a strenuous and all-out effort. In their eyes (setting aside partisan and anti-FDR motivations), they had saved the concept of a nonpartisan and autonomous civil service commission tasked with protecting—above all else—the merit system.

For Roosevelt and the PCAM members, it was a heartbreaking loss. They had come so close. If only five members had switched their votes, they would have won. A dejected Roosevelt quickly wrote a public letter to Rayburn urging no reprisals against the Democrats who had defected on that roll call (Roosevelt 1969, 1938: 206). Given the results, he did not want further political reverberations, which such punishments would have triggered. A few days later, the president was a bit more reflective on the loss. In a press conference for members of the religious press, he said he was unable to overcome "the kind of false information that this country is up against all the time, engendered by political motives." For example, in response to Father Coughlin's radio attacks, House and Senate members "were flooded with telegrams" that opposed moving the organizational location of the US Office of Education (Roosevelt 1969, 1938: 251). FDR, no amateur at persuasive public relations and communication, simply could not overcome every attack on all the large and small issues either in the bill or that possibly could be affected by it afterwards.

In the larger context, the defeat of the reorganization bill in the House was "the last straw" for Roosevelt in his ongoing battle with southern and conservative Democrats who had been siding more and more openly with Republicans to block his legislative program (Dunn 2010, 13). The House vote was the signal event that firmly convinced FDR to go ahead and try to purge the Democratic Party in the fall 1938 elections. Contrary to popular history, FDR had some wins in his intra-party purge effort (Dunn 2010). But then, in the November elections, Republicans doubled their membership in the House from 89 to 169. They were still in the minority, but they had clearly benefited from their all-out war in 1937–38 on FDR's reorganization effort, including CSC reform.

Congressional Consideration, 1939

After the blowout on the House floor in April 1938, a few of the supporters of CSC reorganization tried to keep the issue alive. The League of Women Voters announced continued support for civil service reform, including a single civil service administrator.[111] Speaking to a conference of civil service organizations, Leonard White urged revival of the idea at all levels of government. The record of commissions, he said, "is not adequate," and he praised the one-person model and predicted a trend of that model being adopted more frequently.[112]

But the opponents were equally vocal. In August 1938, Brookings published a 440-page tome by Meriam on all aspects of personnel management, including an extensive defense of the multi-member CSC (Meriam 1938, chap. 14). Considering recent events, one newspaper ran a front page story on the book's release, including that Meriam felt the three-person CSC "should be retained."[113] The head of the American Federal of Government Employes [*sic*] said at the organization's annual convention that he expected new efforts regarding the "crucial" detail of civil service reorganization and committed to continue fighting against this "paramount question."[114] Speaking at the same convention, Senator David Walsh (D-MA) reprised his efforts to kill the idea of a civil service administrator and stood by that position. Covering his speech, the *Chicago Tribune* continued its practice of referring to the reorganization plan as "the dictatorship bill."[115] Similarly, at the annual conference of the American Federal of Labor, the organization went on record as maintaining its opposition to "such revolutionary changes" as a civil service administrator.[116]

After the November elections, the president continued to push for congressional adoption of comprehensive reorganization, including of the CSC. In December, he met with Gulick, Merriam, and Democratic congressional leaders to map a plan. The tentative consensus was that the effort should start in the House and that the original omnibus bill be divided into four or five single-issue bills, one of which would be the civil service administrator.[117]

By now, there no longer was a PCAM staff in place to prepare briefing materials and talking points on reorganization. Former staffer John Miller, now back at Gulick's IPA, prepared a paper on "Reorganization Fallacies" that could be used by the president's supporters. In the section on civil service, he addressed the claim that a civil service administrator would comprise "one-man rule" over all federal employees. In the current setup, federal employees in the departments and agencies were not under the ongoing supervision or jurisdiction of the CSC. Rather, they worked for a specific department or agency and were subject to that organization's personnel policies and decisions. For example, an employee of the Veterans Administration was under so-called one-man rule, as that agency was headed by an administrator. A civil servant's contact with the CSC was only for appeals relating to firings allegedly made for political or religious reasons. That was the limit of the CSC's current jurisdiction over a federal employee. (Its role was much larger in the pre-hiring phase of civil service.) If an employee were to be released for merit-based reasons, such as performance and inefficiency, no appeal could be made to the CSC. Regarding civil service rules, federal employees were also already under one-man rule in that the promulgation of commission regulations could only be done by the president.[118] Miller was trying to document that claims against the personnel reorganization were not based on the realities on the ground.

Roosevelt's effort to revive reorganization, including of the CSC, got surprising support from a quarter that usually undermined him: *Times* columnist Arthur Krock. Krock, who had written a column during the House debate criticizing the CSC plan, now saw the general reorganization plan as being justified "on its merits, which are many." In an analysis in the Sunday section "News of the Week in Review," he depicted the loss in the House as partly due to "a propaganda campaign full of inaccuracy, hysteria and Republican politics." Now, while he expected some continuing opposition to the CSC reform, he emphasized that previous presidents had supported streamlining the CSC with a single administrator. This was not a Roosevelt dictator idea. He hoped it would pass, notwithstanding the continuing opposition, because experts "have very strong arguments" for it.[119] In the same Sunday section a week later, another reporter noted the major change in atmosphere in the capital about reorganization. Of the frequent charge of "dictator" from earlier in the year, "little is heard today." The only controversy over the overall reorganization plan had narrowed down to two remaining items, he concluded, one of which was the CSC.[120]

Before any new political consensus congealed, Ramspeck quickly weighed in again. He would oppose the CSC reorganization in 1939 as much as he had in 1938. His views had not changed. He said "there is no necessity for dealing with civil service in the Administration's reorganization program." Expanding the scope of the merit system within the federal workforce had no inextricable link to changing the CSC to an administrator. These were separate subjects. The PCAM recommendation on increasing the proportion of federal workers under the classified system could be implemented in separate legislation (coming out of *his* committee), sans the adoption of a civil service administrator. Conservative senator Harry Byrd promptly concurred with Ramspeck about the importance of deleting CSC reorganization from any new bill.[121]

FDR needed to decide if he would force the issue or permit a pared-down bill containing some of the elements of reorganization he still wanted. On January 26, 1939, he met with Brownlow. Later that day, he had a larger meeting that included the members of the CSC. Pragmatist that he was, Roosevelt decided to go for what he could get, even if it was not everything he wanted. He agreed to support a new compromise reorganization bill that would exclude the two most controversial elements of the defeated bill: the civil service administrator and modifications to the GAO. Partly because of that, the political landscape of 1939 was as different as night and day compared to the 1938 floor flight.

As eventually presented, not only was the civil service administrator plan deleted from the new bill, but the bill explicitly prohibited the president from using any of the new reorganization powers the bill would delegate to him to affect the CSC in any way. The commission was added to a long list of exempt agencies in the bill, all of which were political sacred cows to some member or another. They included the Employees' Compensation Committee (which had been defended vociferously when Hoover sought to merge it into the CSC in his 1932 post-defeat reorganization plan [chap. 1]), Veterans Administration, Army Corps of Engineers, Coast Guard, GAO, Maritime Commission, and all the regulatory commissions (US House 1939a, 2, 5).

When the House bill came up for floor debate, one member tried to reopen the issue. John Nichols (D-OK) proposed a floor amendment to delete the CSC from the agencies exempted from the reorganization bill. He called it "the one department of Government that needs reorganization worse than another other." Ramspeck swatted it down, as did the bill's floor manager. The amendment really didn't stand a chance and was easily defeated.[122] The House and Senate passed the now-relatively noncontroversial bill by comfortable margins.

When the president signed the bill into law in early April 1939, the idea of replacing an autonomous civil service commission with an executive-controlled personnel manager now appeared to be dead.

Not quite.

3
FDR Constructs a Personnel Management Apparatus, 1939

Now what—if anything? Was the language of the new reorganization law the death of the idea of presidential personnel management as the replacement for a merit system protected by an independent CSC? For the wily Roosevelt, there were different ways to skin a cat. There must be *some* way to do it. Or, at least, to move the (public administration) ball down the field to get as close as possible to Roosevelt's original goal.

Establishing the Position of a Presidential Assistant for Personnel Liaison, April 1939

In part, the idea for a presidential personnel aide harkened back to Meriam's opposition in 1937 to a civil service administrator. Meriam had balanced that with support for a White House staffer who would be a liaison with the CSC and others involved in federal personnel management. Meriam emphasized that his interpretation of the meaning of the term "liaison" excluded giving the liaison officer any power *over* the CSC (chap. 2).

Meriam notwithstanding, "liaison" was a classic FDR term for his approach to public administration. It could mean *anything*. It was a nebulous weasel word that had the benefit of not sounding like a delegation of power. In the public management jargon of the day, it did not sound like a "line" function, in the chain of (civilian) command and directly overseeing those farther down the hierarchical pyramid. Rather, "liaison" sounded more like "staff," the antonym to "line," meaning that it was limited to an advisory role and with no power over anyone.[1] In the sink-or-swim world of FDR's presidency, if someone with a vague title such as liaison could leverage and maneuver that into possessing real power over others, fine. If he could not, well, OK, too. Failure was an option. Roosevelt believed in a kind of competitive administration, of letting underlings with overlapping and fuzzy duties and titles duke it out (Reeves 1973). Competition either meant all important decisions would have to be pushed up to his desk to resolve or that one of the two would prevail over the other. Getting results would be all that mattered. (Coordinator was another inoffensive title with little official meaning—for example, FDR's Coordinator of Information, which eventually morphed into the CIA.)

It will be recalled that, even before Meriam's report in late 1937, Brownlow also had in mind a slightly different arrangement involving presidential personnel liaison. When he testified before Congress in early 1937—when the proposal for a civil service administrator was still very much part of the plan—Brownlow was asked why he was separately recommending *six* new administrative assistants ("with a passion for anonymity") for the president? He described six rubrics of a president's work, one of which was personnel management. Brownlow suggested at the congressional hearing that one of the six administrative assistants should be assigned the responsibility for *liaising* on personnel matters occurring throughout the executive branch (chap. 2).

Roosevelt wanted to move quickly after signing the Reorganization Act in early April. Even though PCAM as a formal body had expired and its staff scattered to the winds, FDR asked its three members to come to the capital to help him draft a very comprehensive formal reorganization plan to be submitted to Congress and subject to a legislative veto (Brownlow 1958, 413–15). Regarding personnel management, they wanted to maximize whatever could be done without violating the prohibition on touching the CSC. Brownlow recalled his congressional testimony and quickly realized that assigning personnel matters to a presidential administrative assistant was wholly consonant with the new law. Now he could move it toward implementation. Even though Brownlow had conceived of the presidential personnel liaison function in a very different context (i.e., including a civil service administrator), the original idea was still a viable structural and functional approach. "Liaison" became the magic word to get around the legal fence protecting the CSC.

The persistence at including personnel in the implementation of reorganization reflected in part PCAM's and the president's larger belief that there were three generic managerial functions that encapsulated the chief executive's responsibilities: budgeting, planning, and personnel. So, in parallel to designating a presidential assistant with a personnel liaison portfolio, the organizational entity that FDR created as his institutional executive office should have units relating to budgeting, planning, and personnel.

At the end of April, Roosevelt sent Reorganization Plan No. I to Congress. Part of it established the Executive Office of the President, transferred the Bureau of the Budget from Treasury into EOP, and recreated the National Resources

Committee into another component agency within EOP, to be called the National Resources Planning Board (NRPB). What of personnel management in the EOP? FDR did not fully tip his hand. The formal reorganization plan had no sections relating to personnel management, if only because the president's new reorganization powers excluded the CSC. But in his cover message, he made sure that "Congress was placed on notice" (Roosevelt 1969, 1939: 504) of his intent to designate one of his new assistants to handle personnel management:

> Because of an exemption in the [Reorganization] Act, it is impossible to transfer to the Executive Office the administration of the third managerial function of the Government, that of personnel. However, I desire to inform Congress that it is my purpose to name one of the administrative assistants to the President . . . to serve as a liaison agent of the White House on personnel management.
>
> In this manner, the President will be given for the first time direct access to the three principal necessary management agencies of the Government. None of the three belongs in any existing Department. (Roosevelt 1969, 1939: 251)

This sounded inoffensive enough. And given that this announcement was within the president's message to Congress, which merely transmitted the plan, and was not within the plan itself, there could be no basis for exercising a legislative veto on that count.

Both houses of Congress passed Plan No. I (more precisely did not exercise a legislative veto), and it was scheduled to go into effect on July 1, 1939.[2] In May, FDR submitted Plan No. II, also containing multiple proposals including some that further affected the proposed EOP, but similarly lacking any language relating to personnel management or presidential personnel liaison. It, too, was passed by Congress.[3]

Reshaping the Civil Service Commission, June 1939

Compared to the fast progress he was making regarding strengthening the president's central managerial functions of budgeting and planning (in Reorganization Plan No. I), FDR acknowledged that the personnel part of his post-Brownlow management program was only "limping along."[4]

By nice timing, the Republican member of the CSC, Samuel Ordway (who had opposed the reorganization [chap. 2.]), announced his resignation in May.[5] New BOB director Harold Smith suggested that the opening created an opportunity for something of a political triple play: replace Ordway with someone nominally Republican but sympathetic to the president's personnel management agenda, persuade current CSC president Harry Mitchell to step down as president (but remain on the commission), and then get the new member elected president. If they could maneuver that, Smith told the president, the new CSC president "would for all practical purposes be the Administrator" of civil service, exactly what PCAM and Roosevelt tried for. In Smith's scenario, FDR could "accomplish all that he had in mind with respect to civil service in a relatively short time."[6] For all intents and purposes, it would be the equivalent of a civil service coup d'état—and fully legal, to boot. FDR was intrigued, but noncommittal.

The key was to name the right person. For the next month and a half, Roosevelt and his staff spent significant amounts of time searching for that perfect nominee. Smith suggested Frederick Davenport, then head of the revitalized federal Council of Personnel Administration (CPA), which consisted of the chief personnel officers of all federal departments and agencies (chap. 4). When the issue of the CSC appointment came up, Roosevelt invited "Freddie" to the White House for lunch to talk it over. Davenport told the president said he would accept the CSC appointment on condition that he would immediately become CSC president. As much as FDR was hoping that Mitchell might take the hint to step down, the president "notoriously disliked firing anyone" (Kaiser 2014, 139).[7] Reflecting that reluctance, FDR appeared in his conversation with Davenport to back off from forcing the issue with Mitchell.[8] In that case, Davenport later told Brownlow, he would prefer to stay at CPA.[9]

In the meantime, longtime civil servant and personnel expert William H. McReynolds, administrative assistant to the secretary of treasury, called Smith and suggested Arthur S. Flemming, then director of the new School of Public Affairs at American University in Washington. McReynolds described Flemming as "a practical, hard-driving person who would get something done" in the CSC. Smith promised to pass the idea along to the president the next time the subject came up.[10]

FDR returned to the recruitment of a CSC nominee when he met with Smith on May 31. Ordway had sent the president two letters with lists of potential replacements. His list included seven men, which Ordway presented in order of his preference. Flemming was first. FDR discussed the names on the list with Smith. He asked Smith for his opinion of one of the other men on the list. Smith said that the person was "one of the outstanding technicians in the county," but did the president want a technician? Or perhaps FDR wanted a bigger picture person, "one of more general background for this kind of position." In other words, did he want a detail-oriented bureaucrat or a public administration generalist who would be a leader in larger policy matters? Typically, without answering, FDR asked Smith to consult with the three former PCAM members and with Leonard White for their reactions to Ordway's list.[11]

Brownlow told Smith that he (Brownlow) and White both recommended

Flemming as far superior to other names on the list. But was Flemming a Republican? This was no small detail, as Ordway (and White) had occupied the Republican slot on the commission, with the other two continuing members both Democrats.[12] Smith also talked again to McReynolds, who continued to prefer Flemming, especially because he had "drive" along with "a quiet way of getting things done."[13] Similarly, Gulick told Smith that he, too, thought Flemming was the superior candidate, in part because he had "a high appreciation of the personnel problems of the Federal Service"—in other words, Flemming saw the subject as a personnel management issue, not as small-bore CSC-style narrow concerns relating to control, rules, and procedure. Smith submitted a memo to the president summarizing his consultations and also confirming that Flemming was a registered Republican.[14]

In reaction to the memo, Roosevelt told Smith that he (the president) continued to consider personnel management as "a field in which he was very much interested as part of the management problem," meaning that he shared the PCAM-derived view of budgeting, planning, and personnel as the three major management functions whereby a president could ride herd over the executive branch. FDR authorized Smith to interview Flemming for the job. Ever the politician, the president asked Smith to find out what state Flemming was from.[15] Members of Congress closely scrutinized where presidential nominees came from, ever ready to feel their state was being slighted or protest if a nominee from their own state was anathema to them politically. Geography was especially sensitive when it came to personnel matters because Congress insisted that appointments to nonclassified positions had to be apportioned fairly by state. They were quick to complain that their state was not getting its share of appointments. So Flemming's state of origin was no small detail either when it came to Capitol Hill politics.

Smith then interviewed Flemming. Flemming told him that he was interested in the CSC position if offered and that he would be able to obtain a leave of absence from American University for the duration.[16] But after Smith sent a memo to the president updating him on Flemming's willingness to accept the appointment, FDR was not yet ready to act. (Procrastination was another of his managerial and political traits.)

It turned out FDR was also thinking about another potential candidate. Clarence Dykstra, who had a doctorate in government, had served as city manager of Cincinnati from 1930 to 1937. Brownlow, as a fellow city manager, thought very highly of Dykstra and hoped to recruit him for one of Brownlow's projects, perhaps as PCAM staff director and/or as Brownlow's successor as head of PACH. In 1937, Dykstra left Cincinnati and resumed his academic career as chancellor of the University of Wisconsin (which then consisted only of the Madison campus). Indicating his commitment to good government and the professionalization of public administration, he also served as (volunteer) president of the National Municipal League, a strong supporter of the merit system and independent civil service commissions in city government.

In late June 1939, the president called Dykstra and offered him the CSC position.[17] Dykstra demurred. He said that the University of Wisconsin was then under attack by Republican governor Julius Heil, a conservative businessman. Smith followed up on FDR's call with his own sales pitch, telling Dykstra that he really "was the man he [FDR] wanted." Dykstra replied less ambiguously than what he had said softly to the president, that he felt an obligation to the Wisconsin faculty not to abandon them when the university was under fire.[18]

Finally feeling he had thoroughly explored all the possible candidates for a kind of de facto civil service administrator, on June 23, Roosevelt announced the nomination of Flemming to the CSC. At 34, Flemming would be the youngest commissioner since Theodore Roosevelt, who had been appointed when he was 30.[19] Even though Flemming did not become the CSC president,[20] the informal messages from the White House were that Flemming would be *primus inter pares*, the go-to and lead member of the commission, the major channel of communication with the president, and the one whose internal CSC work should be seen as the closest reflection of the administration's wants and desires in personnel management.

Within three months, Smith felt Flemming had already proven himself. After a productive meeting with Flemming in September, Smith observed that Flemming's "aggressiveness in improving the situation appears to prove that he was an excellent appointment."[21] BOB assistant director Donald Stone was pleased to describe Flemming as quickly becoming the "de facto chief administrative officer of the commission" (Stone 1983, 33). Just after WWII ended, the author of an article in *Harper's* wrote that "the commission actually is run" by Flemming (Fischer 1945, 365). A year later, an article in *American Political Science Review* commended Flemming's "aggressive leadership" of the commission since being appointed (McDiarmid 1946, 1079). Later academic observers agreed. Van Riper concluded that "many of the advantages of a single administrator were gained" by Flemming's role inside the commission and through his relations with the presidency (Van Riper 1958, 365). Harris (the former PCAM staff director) applauded Flemming's "dynamic and untiring efforts" to make the CSC more fleet-footed and adaptable, especially during WWII (Harris 1964, 172). Harris also pointed to Flemming's "effective intervention" to prevent some ill-advised legislation from passing in Congress (171).

A final, though imputed, signal of Flemming's likely effectiveness can perhaps be deduced from the memoirs of Harry Mitchell, CSC president *during* Flemming's membership on the commission. Mitchell makes no mention whatsoever of Flemming (H. Mitchell 1985). It seems reasonable to expect that Flemming's name would naturally come up, surely at least once, if only as a glancing reference to a colleague on the commission. Flemming's invisibility in Mitchell's memoir is perhaps a signal of Mitchell's unhappiness with Flemming's special relationship with the White House, feeling it should have been him (Mitchell) who was closest to FDR. Given the gossipy-ness of Washington, Mitchell may also have heard of the scheme some White House aides were hatching to ask him to step down as CSC president, even though it never came to fruition. Maybe Mitchell got a small measure of revenge by trying to write Flemming out of Mitchell's historical narrative.

William McReynolds as Personnel and Efficiency Expert Before 1939

Roosevelt was proceeding relatively quietly, but systematically, to construct his version of the next-best architecture for presidential personnel management without violating the law. Next up was selecting the administrative assistant who would be the president's liaison for personnel management. As far back as 1937, Treasury official William H. McReynolds had been rumored to be on the short list if Congress were to approve the PCAM recommendation for six new administrative assistants to the president.[22]

McReynolds had been in the federal service since 1906. Born in 1880, he grew up on the family farm in Kansas. He attended public schools, but it is not clear if he graduated or even attended high school—probably not (Macmahon and Millett 1967, 27).[23] In 1902 (about age 22) he moved to Michigan to clerk for a lawyer and study for the bar (though he never completed the process). That may have been why, later in his career, he was sometimes referred to as "Judge" McReynolds, although the honorific likely also related to the seemingly endless number of administrative conflicts that he calmly adjudicated.[24] Throughout his working career, McReynolds was also known by other nicknames, including Bill (Roosevelt 1972, 22: 215; Stone 1983, 32),[25] Mac (Roosevelt 1972, 15: 391–92),[26] Mr. Mac (Emmerich 1950, 21),[27] and Mr. Mack.[28] For formal correspondence, as was the custom at the time, he sometimes only used only the initials of his first and middle names: W. H. McReynolds or Wm. H. McReynolds.[29]

In 1906, he took a civil service exam and was hired by the Post Office Department as a clerk for its inspection service in Washington. There, he engaged in studies on organization and procedure to improve operations and efficiency. In 1913, with an emerging reputation in efficiency studies, he transferred to the CSC's new Division of Efficiency, created by Congress to develop efficiency ratings for federal employees and engage in more general efficiency investigations (Lee 2006).

In 1916, Congress recreated the division into an independent Bureau of Efficiency (BOE), and McReynolds rose to become its assistant chief.

Bureaucratic infighting between BOE and the CSC regarding the effort to conduct position classifications for the entire federal workforce forced Congress to step in in 1923. It created a Personnel Classification Board consisting of BOE, CSC, and—as chair to break ties—BOB. In 1930, after another congressional intervention, McReynolds became the director of the Classification Board, independent of both BOE and the CSC.[30] McReynolds managed to stay out of the fierce bureaucratic and political gunfights between the two agencies. He testified before Congress in 1932 on Congressman Cochran's bill (largely reflecting President Hoover's recommendations) to consolidate the Personnel Classification Board, BOE, and CSC into a Civil Service Administration (chap. 1). McReynolds demonstrated his mastery of the details of personnel management with testimony that was detail-oriented, well informed on all matters that the board had acted on, nonpolitical, and deferential to Congress—though he was willing to argue back when he felt the facts were being misstated (US House 1932b, 55–59).

During the Hoover administration, McReynolds had a few personal meetings with the president while working on several personnel-related projects, including an evaluation of proposed across-the-board pay raises for military officers (McReynolds 1949, 1–2). After being defeated for reelection, Hoover decided to make one last effort at comprehensive reorganization (chap. 1). The budget director arranged for McReynolds to be temporarily transferred (in federal personnel lingo, detailed) to BOB for the duration. McReynolds helped prepare and draft some of the proposals.

When the reorganization plan came before Congress, one member complained that it folded the General Land Office into USDA and opposed the change. He blamed it on McReynolds, claiming McReynolds had drafted the section without consulting anyone (i.e., the congressman and his allies) and that McReynolds had no factual basis to justify the change. When the congressman informally confronted McReynolds in the hallway, McReynolds—unintimidated, cool, and fact-based—simply replied that the proposed transfer was based on "a theory" that like activities should be in the same agency (US House 1932d, 75). When the committee reconvened its formal hearing, the congressman moved to force McReynolds to testify, but the committee chair refused (89). The incident did not appear to degrade McReynolds's reputation as a technocrat, and perhaps even increased it.

These and other activities also made McReynolds something of a public figure, certainly an important one to the large audience of federal employees in Washington and their protectors on Capitol Hill. As a consequence, the *Washington Post* occasionally covered his activities and involvements.[31] One front-page article characterized him as "an authority" on personnel matters.[32] At least once, he was mentioned in the headline, further indicating his standing and stature as a public figure.[33]

After his temporary posting to BOB ended, McReynolds needed to find a new position in federal service. In early 1933, just before Roosevelt's inauguration, Congress passed a law abolishing BOE, so McReynolds could not return there. But his reputation as a technocrat who could deal with highly detailed matters, especially personnel, served him well. Henry Morgenthau Jr., a gentleman farmer-neighbor to FDR who had served in FDR's gubernatorial administration, was appointed to chair the Federal Farm Board (quickly retitled the Farm Credit Administration). New to the Washington bureaucracy, Morgenthau sought—as he had done in Albany—to put together a small team of staffers who were experts in their areas upon whom he could rely (Levy 2010, 228, 230).[34] He promptly hired McReynolds as his administrative assistant. McReynolds proved himself invaluable to Morgenthau. He "handled all matters of personnel and budget with a nonpartisan efficiency that charmed Morgenthau" (Blum 1959, 81). The first time Morgenthau took McReynolds with him for a meeting with the president, Morgenthau began a formal introduction. FDR cut him off. "Don't introduce me to Mac. The last time I saw him was in [WWI] . . . when he argued with me about supplies and accounts and damned if he didn't have his way" (McReynolds 1949, 2). From then on, FDR occasionally called on McReynolds to handle complicated or delicate personnel and administrative issues.

In late 1933, FDR appointed Morgenthau as his second treasury secretary.[35] Morgenthau took McReynolds with him, making him administrative assistant to the secretary. Morgenthau's first act as secretary was to issue a formal policy clamping down on administrative laxness. From now on, all contacts with reporters had to be through the secretary's office (raising howls from the press, who thrived on back-biting leaks) and "all administrative matters, including personnel and budget, shall be handled by Mr. William H. McReynolds."[36] At Treasury, McReynolds epitomized the characteristic Brownlow later called "a passion for anonymity." McReynolds eschewed a public profile, handled all matters assigned him in detail and with dispatch, deferred to the guidance of the secretary, and generally showed his loyalty and diligence. The hostile *Chicago Tribune* described him as "practically an unknown in the New Deal except as a man Friday for the treasury secretary."[37]

Descriptions of McReynolds conveyed his personality. Two public administration academics described McReynolds as "tight-lipped, skeptical, winding himself up like a slow pitcher, [and] can afford to be more doubting than positive" with Morgenthau (Macmahon and Millett 1967, 142).[38] A syndicated column said he was a chain smoker and "credited with knowing more about the intricacies of government than anyone in Washington."[39] An article in the *Post* marking the 57th anniversary of the CSC noted that McReynolds spoke so softly it was nearly an "inaudible drawl," but his soft-spoken presentation hid "one of the keenest minds on personnel problems."[40] In 1939, based on the recommendation of a committee of forty personnel and public administration experts, American University (where Flemming headed the public affairs school) awarded McReynolds an honorary doctorate in law. He was viewed as a "model career civil servant" who had made an "outstanding contribution to sound governmental administration."[41]

BOB director Harold Smith called him "one of the ablest administrators in the Government."[42] Brownlow concurred. During the confidential work of PCAM in 1936, he consulted often with McReynolds, who Brownlow credited as one of three of "perhaps the ablest career administrators in government." Staff director Harris and other committee staffers also talked to McReynolds "almost daily" (Brownlow 1958, 372). Harris described McReynolds as one of the "leading civil servants in Washington" who "was a person of a very good judgment and a very good person to act as a go-between." On the other hand, Harris said, McReynolds "wasn't a very imaginative sort of fellow" and "was not the kind of man who would think of jobs for his employees" (Harris 1983, 21, 79). Emmerich, a PCAM staffer and later a public administration professor, wrote that McReynolds was "one of our great civil servants" (Emmerich 1950, 20–21). Years later, he further described McReynolds as "shrewd" and one of a handful of those careerists who gained FDR's trust for their competence (Emmerich 1971, 79).

These descriptions and characterizations suggest McReynolds was something of technocrat who worked on the problems in front of him. That was precisely the kind of personality that Roosevelt sensed he would need to develop a White House liaison role in personnel management: someone who could build such a role from scratch without making enemies or having a controversial public profile. Being somewhat plodding, detail-oriented, and conscientious were, in this case, good qualities.

Appointing McReynolds as Presidential Administrative Assistant for Personnel Liaison, July 1939

McReynolds was so involved in PCAM's work that he was one of only four staffers invited to be present when FDR briefed congressional leaders at the White House in early 1937 on the upcoming reorganization report (Emmerich 1971, 206).[43] When the reorganization plan was bogged down in Congress, Roosevelt continued to give McReynolds personnel-related assignments. For example, on January 31, 1939 (before the passage of the Reorganization Act), the president met with him one-on-one. They discussed the upcoming presidential announcement establishing a task force to develop a civil service system for professional, scientific, and technical career tracks. Given that its scope included government lawyers, FDR appointed two Supreme Court justices and the attorney general to the committee, along with McReynolds and Leonard White (and two senior businessmen). That McReynolds was one of seven members of a study committee which included two Supreme Court justices and a Cabinet member indicates his high standing in FDR's eyes. The president's announcement described McReynolds as having "long years of experience with the practical operation of the civil service," including his current role at Treasury, where he "supervises and directs the selection and promotion of the largest single unit of personnel" in the executive branch (Roosevelt 1972, 13: 99).

In the run-up to Roosevelt's nomination of Flemming to the CSC (recounted earlier in the chapter), there was speculation in the press that the position might go to McReynolds. He quickly batted it down, saying flatly said he was not interested because it would force him to give up his own civil service status.[44] With that out of the way, McReynolds was an active participant in the round robin of consultations with White House staff about the CSC vacancy. In one of Smith's meetings with the president about the vacancy, when McReynolds's name came up, Roosevelt waved off consideration of McReynolds for the CSC because the president "had in mind using McReynolds as a liaison man."[45]

Smith interpreted that conversation as reflecting FDR's thinking as relatively firm. So, when Smith continued his consultations about the CSC vacancy with others, the subject of McReynolds's future role came up. Brownlow and White told him that "by all means" McReynolds should be named by the president as "his liaison man with Civil Service." In fact, they felt appointing McReynolds to that position was "probably more important" than who would be the new CSC member.[46] Now more confident that FDR would name McReynolds to a coordinating position, Smith made a point to keep in touch with McReynolds about the CSC vacancy because "it was important to have on the Commission a person in whom McReynolds has confidence."[47]

Based on these interactions, Smith continued thinking well of McReynolds. In a meeting with the president about the liaison role, "I told him frankly that I thought McReynolds would be tops in that position."[48] While working on the CSC vacancy with McReynolds, Smith wrote in his diary that "I knew his judgment would be good" in making a final recommendation.[49] Smith also liked another aspect of McReynolds's personality and skills. He saw that McReynolds was not an empire builder who would be constantly fighting turf wars. Just the opposite. That a budget director would be involved in a CSC appointment did not bother McReynolds. He was a team player and glad to work with Smith. For Smith, this was an important detail. He knew that personnel matters were also inevitably budget issues. Also, Smith was about to expand BOB to include a management research unit. That new BOB unit, too, might get involved in studies and recommendations relating to personnel management, structure, and procedures. Smith felt confident that McReynolds's work as presidential personnel liaison would not lead to bureaucratic in-fighting about BOB's proper role and involvement. The two could work well together, each understanding that the other must have a role regarding major personnel matters that overlapped their separate portfolios.[50]

FDR's two reorganization plans approved by Congress, including the six new presidential assistants, were scheduled to go into effect on July 1, 1939.[51] In the months leading up to July 1, Washington was abuzz with rumors about who those six might be. In May, a reporter for the *Post* accurately predicted that McReynolds was on the short list of finalists.[52] (On June 21, McReynolds met with the president as part of a larger group of Treasury officials, including Secretary Morgenthau. The meeting was about a Treasury-related policy matter, but it is possible that, during the course of the meeting, FDR told McReynolds and his boss of the impending appointment.)

On July 12, Roosevelt made it official with a request that a formal commission of appointment be executed for McReynolds and two others.[53] The White House press secretary then issued a press release of his action. Press coverage noted that McReynolds's main duty would be as "adviser on all civil service problems" and to "handle questions relating to personnel and administrative procedure."[54] Another article characterized him as "like the type of man turned out by the English government, the civil servant who carries out his job unobtrusively and efficiently no matter what regime he may be serving."[55] It was a perfect description of McReynolds's work orientation and nonpartisanship. It was also one of the goals of the nascent field of public administration as nurtured by Brownlow and Gulick. For them, the British model was prized.[56]

The White House announcement noted that McReynolds would retain his civil service status so that he would continue to qualify for a pension when he retired.[57] At the time of his appointment, he was 59 and had been a federal civil servant for more than three decades, beginning in 1906.[58] Given the average longevity for American white males born in the 1880s was about 65 (Blacklow 2007), McReynolds was at an age and stage of his career when most people were ready to slow down and prepare to retire. Instead, he accepted a position in the high pressure and intense environment of the White House. Some press coverage noted his age, saying he was the "eldest" of the president's administrative assistants.[59]

There was one hitch for McReynolds and all the other staff now part of the new Executive Office of the President: there was no office space to move into. The White House proper was full, so, planning ahead, FDR asked Smith to obtain office space in the federal building immediately west of the White House, with only a narrow alley in between. At the time, it was called the State, War, and Navy Building.[60] The president wanted it to house at least the six new administrative assistants and the three central managerial agencies conceived by PCAM: budgeting, planning, and personnel.[61] (A reminder that from 1921 to 1939, BOB was formally part of Treasury [even though under the direction of the president] and therefore located in that department's building, a block east of the White House.)

Part of accomplishing FDR's assignment to Smith of obtaining presidential office space in the building was relatively easy, as the War Department was on the verge of moving to its own new building.[62] But Smith ran into an obstinate refusal by the State Department to cooperate. Departmental officials, all the way up to Secretary Cordell Hull, insisted that the department could not yield a single office in the building nor move any files out of the building. Not only were all of the rooms being actively used by the State Department, but they could not operate efficiently and in integration with the rest of the department if any staff or files were placed in a more distant building. *All* needed to be right there. Similarly, the State Department claimed that all the files then in the building were quite current and relevant to the daily work of the department. Every file needed to be accessible quickly.

Smith, the patient but persistent bureaucrat, reported back to FDR that the State Department would not yield a single office nor empty even one file room. The president told Smith to convey back to State officials that if they did not voluntarily vacate at least some offices and file rooms, he (the president) would personally come over to the building and decide which rooms occupied by State did not absolutely have to be at that location. These back and forths happened three times. Each time, State would not budge.

Finally, Roosevelt made good on his threat. On July 25, he had the Secret Service take him to the building and directed Smith, Secretary Hull, and Under Secretary Sumner Welles to meet him there. Smith described the hilarious scene of the president in his wheelchair with a map of the building plan and room assignments on his lap. For nearly two hours, the president roamed the building. Smith recalled:

> I observed with some amusement that Sumner Welles was making strenuous efforts to maintain not only his own dignity but the dignity of the State Department. When the President would ask to see in a room, although Sumner Welles would be a few feet from the door, he would not open it but would ask that it be opened by the Budget Officer of the Department or some other staff person. The President went into a number of rooms where there were files and would request how current the files were. When

> it was explained that they did not go farther back than 1928 or 1920 or some such date the President would then say, "Let me see what is in the files." His wheel chair would be put up alongside the files and he would open the drawers, much I think to the surprise of the State Department people. The first file he opened dealt with wild horses in China. He wanted to know if they considered that a current file. . . .
>
> He also went through the offices . . . of the Passport Division. He asked in detail the procedure for handling passports and for filing passports. He apparently felt that this Division was so separate in its work from other Divisions of the Department of State that it might well be housed in an outside building if it needed to be moved to make room for the Management Agencies. All the while he was making the inspection he was doing a certain amount of wise-cracking which relieved, to some extent, the tension inherent in the situation.[63]

Even after that, the State Department still fought an obstinate rear-guard action with Smith to maximize the space it would keep in the building.[64] More than a month after the president's inspection, McReynolds inquired of Smith if he could finally move into his new office? Smith said it was still not ready, but should be relatively soon.[65] In the meantime, the new presidential administrative assistants were assigned temporary office space elsewhere in the State Department's building.[66]

Establishing the Liaison Office for Personnel Management in the Executive Office of the President, September 1939

By late summer 1939, Roosevelt had already notified Congress in his April message transmitting the first reorganization plan that he intended to create a role in the new executive office for personnel management liaison and then had appointed McReynolds as an administrative assistant with responsibility for such liaison.

The president dropped the last shoe in early September. After July 1, the Executive Office of the President and the central managerial agencies within it had been in a kind of legal limbo. They existed due to the reorganization plan having gone into effect, yet they still had not attained full actualization and operation. Partly as a result of Hitler's invasion of Poland on September 1, 1939,[67] Roosevelt felt that the timing was right to fully implement the new EOP. The executive order doing that could therefore be presented, in part, as a reaction to the beginning of the war. The war necessitated being sure that the president had a modern and flexible institutionalized structure under him to respond to the emergency situation however it may unfold.

On September 8, 1939, Roosevelt issued Executive Order 8248 to complete the reorganization process of presidential powers that had begun with PCAM in 1936. The order fully established the Executive Office of the President and placed five agencies within it: the White House Office (including the six new administrative assistants), BOB, NRPB, the Office of Government Reports, and a new entity, the Liaison Office for Personnel Management (LOPM).[68] The executive order identified BOB, NRPB, and LOPM as constituting "the three principal management arms of the Government," specifically noting that the three agencies would be responsible for unique tasks, "none of which belongs in any department but which are necessary for the over-all management of the Executive Branch."

In general, LOPM would provide for "coordination of the administration of personnel." It was assigned two specific duties. First, it would assist the president in relations with the CSC. The order pointedly noted that CSC proposed regulations could only be promulgated by the president, thus highlighting the president's pre-PCAM and longtime statutory role in overseeing and approving (or not, as the case may be) CSC's formal policies and operations. Second, LOPM would assist the president in relations with the personnel offices of the departments and agencies of the executive branch (Roosevelt 1969, 1939: 493–95). While not mentioning it specifically, this would also necessarily encompass the Council of Personnel Administration (CPA), which consisted of agency personnel officers and a small staff headed by Davenport.

The head of LOPM would be the presidential administrative assistant tasked with the personnel management portfolio. While his senior title would continue to be administrative assistant, his other title, to use at his discretion, was liaison officer for personnel management.[69]

In the press release explaining the executive order,[70] Roosevelt emphasized that these EOP agencies have "to do with the overall management and central direction of the Executive Branch" by the president. The components of EOP were intended to give him a "compact organization" and to be "the regular management arms of the President" (Morstein Marx 1947, 17). More specifically regarding LOPM, Roosevelt later wrote[71] that he wanted LOPM to exist so that it would have "ample opportunity to collaborate with the Bureau of the Budget and the other managerial agencies" regarding personnel management issues. In particular, he wanted to see "personnel policies be more speedily and more carefully directed toward attracting and retaining a high brand of men and women in the federal service" (Roosevelt 1969, 1939: 504).[72]

In a Rooseveltian flourish, the executive order contained a sleight of hand. The description of the role of the six administrative assistants stated unequivocally and soothingly that they would be "personal aides to the President and shall have no authority over anyone in any department or agency. . . . In no event shall the Administrative Assistants be interposed between the President and the head of any department or agency" (Roosevelt 1969, 1939: 492). Yet, in reality, FDR was expecting Administrative Assistant McReynolds, as liaison officer for personnel management, to do exactly that when it came to the CSC and the CPA.

In mid-September, Smith looked back on what Roosevelt had accomplished in reorganizing and strengthening presidential personnel management during the year, notwithstanding the Reorganization Act's ban on touching the CSC. He concluded with great satisfaction that the time and effort had been well spent and worthwhile. McReynolds and Flemming were excellent appointments on their own individual merits, but even more importantly as a collaborating duo. With the two men now in place (and with LOPM, however modest, just established) he felt that "great improvements can be made" from now on in presidential personnel management.[73] A few years later, White reviewed what Roosevelt had done in the personnel arena in 1939 despite the legal ban on any reorganization touching the CSC. He was pleased, calling the results "a neat tactical move, [which] gained some of the advantages of a single administrator" of personnel (White 1945, 142).

4
The Liaison Office for Personnel Management in Operation, 1939–1941

The founding of the American Society for Public Administration (ASPA) in late 1939 was in part an outgrowth of PCAM, the Reorganization Act of 1939, the establishment of the Executive Office of the President, and the appointment of Harold Smith as BOB director. All pointed to an emerging new field of public administration. Brownlow, Gulick, and Smith, along with William Mosher, first dean of Syracuse University's new Maxwell School of Citizenship and Public Affairs (the first to grant the degree of Master of Public Administration [MPA]), all believed that this new area of expertise was a joint endeavor of academic researchers and high-level practitioners. Before then, the standard template of professional organizations in the United States was for either an association limited to professors specializing in that field or a membership association of practitioners. ASPA was designed as a professional membership organization for both academics and practitioners (Lee 2014).

For the second ASPA conference (which ran concurrent with the annual meeting of the American Political Science Association) in Chicago in December 1940, Brownlow, Gulick, and Harris (who had been the PCAM staff director) convened a panel on the new EOP and invited the heads of the six EOP agencies to make presentations (Colegrove 1941, 128). The presenters then reformatted their talks into articles, which were published as a symposium on EOP in the second issue of *Public Administration Review*. McReynolds's article summarized the mission and work of LOPM (McReynolds 1941).

He reviewed the history of the relationship of the CSC with presidents and recounted the PCAM fight to reorganize that relationship. Turning to the activities of LOPM since its creation in 1939, he said he "periodically meets" with the CSC and then briefs the president on important developments (124). This intermediary role reduced the "delay attendant" to meetings of the commission with the president (125). He also related his work with the personnel officers of the departments and agencies, as well as with the Council of Personnel Administration (CPA). McReynolds made a point of emphasizing that many of those latter activities and issues were wholly beyond the jurisdiction of the CSC, thus highlighting the need for *presidential* coordination of personnel management.

The article also discussed LOPM as a component of EOP. McReynolds said that this facilitated "ready and easy access to the other managerial agencies" of the president. In particular, he praised the close coordination between LOPM and BOB, given that "many personnel matters have major budgetary implications" (125). He diplomatically contrasted this new harmonious cooperation with the preceding dynamic, when BOB and CSC had "not kept in close touch with each other" (125). Finally, McReynolds reported that he had "direct access" to the president (126) and that FDR was committed to never acting on any civil service and personnel management matters "without obtaining the advice and recommendation" of LOPM (125). Overall, McReynolds depicted LOPM as a de facto presidential personnel agency that "accomplished many, though not all" of PCAM's recommendations (125).

However, McReynolds was relatively skimpy in his article on specific policy areas LOPM had been involved in since September 1939. This was probably partly a reflection of the short time LOPM had been in operation, the length limitations of a journal article, and likely the nature of personnel management, namely that there were few topics with a clear start date and an equally clear end-of-story resolution. This chapter reviews LOPM's work from its establishment September 1939 to the US entrance into WWII in December 1941. It first presents a sketch of LOPM as an agency, its relations with the CSC and the president, and then summarizes some of the major substantive policy areas McReynolds and his staff were involved in during that period.

LOPM Administrative Sketch: Status, Funding, and Staffing

Compared to the paperwork and appointments involved in creating LOPM (chap. 3), now came the hard part: how to fund the operations of this new agency on an ongoing and permanent basis. This was no minor detail. Congressional rules limited routine annual appropriations bills for agency operations to entities with statutory status (i.e., those that had been created by law). This was not a problem for three of the five EOP agencies; the Bureau of the Budget had been created by a 1921 law, the NRPB had a very tenuous statutory status as the organizational metamorphosis of the 1931 Federal Employment Stabilization Board (Clawson 1981), and the White House Office (especially the six new presidential administrative assistants) was sanctioned by the 1939 Reorganization Act. The funding for these statutory entities was routinely included with the non-Cabinet agencies covered by the annual Independent Offices Appropriation Bill.

What of the other two, OGR and LOPM? The White House initially presented the argument to Congress that this pair of new EOP agencies also had a legal basis and congressional endorsement because they were created by a formal reorganization plan that was subject to a legislative veto. Both houses had held floor votes on whether to veto FDR's reorganization plan and decided not to. Wasn't this the legislative equivalent to congressional authorization? The argument did not fly. From a strict interpretation of parliamentary rules, to be eligible for an appropriation, an executive branch entity had to be created by a *bill* that became a *law*.

For a short-term solution, FDR could fund these two EOP agencies through discretionary presidential funds approved by Congress. So, he initially funded OGR the same way he had funded its predecessor, the National Emergency Council, through allocations from emergency relief funds (Lee 2005a, chap. 5). Later, with the emergency funding of the national defense buildup after the beginning of WWII in 1939 (Pearl Harbor wasn't until December 1941), he continued to have the option of this backdoor funding approach.[1] FDR was, in a sense, lucky with the timing of WWII. Congress approved enormous lump-sum appropriations bills to be allocated at his discretion (Lee 2012a, 86).

For one of the two non-statutory EOP agencies, OGR, FDR decided to bite the lawmaking bullet. He proposed legislation to authorize OGR, thus making it eligible for funding in the Independent Offices Appropriation Bill. He overcame enormous political obstacles and persuaded Congress to pass a law giving OGR a statutory legal foundation (Lee 2005a, chap. 5). The legislative battle over OGR's statutory status was viewed at the time as second only in political significance to the fight over passing Lend-Lease. That made any legislative effort to authorize LOPM a near impossibility. Once could almost hear the opposition claiming that authorizing LOPM was the first step in undoing the Reorganization Act's prohibition on touching the CSC. Such a political context would make a bill a nonstarter.

But other maneuvers, such as the subterfuge of funding LOPM from emergency relief bills or trying to pass new legislation, were not necessary either. As an administrative assistant to the president, McReynolds's salary and the costs of running his office, which included his immediate clerical and administrative staff, could be funded by appropriations authorized by the Reorganization Act of 1939 for the White House Office. So this new and modest presidential personnel liaison agency would be wholly encompassed in McReynolds's (somewhat extended) office staffing and budget. At that point, there was no need for funding anything else and no need to draw further attention to LOPM.

Sometimes, in politics, a low profile reduces the awareness and perceived importance of a target. This was likely one reason that the title McReynolds almost always used on his official correspondence was "Administrative Assistant to the President" rather than "Liaison Officer for Personnel Management."[2] This approach also helped shelter LOPM a bit from political attacks because it reduced familiarity with the new agency. When Senate Republican leader Robert Taft (R-OH) criticized the burgeoning EOP, he pointedly mentioned that many of its new agencies were only presidential in their legality (established by executive orders) and lacked any statutory standing or legitimacy. Going through the list of EOP entities, when he got to LOPM he said, "I do not know what that is."[3] From the White House perspective that was probably a good thing, so as not to revive the fight over presidential direction of personnel management.

Before long, however, McReynolds's workload was getting beyond what he could handle personally. LOPM needed more than his own executive assistants and secretaries. It needed a modest level of additional professional staffers who were at higher management levels to be able to handle complicated policy and coordination roles. In spring 1940, McReynolds asked the postmaster general to detail a staffer from the department's Investigation Service (where McReynolds began his own federal career) to assist in a project. The postmaster assented to a brief assignment outside the Post Office Department, but not on an indefinite basis.[4] A few months later, McReynolds made a similar and successful request to USDA.[5]

LOPM Consultant G. Lyle Belsley, 1940–1941

A somewhat longer-duration staffing solution presented itself in May 1940. As a result of the worsening war situation in Europe (and, to a lesser extent, East Asia), FDR wanted to increase the country's preparedness for any military eventuality. Signing an administrative order, he activated the sixth and standby EOP agency, the Office for Emergency Management (OEM). Then he created the National Defense Advisory Commission (NDAC), vaguely within OEM.[6] The commission was a kind of exoskeleton of the plodding old-line departments and agencies in the executive branch for all matters dealing with national defense. It was a typical FDR action: an ad-hoc solution, confusing in terms of power and authority, and only vaguely structured. Best of all, it was wholly under his control because it existed solely under the authority of his September 1939 executive order establishing EOP and its constituent agencies, not any congressional statute (Lee 2012a, 24–28).

The president then appointed McReynolds as his liaison officer to NDAC, in addition to his continuing LOPM responsibilities. (Note that McReynolds was neither the *director* of NDAC nor its coordinator, merely a liaison. He gradually became the commission's secretary, largely playing a ministerial role, though occasionally making suggestions and offering observations during formal commission meetings.) To fund NDAC, Roosevelt allocated monies from the large presidential discretionary fund that Congress had recently passed for purposes of increasing national defense. McReynolds, in turn, shrewdly employed a Rooseveltian tactic and used a small amount of that money in July 1940 to hire a new full-time staffer with extensive personnel management experience. G. Lyle Belsley was funded by NDAC money and therefore formally worked for it, ostensibly as "Consultant in Public Administration." Additionally, he was hired to do "liaison work with the departmental personnel offices," clearly more of an LOPM-related assignment than a national defense one.[7] In any event, as a direct report to McReynolds, he worked on personnel matters for LOPM. There were, of course, many personnel management problems associated with the work of NDAC. Who could say if handling them was really only LOPM-related and had absolutely no possible connection to NDAC's *raison d'être*? For example, in 1941, Belsley gave a talk at a personnel conference on "Personnel Problems and National Defense."[8] That neatly covered the jurisdictions of both LOPM and OEM/NDAC.

Belsley had a deep familiarity with government personnel management. In the late 1920s, he had worked for McReynolds at the Personnel Classification Board and then moved to the Farm Credit Administration as its director of personnel (probably with McReynolds's endorsement). In that capacity, Belsley testified at one of the hearings of the Commission of Inquiry on Public Service Personnel (Commission 1935a, 566–579). During this period, he received a doctorate in economics and public administration from the Brookings Institution (and likely got to know Meriam at Brookings's Institute for Government Research).[9] In the mid-1930s, he was appointed as executive director of the Civil Service Assembly of the United States and Canada, one of Brownlow's PACH-affiliated agencies (Gaus and White 1935, 447). At the assembly, he was exposed to the strengths and weaknesses of the many CSCs at the state and local levels, including their structures and policies. He took a brief leave of absence to serve on the PCAM staff and helped draft its recommendation to reorganize the CSC into a presidential agency (chap. 1). Belsley clearly was an intimate of the public administration activists, including Brownlow, Gulick, White, and McReynolds, all of whom were interested in an updated version of civil service reform, in particular a greater role for the chief executive.

Historical records were remarkably inconsistent—probably deliberately—about whether Belsley was formally assigned to NDAC or LOPM. For example, in April 1941 Belsley opaquely identified himself as "currently on the staff of the Executive Office of the President," which could have referred to LOPM or OEM/NDAC.[10] On several occasions, he engaged in correspondence that was filed in LOPM's office records, but he used no formal title in signing the correspondence, thus leaving his affiliation ambiguous.[11] When McReynolds had to cancel participating in the EOP panel at the ASPA conference in December 1940, Belsley attended and read McReynolds's LOPM and OEM/NDAC papers on his behalf at the panel session (Colegrove 1941, 128).

Irrespective of the formalities of his funding, Belsley functioned more as de facto LOPM staffer than an NDAC one. For example, in March 1941, he spoke at a meeting of ASPA's New York metropolitan chapter. He was identified as "assistant to the Liaison Officer for Personnel Management" and spoke on "the personnel agency as a tool of management"—a topic wholly unrelated to NDAC.[12] On another occasion, Belsley reported that when he took a leave of absence from the Civil Service Assembly in mid-1940, it was to work as "Assistant to William H. McReynolds, Liaison Officer for Personnel Management."[13] Those on the outside also thought he was part of LOPM. For example, correspondence from the CSC was addressed to Belsley at LOPM.[14] Belsley was also able to add another secretary to McReynolds's office payroll to help with the work he was generating, thus slightly expanding the secretarial support for LOPM.[15]

McReynolds's clever arrangement to add a professional personnel expert to LOPM staff while charging it to OEM/NDAC had to end in April 1941. That's when FDR relieved him of his double-duty and appointed Wayne Coy in his place. By now Roosevelt had recreated NDAC into the Office of Production Management (also within OEM). As the national defense program expanded, it required more and more the exclusive attention of a full-time executive official (and then some) who was oriented to organizational management. In other words, the position was becoming more "line" than "staff."[16] Coy promptly hired Belsley as *his* assistant.[17] Even though McReynolds was the good soldier who had demonstrated his loyalty to FDR in accepting the NDAC role, its work did not reflect any particular expertise on his part.[18] So, McReynolds was likely glad when relieved of that second assignment, even if that meant losing Belsley's services to LOPM.

LOPM Consultant Guy Moffett, 1941–1944

When FDR formally notified McReynolds of the transfer of the defense coordination role to Coy, he made of point of emphasizing that he hoped McReynolds would redouble his work "as Liaison Officer for Personnel Management." The president noted some of recent personnel-related developments that he hoped McReynolds would now have more time to get involved in. He also said he wanted

McReynolds to oversee "the many acute personnel problems arising out of the defense program."[19] Here was a signal that FDR had not changed his thinking about the need for a presidential role in personnel management and that he wanted LOPM to continue functioning with vitality.

A few months later, in September 1941, McReynolds replaced Belsley with Guy Moffett. This time, the replacement staffer formally worked for LOPM as a "consultant." This title had a Rooseveltian ring, as it implied that it was not a permanent staff position. No one could criticize LOPM for starting to build an empire of bureaucrats who would impinge on the congressionally protected CSC. Rather, the title implied a shorter-term duration and a close link to specific assignments, rather than having permanent personnel management duties.

McReynolds worked the official channels to make this happen. First, he sought Smith and BOB's support for additional funding/staffing for LOPM. Here was one of the benefits of the close working relationship between BOB and LOPM compared to that of BOB with CSC. In September 1941, Smith recommended to FDR to approve transferring $34,000 to LOPM from the president's discretionary national defense appropriation for FY 1942. The purpose of the transfer was for the hiring of a small staff who would be "making personnel studies in connection with the national defense." Some likely projects included employment and training programs for industrial production, defense training programs, and the expansion of the classified civil service system (i.e., the CSC's scope) to include more federal employees, especially those in field services. The same day he got the recommendation from Smith, FDR signed the authorization letter.[20] (Such presidential allocations of discretionary funds were a serious and formal matter. Later that year, for example, the allocation to LOPM was included in a report to the House Appropriation Committee as it was considering the FY 1943 Independent Offices Appropriation Bill, the bill which included the annual funding for the White House, BOB, and CSC [US House 1941, 1123].)

Two weeks later, McReynolds asked the president to appoint Moffett as LOPM consultant. In his cover memo, McReynolds reminded the president of his earlier familiarity with Moffett during WWI and carefully explained that he hoped to hire Moffett at a relatively high salary so that Moffett would be considered senior to the many "government officers with whom he will be dealing."[21] In other words, in status-conscious Washington, Moffett needed to be the big dog in the room in order to obtain the cooperation of other federal staff. The problem was that, given CSC and congressional limitations on grade classification categories and in-grade salary limits, only a presidential appointment could overcome those rules and regulations. Showing his confidence in McReynolds's judgment, Roosevelt signed the letter the same day.[22]

There is great significance in FDR's signing the letter of appointment of Moffett. It highlights how differently the president viewed McReynolds from his other five administrative assistants. According to Seidman, around this time, another of the administrative assistants, James Rowe, asked Roosevelt to approve the hiring of an assistant to Rowe. FDR declined, saying that "if he was unable to do his job without assistance, he was not doing what the president wanted him to do" (Seidman 1998, 56). By that, the president was emphasizing that the new administrative assistants were *staff*, not *line*. They did not supervise anyone, they did not order Cabinet secretaries around, and they were not within any kind of a civilian equivalent to the military chain of command. They were merely advisors. Had Roosevelt reacted the same way to McReynolds's request to appoint Moffett, then FDR would have emphasized the same point as he made to Rowe, namely that McReynolds was to confine himself to being a staff advisor. By approving the hiring of Moffett, Roosevelt was differentiating between Rowe's and McReynolds's roles, even though they were technically equals. In FDR's eyes, McReynolds and his small LOPM were line, there to oversee and, literally, manage the CSC and all other components of the executive branch's personnel system (such as the Council of Personnel Management). It was a subtle, but powerful, expression of how strongly FDR wanted the president to be in charge of federal personnel management.

Like Belsley, Moffett had an extensive background in public administration and personnel.[23] A longtime figure in civil service reform and good government, he had joined the CSC in 1909 and was promoted to assistant to the chief examiner in 1916.[24] During WWI, by now the CSC's chief examiner, he had some modest interactions with Assistant Navy Secretary Roosevelt to help expedite recruiting and hiring for the navy yards.[25] By the mid-1920s, Moffett was a senior official at the CSC, including the commission's representative on the Personnel Classification Board, where McReynolds was the staff director.[26]

In 1929, Moffett resigned from federal service and was hired on the funding side of the good government movement, becoming a grants officer at one of the Rockefeller philanthropic funds in New York. There, he was the point man for the family's longtime support for the professionalization of public administration. This commitment had begun in 1914, when John D. Rockefeller Sr. offered relatively generous and permanent funding to the New York Bureau of Municipal Research, but with the key caveat that its work be nonpolitical and noncontroversial (Lee 2013b, 523–24). He wanted to promote a merit-based and expert-staffed government employment system that was independent of political spoils and patronage jobs. Similarly, Rockefeller wanted to increase the quality of the public service, its training, and its professionalism, and see that it be based on scientific methods as discovered through rigorous research (Lee 2014).

At the Rockefeller philanthropic funds, Moffett was the behind-the-scenes funder for the new professional infrastructure that Brownlow, Gulick, and others were constructing. Moffett provided the financing for the Public Administration Clearing House (PACH) in Chicago, the construction of the "1313" building next to the University of Chicago campus to serve as a kind of capital and headquarters for public administration, and the development of professional associations for many of the specialized silos in government. He was also a generous supporter of civil service professionalization, including the Civil Service Assembly of the United States and Canada (where Belsley worked) and Bureau of Personnel Administration (Brownlow 1958, 221–25, 237, 257, 280, 302, 314).[27] In the run-up to PCAM, he had funded the predecessor Commission of Inquiry on Public Service Personnel. Moffett was also a funder of some other key developments in public administration, including the Committee on Public Administration of the Social Science Research Council (the latter also a Rockefeller project) and the study of the work of the Governmental Research Association, which directly catalyzed the creation of ASPA in 1939 (Lee 2014).

Moffett also had a relationship with BOB's Smith, since both were seeking ways to improve the quality of government.[28] For example, Smith suggested to FDR that the president endorse a project promoted by Moffett and others "to explore the possibilities of closer integration of various social programs as between federal, state, and local agencies."[29]

In 1940, when McReynolds was serving in his dual roles of LOPM and NDAC, he asked Moffett to prepare a study on a similar subject, how the commission could accomplish greater state and local cooperation with the new national defense mobilization effort (Advisory Commission 1946, 34; National Archives 1955, Doc. 20). The commission discussed the Moffett report at its July 17, 1940, meeting. In McReynolds's dry official minutes of the commission meeting, "it was expressly understood that it did not constitute approval of the Moffett report as some of the Commissioners had reservations with respect to certain things in the report" (Advisory Commission 1946, 48). In June 1941, Moffett retired from the Rockefeller philanthropic funds.[30] His retirement was short-lived, with McReynolds arranging in September for the president to appoint him to LOPM.

Liaising with the Civil Service Commission

FDR had wanted to terminate the independent, autonomous, and bipartisan three-member CSC and replace it with a civil service administrator who would function in the HR sphere comparable to the president's budget director. After more than two years of fierce political battle, Congress had prohibited FDR from doing so by banning use of his new reorganization powers to make any modifications whatsoever in the CSC (chap. 2). Given this seemingly fixed statutory environment, a central perspective for this inquiry is what, if anything, LOPM was able to accomplish to come closer to FDR's personnel management goals while the CSC continued to exist and operate in an unchanged legal environment. Therefore, this review of LOPM's record of performance in its initial years of existence necessarily begins with its key role, LOPM's interactions with the CSC.

It turns out that LOPM made a world of difference. For all intents and purposes, the CSC was now subordinate to McReynolds and, in management lingo, the commission had become his direct report. He had a regular standing appointment with the commissioners in his office on Tuesdays to go over any business they wanted to raise or he wanted to discuss.[31] At those meetings, for example, the commissioners would submit to him drafts of executive orders they hoped the president would issue. If McReynolds (and BOB) approved it, he submitted it to the president for signing.[32] Sometimes McReynolds would meet with FDR, talk it over, and then give feedback to the CSC, for example explaining why the president declined to issue a proposed executive order.[33] This relationship was so much more than merely coordinating and liaising. McReynolds was operating as the commission's boss.

McReynolds did not limit his contacts to the commissioners. He routinely bypassed them and worked directly with senior staff of the commission, such as its executive director, chief examiner, and assistant chief examiner. To convey his views even more thoroughly to the commission staff, he sometimes spoke at in-house conferences the commission organized for its staff, such as a conference of its regional managers.[34] To influence the selection and quality of future senior CSC staff, he agreed to serve on a CSC committee revising the position classifications for those roles.[35] Indicating his power, at least once McReynolds drafted a document and directed a senior CSC official to submit it to CSC president Mitchell for signing.[36] Similarly, Belsley was in close contact with the CSC's coordinator and director of training regarding its inter-agency initiatives and committees, including its in-service training of personnel staffers throughout the executive branch and regarding the training facilities operated by departments and agencies.[37]

After trying to untangle a difficult personnel-related case in the Justice Department, McReynolds in an aside expressed exasperation with CSC staff who continued to reflect the narrow, negative, and regulatory mentality that PCAM had complained about. He said that, instead of the culture of flexibility and problem-solving that he and Flemming were trying to inculcate, he continued to see "the disposition to be somewhat belligerent and not a little bossy."[38]

McReynolds also now had a role regarding CSC budgeting and appropriations. For example, Smith asked him for feedback on CSC budget request for FY 1941. McReynolds endorsed it with suggestions for two minor revisions.[39] In an article in the first issue of ASPA's *Public Administration Review* in the fall of 1940, Flemming frankly described the impact of the new presidential intermediary role. Now, "*through* the President's liaison officer for personnel management, William H. McReynolds, important assignments in connection with the nation's over-all recruiting problems have been *given* to the Commission" (Flemming 1940, 25, emphasis added).

Summarizing his work with the CSC in mid-1941, McReynolds felt that the commission had become much more flexible, fast-acting, and responsive. In his view, the CSC "has made many changes in its administrative and technical practices to meet the practical personnel needs with which the departments and agencies of the Federal Government are faced as a result of the present emergency."[40] Here was an indication that McReynolds's role had become tantamount to that of the presidential central personnel manager that PCAM recommended and Congress prohibited. He was shaping and molding the CSC to reflect a closer link to the president's personnel perspective than that of an autonomous, regulatory, and policing CSC.

Indicating at least something of a differing perspective, CSC president Harry Mitchell's memoirs omit any mention whatsoever of McReynolds, LOPM, Belsley, or Moffett (Mitchell 1985). If McReynolds's and LOPM's role was as extensive as described above, then their absence from Mitchell's memoirs is odd, unlikely to have been happenstance. It is probably fair to interpret their invisibility as reflecting Mitchell's unhappiness with being subordinated to McReynolds rather than having direct, routine, and regular contact with the president personally, as had been the case before LOPM.

LOPM as a Presidential Agency

Besides McReynolds's multiple contacts with FDR as the president's intermediary with CSC (preceding subchapter), he had many other contacts with the president, at times in person, at other times through aides and consultations with other EOP agencies. Sometimes, Roosevelt would initiate a meeting with McReynolds to discuss a personnel matter on his mind[41] or to hear differing views of McReynolds and another staffer on a personnel policy issue and then decide what to do.[42] McReynolds met one-on-one with the president three times in 1939 after his White House appointment;[43] five times in 1940 (two with BOB director Smith; some of these likely covered NDAC business);[44] and twice in 1941.[45] One of the 1941 meetings was to discuss the controversial topic of creating a civil service career ladder for lawyers. James Rowe, another of the six presidential administrative assistants and a lawyer, also attended that meeting.

During all of McReynolds's service to FDR, he could recall only once when the president neglected to consult with him for feedback in the decision-making process for matters touching on personnel management. It was, he said, an executive order relating to creating a new temporary agency dealing with national defense. For a Saturday meeting with the president, the attorney general had brought with him a draft executive order that the Justice Department had prepared for FDR's signature, assuming he approved of the final version. Indeed, the president signed it on the spot, neglecting to ask McReynolds for input. As soon as McReynolds saw the just-promulgated executive order, he told the president that it was missing a provision dealing with the civil service status of the employees of the new agency. FDR agreed and had that detail addressed in the next relevant executive order (McReynolds 1949, 3).

However, the frequency of meetings between McReynolds and FDR during this period gradually decreased. They were increasingly conducting their business in writing. In mid-1940, McReynolds explained that "the President is so tied up I am not getting at him very much."[46] Two likely reasons were war developments (Germany's invasion of northern and western Europe) and domestic politics (would FDR run for a third term?). Another explanation could be FDR's increasing trust in McReynolds's judgment and reflexive approval of McReynolds's recommendations and decisions. However, that they were meeting less frequently was not to say they were barely ever meeting. FDR was a voracious reader, but also gregarious, enjoying meetings and the chance for fuller discussion of issues.

At other times, the president conveyed messages to McReynolds through Smith (who met with FDR much more frequently and on a wide range of subjects).[47] Sometimes Smith asked McReynolds's input on drafts of policy memos to be submitted for the president's approval.[48] McReynolds was also routinely in direct touch with other BOB officials giving his input on personnel-related policy and budget decision-making.[49] Donald Stone, in charge of BOB's administrative management efforts, recalled that McReynolds had a very good working relationship with BOB staffers who had responsibilities that overlapped with personnel management (Stone 1990, 7).

Other presidential aides also conferred with McReynolds as they were preparing reports to the president, such as if FDR should threaten to veto legislation containing a personnel-related section that McReynolds had opposed and worked against.[50] Routinely, the president referred letters he received on general personnel policies to McReynolds, so McReynolds could draft replies or reply directly.[51] FDR also passed on to McReynolds correspondence asking for help on a personal employment matters. This kind of correspondence was essentially casework. McReynolds took these referrals seriously and tried to help, although sometimes unsuccessfully.[52]

As LOPM head, McReynolds became the president's representative to the executive branch on all manner of personnel subjects. He routinely issued memos to the heads of all departments and agencies in the name of the administration with directives, requests, and explanations on HR and CSC matters. Examples included requesting cooperation with a survey on recruiting for civil positions in the national defense program and a punch-card data collection project on the qualifications of federal employees.[53]

Liaising with the Council of Personnel Administration

President Harding and then Hoover had created a council to promote and coordinate personnel management in executive branch departments and agencies (chap. 1). At first as president, Roosevelt let it atrophy. Then, in 1938, in the midst of the reorganization fight over a presidentially appointed civil service administrator, he revived Hoover's Council of Personnel Administration (CPA). It was part of an executive order significantly expanding the scope of the classified system to more federal employees (as recommended by PCAM).[54] The council's members were the personnel directors of almost all federal agencies, along with representatives of BOB and CSC.

FDR pointedly did not make his revived CPA part of the CSC, but rather independent of it. This was a small but deliberate action that highlighted that the CSC's legal jurisdiction did not encompass all personnel matters in the executive branch (as FDR's legislative opponents implied)—another detail justifying a presidential personnel agency. By reviving CPA, FDR was signaling the importance he (and PCAM) put on professionalizing personnel management throughout the executive branch. He wanted every major federal establishment to have a personnel officer who was qualified and trained for that role, and for all those officers to have a venue to work cooperatively to enhance the quality of personnel management throughout the federal government.

About six months later, Roosevelt appointed Frederick Davenport as the (salaried) chairman the CPA.[55] Davenport was a longtime good government activist and progressive. He was a faculty member in political science at Hamilton College in upstate New York and later played a major role in developing the mission of the Maxwell School of Citizenship and Public Affairs at Syracuse University. He was so involved in planning the new school that he was invited to be its first director. (He declined.)

Outside the academy, Davenport was active politically. Reflecting pre-FDR partisan political alignments, the Democratic Party was in large part the conservative, machine, and racist party. Davenport was a Theodore Roosevelt progressive and was elected as a Republican to several terms in the state senate. When

TR bolted in 1912 to run for president as the Progressive Party's nominee, Davenport followed him out and helped fill out the ticket as the party's candidate for lieutenant governor. (He lost.) After the disintegration of the Progressive Party, Davenport returned to the Republican Party and was elected in 1924 to Congress from upstate New York and reelected to three more terms. He was defeated in the Democratic landslide in 1932 (Teti 1966).

As progressive-oriented reformers in New York state politics, Davenport and FDR were a kind of political version of fraternal twins: FDR was in the progressive wing of the Democratic Party while Davenport was in the counterpart faction of the Republican Party. Indicating his good opinion of Davenport, Governor Roosevelt had named Davenport to an advisory commission on the idea of a St. Lawrence River seaway (Davenport 1952, 92). After losing his congressional seat, Davenport stayed in Washington, DC, and became active in good government and civil service reform efforts. In 1934, he founded and led the National Institute of Public Affairs, which focused on training college graduates for federal careers in public administration (89–92). The institute was part of the increased focus by Brownlow, Gulick, et al., to improve the federal government by training and hiring men with public administration education. It was funded, of course, by Rockefeller philanthropies (Reining and Stromsem 1942, 190). So, when FDR appointed Davenport to head the CPA in 1939, Davenport was already a longtime and respected member of the loose network of activists seeking to strengthen and professionalize public administration in the federal executive branch.

Funding the Council

As was becoming somewhat typical for FDR's efforts to institutionalize some of his executive-based creations, there was a problem getting funding from Congress. In the spring of 1939, a few months after his appointment, Davenport was on Capitol Hill testifying in favor of a congressional appropriation for CPA as part of the Second Deficiency Appropriation Bill (US Senate 1939a, 58–60). To bolster Davenport's testimony, FDR even sent a formal message to Congress addressing the topic of funding for CPA, seeking $15,000 for it (US Senate 1939b). It was all for naught. Congress did not include any funding for CPA in that bill.

But FDR was not willing to give up on his comprehensive approach to personnel management and reform. He asked McReynolds, now on board as his White House personnel advisor, to help. McReynolds made several recommendations, all intended to have the effect of demonstrating to Congress the need for CPA and, more generally, for every department and agency to have funding for a professional personnel director and personnel office.[56] In mid-year, the administration tried again in the next emergency funding bill, the Third Deficiency Appropriation Bill. Again, Davenport faced hostility from congressional appropriators (US House 1939b, 414–18). Eventually, Congress approved one-time funding of $22,700 for CPA for FY 1940.[57]

Getting permanent and ongoing funding in the annual spending bill was quite another matter. CPA faced the same problem as NRPB and OGR, all three having been created by executive order, not by statute. Therefore, even though the Democratic majority on the House Appropriations Committee was willing to try to fund CPA, a Republican point of order on the floor successfully knocked funding for it out of the Independent Office Appropriation Bill for FY1941 (US House 1940a, 978–1029; 1940b, 9).[58]

This was considered major news, another setback for FDR's effort to restructure the executive branch and presidency.[59] At his next press conference, FDR was asked about the House action. He vigorously defended the three non-statutory agencies. He displayed a detailed knowledge of CPA's purpose and activities so far: "It has brought in together personnel officers from every department of the Government . . . accomplishing a uniform policy of employment in the Government. He [Davenport] is preventing the stealing of one man in one department by another department. They are working out systems of promotion according to merit. . . . This Council of Personnel Administration is giving everybody a square deal on merit. It will improve the Government service" (Roosevelt 1972, 15: 91–92).

FDR then dispatched McReynolds to testify at the Senate hearing on the bill to appeal for restoring the CPA funding that the House had stripped out. Appearing both as administrative assistant to the president and as liaison officer for personnel management, McReynolds tried to clear up misconceptions about CPA. First, it was an "association of personnel officers" who benefited their own agencies by having a forum to interact with their peers; CPA did not duplicate the responsibilities of the CSC (which were largely limited to recruitment, examination, and appeals), and the small CPA staff engaged in modest research projects to improve the quality of federal personnel management across the board (US Senate 1940, 101–02). Nonetheless, the Senate declined to fulfill the president's request. Instead, it added about $25,000 to the CSC appropriation, "for the work formerly performed by the Council for [*sic*] Personnel Administration."[60]

McReynolds continued trying to find a way to fund the CPA. FDR suggested he work to persuade the conference committee to change the wording of the Senate version. Their goal was to save the CPA and, especially, to prevent it from being subsumed by the CSC. McReynolds phoned the chairman of the House conferees (who was the chairman of the appropriations subcommittee for the Independent Offices Bill) and made the argument that, as an association of departmental personnel officers, CPA was an *executive*-related activity. He said that its interests and activities were divorced entirely from the CSC's limited personnel management role. Also, if the CSC were to be seen as controlling CPA, the departmental personnel officers would likely shy away from active involvement because they would no longer see it as a voluntary association of their peers. In lieu of the Senate language, McReynolds suggested revising it to expressly permit the CSC to *participate* in the CPA.[61] Despite McReynolds's active lobbying and the president's strong support, they failed again. CPA could continue, but only within the CSC (Kammerer 1951, 338).

Trying to rescue some semblance of the independent CPA before the expiration of its current funding through June 30, 1940, McReynolds suggested to FDR that the two CPA staff members could shift to the payroll of the CSC without much problem. But he strongly opposed having Davenport, as CPA chair, also be on CSC payroll. That, he said, would undermine the very purpose of CPA as independent of the CSC and as a voluntary council of departmental personnel officers. Instead, he asked the president to approve rehiring Davenport as a staff member within McReynolds's office. First, McReynolds consulted with Brownlow to see if this would be consistent with PCAM's goal of a stronger presidential role in personnel management. Brownlow agreed, and McReynolds reported back to the president that such a hiring "would certainly conform to the pattern laid down in the report and recommendations of your Committee on Administrative Management." BOB director Smith also liked McReynolds's idea, as he too saw the importance of a central presidential personnel agency to parallel the budget agency. FDR, always seeking to reach his goals no matter how crooked the path may be, okayed the idea.[62]

In tandem with McReynolds's administrative maneuvering about Davenport's official home, FDR signed an executive order on the first day of FY 1941 that controlled how the CSC would treat CPA (now that it had been merged into the CSC). This was a shrewd use of the longstanding civil service law that CSC regulations could only be promulgated by the president. (These were routinely in the form of executive orders.) By careful drafting of Executive Order 8467, Roosevelt was ostensibly merely implementing his duty to issue formal CSC policies and operations. In this case, he made the most of it—and then some. The executive order directed the CSC to recreate CPA in the form, mission, and membership as the *status quo ante*. According to the *Post*, what FDR accomplished through this use of his powers was that the council "Rises Like Phoenix."[63]

The executive order also controlled how tenuous the link between the CSC and CPA would be. Essentially, the order negated the CSC's new de jure jurisdiction over CPA and retained the de facto independence of the CPA from the commission. FDR and McReynolds were so successful in distancing CPA from the CSC that CPA's letterhead was unchanged from before. At this point, the

CPA stationary contained no overt reference to its CSC link, funding, and administrative home.[64]

As a result of these presidential interventions, up to Pearl Harbor (in December 1941, so halfway through FY 1942) CPA continued functioning as before. It was a major forum for inter-departmental coordination of personnel management issues, especially the many subtopics which were wholly outside the CSC's jurisdiction. The council's members continued to consist of the personnel directors of all Cabinet departments, independent agencies, and the regulatory commissions.[65] As alluded to by FDR in his press conference, CPA's ongoing work contributed to the principles that the federal government was a unitary employer and that agencies needed to develop and coordinate consistent and professionalized personnel management policies. While modest in scope and size, CPA advanced PCAM's recommendation for more centralized and presidentialized personnel management.

Other Personnel Management Matters

McReynolds was involved in many other policy matters regarding personnel management from 1939 until Pearl Harbor, including veterans' points, employee manuals, employment of African Americans, and draft deferments.

Veterans' preference points in federal hiring were a politically touchy subject. Most personnel professionals disliked them because they distorted the results of eligible candidates who could be hired for a particular position. However, most elected officials sought to show solidarity with veterans and did not want to be on the wrong side (politically) of a controversial issue like that. The National Civil Service Reform League and the League of Women Voters wrote FDR in favor of limiting the scope of veterans' points, as did Leonard White. McReynolds drafted replies for the president that were neutral on the policy, merely committing LOPM to consulting with the CSC and Veterans' Administration, as well as "private organizations interested in this matter" (i.e., veterans groups).[66] All that McReynolds would commit to on behalf of the president was that "a careful study will be made and you will be further advised."[67] Ultimately, the president did not sign any executive orders with major changes in CSC regulations relating to veterans' preferences.

LOPM participated in preparing policy manuals and guidebooks for federal employees and supervisors containing the rules and regulations affecting working conditions such as hours of duty, holidays, and leave policy.[68] The most controversial issue was leave for purposes of voting (for civil servants who resided outside the District of Columbia). There was no formal or consistent policy on that, though McReynolds usually advised supervisors to be flexible in order to permit federal employees to vote.[69]

McReynolds was the president's point man on issues relating to federal employment of African Americans. In general, while FDR supported the principle of equality, he sought to maintain a low profile politically on civil rights issues, if only to avoid provoking retaliation from Democratic southerners who largely controlled Congress and were willing to hold up unrelated issues to pressure the president against civil rights initiatives (Kaiser 2014, 226–31). The case of equal—or at least fair—treatment of African Americans who worked for the federal government (as opposed to corporations holding federal contracts) was a more narrow issue and directly related to the president's own claimed predominance in federal personnel policy and management. For example, in early 1940, McReynolds met with FDR and talked about the "possibility of appointing [a] colored representative to work with the Civil Service Commissioners to handle matters relating to colored employees."[70]

The conversation with the president partly led to McReynolds's request that CPA's Davenport create a Committee on Race Relations in the federal workforce.[71] The committee's eventual report, "Problems of Minority Groups," confirmed instances of discrimination against African American federal workers. Now what? McReynolds asked Davenport if perhaps CPA would issue a letter to all departments and agencies reminding them of the importance of nondiscrimination in the workplace. Davenport demurred, saying it would be more helpful if the letter came from the president.[72] McReynolds agreed and recommended to FDR to sign and issue such a letter, which McReynolds drafted.[73]

Two days after Labor Day 1941, FDR signed the letter. In a nod to Labor Day, he noted his awareness of "possibly some lack of sympathetic attitude" towards minorities, especially regarding "employment and assignment of negroes in the Federal Civil Service." He asked that personnel policies of departments and agencies assure "the doors of employment are open to all loyal and qualified workers regardless of creed, race, or national origin." He concluded with a directive to do so "speedily and effectively."[74] For Roosevelt, it was a relatively assertive public involvement in issues relating to African Americans. Given the context, his letter prompted significant coverage in the majority and minority press.[75]

The enactment of the (peacetime) draft portended major issues with regard to its impact on federal employees. McReynolds quickly issued a formal directive to federal agency heads on the likelihood they would receive many requests from their employees for draft deferments. Proactively, he suggested each agency personnel director prepare for such developments and have a uniform policy in place on handling deferment requests. In particular, he urged becoming familiar with the (new) Selective Service regulations relating to justifiable and unjustifiable deferments.[76]

Finally, LOPM was involved in the routine contacts and correspondence between outside groups and the White House. For example, for the annual conferences of civil service organizations, McReynolds drafted greetings from the president to the conference attendees, generally summarizing the administration's record in promoting a strong, apolitical civil service system during the preceding year.[77] LOPM also maintained contact with the network of public administration professionalizers, faculty, and activists who sought to continue studying federal personnel matters and wanted to confer with McReynolds, submit relevant reports, obtain his participation in a study, or help facilitate a new research project. This was the group that had been promoting improved personnel management beginning with the 1933–35 Commission of Inquiry (chap. 1). McReynolds and Belsley routinely interacted with the Committee on Public Administration of the Social Science Research Council, with Luther Gulick and his Institute of Public Administration in New York, and with Harvard's Pendleton Herring.[78]

As discussed earlier in this chapter, in spring 1940, FDR had named McReynolds as the liaison officer to the new NDAC. At the press conference announcing the appointment, Roosevelt was asked if McReynolds would continue with his presidential duties regarding personnel management. The president's answer was a pithy verbal vote of confidence in McReynolds's first year of LOPM work: "Oh, my, yes; yes" (Roosevelt 1972, 15: 392).

In 1941, looking back on LOPM's record since 1939, Roosevelt was satisfied that he had facilitated the maximum degree of presidential personnel management notwithstanding the legal ban on reorganizing the CSC. He wrote (actually his speechwriter Samuel Rosenman wrote) that "*many* of the objectives have been achieved through this liaison officer" (Roosevelt 1969, 1939: 505, emphasis added).[79] Brownlow's verdict on LOPM's record before WWII was equally positive. He said that it "worked well" (Brownlow 1958, 421). Brownlow was especially pleased with McReynolds interposing himself between the president and the CSC. After the 1939 reorganization, the commission almost never met with FDR as it had before. Instead, all its presidential business was conducted through McReynolds (and Flemming). That was a kind of de facto implementation of PCAM's original recommendation, namely presidential leadership of federal personnel management, including bringing the CSC's side of the personnel-related activities into closer and ongoing harmony with the president's managerial goals for the federal workforce.

McReynolds was more circumspect about LOPM's record of accomplishments. In late October 1941 (only about six weeks before Pearl Harbor), he talked about

LOPM's work since its establishment in 1939. Speaking to the annual conference of the Civil Service Assembly (where Belsley had been executive secretary), McReynolds felt that "much progress had been made" on the federal civil service issues he had been working on, but there were "some weaknesses still evident and we are far from our goal."[80] What were they? In a different document, he hinted at them. First, he wanted strengthen the professionalism and practice of public personnel administration in federal departments and agencies. In particular, he wanted to facilitate the kind of *career service* orientation that PCAM and the Commission of Inquiry had encouraged. McReynolds also wanted to promote careers that were generically federal rather than agency-specific vertical silos. For example, he felt that transfers between agencies needed to be made much more simple and easy to navigate. Second, he wanted to see greater cooperation between the CSCs at the federal, state, and local levels. In this context, too, he wanted to promote a career orientation regardless of the horizontal silos (i.e., different levels of government) that impeded this. McReynolds's long term goal was to "make it possible for persons to move from one jurisdiction to another without meeting too many administrative obstacles."[81]

From an academic perspective and with the benefit of a longer time frame for evaluating its record, Millett complimented LOPM for its record during its initial years.[82] He said it "had considerable vitality" in its first two years of existence (Millett 1959, 281). That was a pretty good grade for a bureaucratic youngster and small operation.

But now for the hard part: World War II.

5
The Liaison Office for Personnel Management in World War II, 1942–1945

Everything changed with the Japanese attack on Pearl Harbor on December 7, 1941, and the congressional declaration of war on Japan the next day.[1] Now the purpose of presidential personnel management took on a new and urgent meaning. As this inquiry focuses on the tension between an independent merit system and an executive-centered HR management, it is not necessary to review the many substantive personnel issues that arose during the war. Given his role as the White House's preferred commissioner, Flemming gave a contemporary overview of the federal government's internal HR and personnel management agenda as it looked to him circa September 1942 (Flemming 1942). These wartime HR issues have also been well covered retrospectively in the postwar academic literature (though it is by now a bit dated) (Van Riper 1958, chap. 14; Kammerer 1951). Paralleling the preceding chapter's attention on the prewar years, the focus of this chapter is on the role of the presidency in personnel management during the war versus that of the ostensibly untouchable CSC. More precisely, what was LOPM's role? Was it indeed political window dressing to salvage appearances after FDR's losing fight during the reorganization battle to create a civil service administrator? Or was it a significant player and presence in the managerial issues that needed to be addressed as the war unfolded?

LOPM Administrative Sketch: Status, Funding, and Staffing

During the war, LOPM had—at least formally—up to five full-time staffers (US House 1943, 847; 1944a, 45). This number did not include McReynolds, who was paid and counted as part of the White House office budget. LOPM's staff included Moffett as a "technical consultant," an administrative assistant, a private secretary, and two secretaries.[2] The two secretaries were formally assigned to LOPM, not to McReynolds as a presidential administrative assistant. This minor detail can be seen as an indication that LOPM was becoming somewhat institutionalized as an agency, at least in the eyes of the administration. The estimate of LOPM's staffing level is probably a bit low because some White House and EOP staff were routinely "detailed" to the presidency while remaining on the payrolls of their home department or agency. McReynolds did this sometimes for LOPM. For example, in late 1944, he shifted his administrative assistant to the payroll of the Internal Revenue Service.[3]

Most of the funding for LOPM came from discretionary allocations the president made from the Emergency Fund for National Defense (US House 1945, 51–52). For FY 1942, FDR transferred $34,000 to LOPM, probably related to the indefinite appointment of Moffett as LOPM consultant (chap. 4). For FY 1943, LOPM received $43,500 in transfers from the president's discretionary account (Treasury Department 1946, 870) and $23,500 during FY 1944 (US House 1944b, 213).

The Russell Amendment

Given its tenuous source of funding and lack of statutory status, LOPM's existence was in danger in mid-1944. Several political issues coalesced into a surprisingly strong rebellion on Capitol Hill that nearly brought down LOPM and like agencies. The controversy started in the Senate, where southern racists were seeking any way to shut down the Fair Employment Practices Committee (FEPC). FEPC had been created by FDR by executive order in 1941. Its mission was to combat racial discrimination by federal contractors (in contradistinction to discrimination against federal employees [chap. 4]). However, FEPC had little legal power, as well as a small staff and budget. Nonetheless, southern conservatives fought it tooth and nail. One of the strategies to kill it was an amendment by Richard Russell (D-GA) during the Senate Appropriations Committee's consideration of the Independent Offices Appropriation Bill for FY 1945. He moved to ban *any* federal spending by agencies created solely by executive order.[4] The committee approved his proposal.[5] Then, during the Senate's floor debate on the bill, it was approved, too.

Russell's indirect strategy to kill FEPC had the political benefit of not being overtly racist (as many of the other efforts to kill FEPC were), but especially because it appealed to a wider audience on Capitol Hill who were protective of a legislature's institutional interests. One of the longstanding anti–New Deal narratives in Congress had been that FDR was acting like a dictator and was expanding the power of the presidency at the expense of Congress. Given the constitutional provision that only Congress could appropriate money, the implication was that FDR was spending money illegally and seemingly unconstitutionally when he created new agencies by executive order, meaning that those entities did not have statutory basis for their existence (and could not be funded by agency-specific annual appropriation bills [chap. 4]). Russell said his amendment was needed "to stop the executive department from legislating. I want to stop this practice of creating agencies that Congress knows nothing about."[6] On another occasion, he said the amendment was needed to stop "the creation of bureaucracies without the consent of Congress."[7]

Two EOP agencies, OGR and NRPB, received the brunt of that generic attack. That was what had prompted FDR to conclude he had to push through Congress a bill authorizing OGR (chap. 4). This perspective was also the basis of the successful congressional effort so far to defund NRPB. Up to that point, Roosevelt had usually found circuitous ways to fund the administrative entities he had created by executive order. Russell's amendment had broad appeal because it represented a principle strongly held on the Hill, regardless of geography, party, or ideology.

While FEPC was at the center of the controversy, about a dozen other executive order–only agencies were caught in the dragnet of the Russell amendment, including LOPM. For the legislators who had fought so hard to exclude the CSC from FDR's new reorganization powers and prohibit a central presidential personnel management agency, LOPM's existence in EOP as an executive order–only agency seemed to be a daily defiance of their accomplishment. LOPM was a symbol and tangible operating example of how the president had successfully maneuvered to achieve partially his personnel management centralization effort, notwithstanding the protection Congress had given the CSC. While LOPM was a minor factor in the public debate over the Russell amendment, pro-CSC legislators would have known and been glad to see it caught up in the larger net and make it disappear from existence. The link between FEPC and LOPM in the Russell amendment was especially obvious to Congressman Robert Ramspeck (D-GA). As chairman of the House Civil Service Committee, he had been the point man in opposing the PCAM plan for a civil service administrator and vociferously defended the model of an autonomous and independent CSC (chap. 2). Now, Ramspeck strongly supported the Russell amendment to defund FEPC and LOPM (and several others) and spoke in favor of it during the floor debate on FEPC.[8]

In conference committee, the House conferees refused to support the Russell amendment and recommended to the House to uphold their position.[9] This recommendation was challenged on the floor of House. FDR's supporters and the Democratic leadership were crushed by a floor vote of 282–46, indicating that Russell had tapped into a deep bipartisan hostility to FDR's executive order–centered approach to public administration.[10] The news media dubbed it a "death sentence" for those agencies.[11]

The president eventually signed it into law[12] because he had, typically, found a way around it. After an appeal from FDR, his allies on Capitol Hill succeeded in effectively nullifying the Russell amendment with another amendment in a funding bill that came up a few weeks later. The 1944 Second Deficiency Appropriation bill allowed continued funding for executive order–only agencies by the president from his discretionary emergency national defense fund. This was LOPM's source of funding, as it was for most of the other executive order–only agencies. The provision was worded in a way that did not seemingly contradict the preceding rider in the Independent Offices bill. It retained in place the ban on use of appropriated funds for executive order–only agencies, but *only* if both houses or both appropriations committees explicitly voted against funding that specific agency.[13] (Meanwhile, FEPC got funded separately after another fierce floor fight a few weeks later on a third bill, the War Agencies Appropriation Act of 1944.[14])

In the last year of the war, LOPM's staffing changed. Moffett retired at the end of September 1944.[15] With the end of the war somewhat in sight and at age 62, he wanted to step out of the pressure-cooker atmosphere of the EOP and live full-time on his farm in Leesburg, Virginia.[16] McReynolds accepted the resignation "with reluctance and regret." He praised Moffett's work at LOPM, saying "There is no one else who could have rendered so effectively the service and support you have so freely given."[17]

McReynolds as Political Appointee

One of the oft-overlooked details of the 1939 Reorganization Act creating the six new White House slots for administrative assistants was that the six were explicitly exempted from the Hatch Act prohibitions on federal employees being involved in politics (Lee 2005, 220n20). Nonetheless, McReynolds shied from open political activity and preferred the role of the nonpartisan expert in the complicated area of personnel policy. (He was arguably still "Hatched" because he retained his civil service status when he transferred from Treasury to the White House.) As a result, when testifying at Capitol Hill hearings, members tended not to treat him as a partisan and ideological representative of the president, but rather as a civil service expert who could help unravel complicated situations in a neutral and fair-minded way.

However, McReynolds once acted in a political role publicly by showing his support for and loyalty to the president. On July 11, 1944, Roosevelt announced at a White House press conference he would run for a fourth term. In the run-up to his announcement, the president had seemed to be less energetic and sharp and, generally, to be in decline. Rumors were rife about his health. In a show of support, McReynolds attended the press conference, along with the other administrative assistants, and sat on the side of the room.[18] Besides demonstrating his political support for FDR, by their attendance, the White House staff were also conveying they believed he was strong enough for another term. After all, if the people who worked with him and interacted with him intimately were indicating by their presence his ability to serve another term, who could argue with the authoritativeness of their witness? It was untrue, of course. Roosevelt was dying, and his powers of concentration, articulation, and long work hours were indeed fading. His hands trembled, his face was sagging, and he had lost a significant amount of weight (Jordan 2011).

Liaising with the Civil Service Commission

The impact of LOPM on the CSC has been one of the foci for this historical inquiry. Did its existence and record bring FDR closer to his goal of presidential personnel management, notwithstanding the legal ban on using his reorganization powers to touch the CSC? Therefore, similar to the discussion of LOPM's role *vis-à-vis* the CSC in its first two plus years of existence (chap. 4), this orientation is again the first to be examined in a review of LOPM during the war years.

Before the creation of LOPM, the three CSC members had occasionally met directly with the president. After LOPM's establishment, these meetings became very infrequent, with McReynolds the liaison between FDR and the CSC (chap. 4). Once WWII started, CSC meetings in the Oval Office ceased entirely. The president was dedicating virtually all of his time to the war. For example, in 1945, Harry Mitchell, still president of the CSC, admitted in a letter to an old friend from his home state of Montana (who was seeking help for his son in the service) that "all our contact with President Roosevelt is *entirely* through one of his assistants, Mr. McReynolds."[19] This letter contradicts Mitchell's odd claim in his memoir that during the war, his White House liaison was a weekly meeting with the FDR's son and aide, James Roosevelt (Mitchell 1985, 231). Mitchell also claimed in his memoir that at least once James was unable to resolve an issue and arranged for a short meeting between the president and Mitchell. However, a review of the president's daily schedule online during the war years indicates no such meeting. Similarly, FDR's daily schedule during the war show no business meetings with James Roosevelt. All calendars documenting his presence are social: shared meals, overnight guest, etc. Also, during part of the war, James Roosevelt served in the military and was stationed outside Washington. (Similar to my previous speculation [chap. 4], Mitchell's historical version seems in part to be a settling of scores and revising the narrative story to a version he would have preferred, as when he failed to mention Flemming, McReynolds, and LOPM at all. For a historian, the credibility of a document written at the time, namely Mitchell's 1945 private letter to a friend, must be given greater weight for accuracy and credibility than his retrospective memoirs.)

During the war, McReynolds and Moffett were in extensive contact with the CSC, in person, in writing, and on the phone. They reviewed all CSC proposed regulations (which by law could only be promulgated by the president) and, if acceptable, forwarded them in executive order format to FDR for signing. Roosevelt routinely signed dozens of CSC-related executive orders during the war based on McReynolds's intermediary role. Examples include special procedures relating to recruitment, placement, and changes in status (9063, February 16, 1942);[20] modifying the conditions for granting classified status (9506, December 12, 1944);[21] and coordination of allocation of field positions subject to the Classification Act of 1923 (9512, January 12, 1945). Regarding that 1945 executive order, McReynolds made sure that the final version of an executive order directed that any instances of non-compliance with the policy enunciated in that particular executive order should be reported to LOPM, rather than the CSC. That detail reinforced to the agencies in the executive branch affected by the order the supreme status of LOPM as the centralized presidential agency for personnel management, higher than that of the CSC.[22]

Besides executive orders, McReynolds also kept a tight rein on the CSC by reviewing and controlling its legislative positions and its annual reports to the president (which the president then sent to Congress and were published). For example, McReynolds reviewed the draft of the report for FY 1944 and required some "corrections." He then "cleared" it for formal submission.[23] This way McReynolds was especially able to control the contents of the section of the report with CSC's recommendations to Congress for HR legislation. He permitted the report to contain only legislative proposals he approved of.[24] Only then did he recommend that the president send the report to Congress. On a different occasion, Flemming wanted to testify against a bill (not emanating from the CSC) at a congressional hearing. Before doing so, he needed McReynolds's OK. Flemming went to McReynolds's office, briefed him on the legislation, and explained why Flemming thought it was a bad idea. At the end of the conversation, McReynolds approved Flemming's plan by telling him, "You've got clearance; go up and tell them."[25]

Some of the topics of routine CSC work that McReynolds actively participated in included conditions under which employees of the War and Navy Departments could take CSC examinations for positions outside their department;[26] proposed legislation affecting retirements at the US Board of Tax Appeals,[27] the format for presentation of payroll deductions on pay statements,[28] temporary appointments to the police and fire departments of the District of Columbia,[29] apportionment of releasing wartime civilian employees,[30] and reemployment rights of veterans.[31] Moffett was similarly involved in overseeing in great detail the work of the CSC, including improving its reporting and record keeping;[32] low-amount retirement interest checks;[33] recruitment efforts for specialized and professional occupations;[34] quality of field inspection reports;[35] and allocation standards.[36] The seeming mundaneness of these subjects indicates how deeply LOPM penetrated the CSC's decision-making and operations and its near total control over the outcomes of relatively ordinary HR policies and procedures.

Therefore, LOPM can be seen as practically the complete lord and master of the CSC whenever the situation seemed to call for it to be so. It had nearly a blank check to speak for the president and insist to the CSC that his preferences be implemented. There was no subject too minor for McReynolds or Moffett to get involved in, raise questions about, or suggest resolutions. At least based on the archival record examined for this study, the CSC never refused to do what LOPM told it to do. FDR had successfully tamed and co-opted the CSC. From an agency that had claimed statutory autonomy and independence in order to protect the merit system, it meekly became part of a centralized presidential personnel management system.

A Plan to Reorganize the CSC

Despite the CSC's responsiveness to LOPM's oversight, McReynolds was still frustrated with the agency's lumbering and inefficient style of operations. Beginning in 1943 and through 1944, he concluded that notwithstanding the commissioners' and CSC staff's efforts to move faster during the war, all "work of a purely administrative character is delayed pending disposition by the Commission. Also, it is possible Commission members are more cautious than necessary, thus bringing about inaction and indecision." McReynolds felt there was a need "for concentration of executive responsibility in one person," specifically a commissioner "who possesses such temperament and ability that he will be able to achieve the desired result."[37] Who? Flemming.

McReynolds proposed that the president issue an executive order designating one commissioner as the "chairman" of the CSC and assigning him all executive powers over CSC staff. This new office of chairman with duties of a CEO would be slightly different from Mitchell's title as CSC president, whereby he merely presided at commission meetings but had no other powers. The new chairman would have all the administrative powers currently exercised by the top professional of the CSC staff, who held the title of chief examiner. Most importantly, the plan would make the CSC chairman "the executive head of civil service responsible to the President."[38] This redesignation of powers, McReynolds felt, would greatly improve wartime personnel management. In fact, the ultimate impact of the change would largely render LOPM moot, although he did not put it that way. (What

McReynolds was proposing would have been a de facto reversal of the agreement Mitchell said he had obtained from FDR in 1933 not to name a "secretary" of the commission, even though the law gave him to power to do so [chap. 2].)

Knowing of the political battles of 1937–39, McReynolds had to proceed cautiously and knew he certainly could not achieve these goals by invoking the president's 1939 reorganization powers. Rather, any action would have to be based on the pre-1939 statutory role that all presidents had *vis-à-vis* the CSC: nomination of members to the Senate, promulgation of rules (through executive orders), and designation of a non-commissioner as CSC secretary. McReynolds talked with Congressman Ramspeck, chair of the House Civil Service Committee (and opponent of the civil service administrator idea), and got his informal assent to do something along those lines. BOB also okayed the idea and helped draft preliminary legal papers to accomplish it if the president decided to approve it.[39]

But McReynolds avoided putting much in writing because he feared that the customary process of what he called "the usual official circulation"[40] might trigger premature opposition, even leaks to the press and attacks from Republicans, Democratic conservatives, civil service defenders, employee organizations, and newspaper editorials and columns. Instead, in one of his very infrequent meetings with the president during the war, he talked it over with FDR on February 19, 1943. The president apparently gave him a very cautious approval to proceed to explore the idea. McReynolds then discussed his plan with Senator James Mead (D-NY), Ramspeck's counterpart. Mead said he was "entirely sympathetic" with the goals of such an executive order if FDR decided to go ahead. McReynolds then prepared for the president's signature two documents: a formal executive order and a letter to Flemming designating him as holding the new office of chairman of the CSC.[41]

Roosevelt never signed either document.[42] The archival record is incomplete and provides no explicit explanation for why he so acted. However, it seems reasonable to speculate that the president felt the CSC's operations with Flemming as a member working closely with LOPM were good enough, that such an executive order might unintentionally bash a political beehive and create unnecessary public controversy (especially when he was running for reelection later in 1944), that by this time FDR was single-mindedly focusing on war strategy, and that he was gradually losing his extraordinary mental capacity for work and multitasking. At the very least, his political instincts would have been better than McReynolds's, and he would have intuitively sensed it was not a good idea politically, even if on the merits McReynolds was right. This failed effort to reorganize the CSC was McReynolds's largest *faux pas* as liaison officer for personnel management, perhaps largely because he was stepping beyond his personnel management role into a political advisor's one, a role for which he was not as well suited.

In summary, how does one score the record of LOPM's wartime oversight of the CSC? In 1944, with the tide of the war having turned, three personnel experts weighed in with assessments of the wartime performance of the CSC and consequently (at least impliedly) their views on LOPM's effort to oversee and improve the CSC. Reeves, the original author of the PCAM report on personnel management,[43] felt that the commission had only modestly improved its operations, flexibility, and speed of action. Who should get the credit for whatever limited progress it had made? Reeves said that it was "not entirely clear" what was driving those improvements, but that it might be due to LOPM's influence and oversight of the CSC (Reeves 1944, 329). The small presidential agency's low public profile and largely behind-the-scenes work made it difficult in the midst of the war for him to conclude definitively that LOPM was the major factor in whatever positives were finally happening at the CSC, but it was certainly a possibility.

A personnel staffer in the War Department concluded that LOPM had contributed "a modicum of coordination in the personnel sphere" that had been lacking before its creation, especially by linking the CSC with the president. For example, thanks to LOPM, the CSC "has received the benefit of closer working contacts with the Executive Office" and, as a result, had been able to play a more constructive personnel management role than before (Mangan 1944, 14).

White, as the longtime supporter of PCAM's recommendations, was the most scathing in his criticism of the CSC's wartime record. He claimed that the CSC's prewar good relationships with Congress (which had been a factor in Congress protecting the commission in the 1939 Reorganization Act) "have deteriorated in the last few years" (White 1944, 65). He urged Congress to act on this dissatisfaction by reversing the "inadequate authority" it had delegated to the president up to now in personnel matters. Congress should approve a "central direction of personnel policy" (impliedly by the president), and the CSC should be reconstructed into "the Office of Civil Service Administration" (68).[44] From his perspective, LOPM may have been somewhat helpful, but it just wasn't enough.

LOPM as a Presidential Agency

Once war was declared, the frequency of McReynolds's personal meetings with the president dropped significantly. During the three plus years of the war, FDR's calendar shows only six meetings with McReynolds.[45] McReynolds's oral history mentioned a seventh, right after the 1944 election (chap. 6). (It is possible, of course, that there were some meetings not listed on the president's formal schedule, chance encounters, casual conversations, and phone calls.[46]) When McReynolds expressed his concern to the president that the lack of contact might lead to McReynolds being wrong about what the president would want, FDR's wry answer was "Wait until I complain, Mac" (McReynolds 1949, 4). This, of course, would have boosted McReynolds's confidence that the president trusted his judgment and that McReynolds could feel a bit freer to speak in the name of the president even without discussing it with him first.

Roosevelt occasionally mentioned McReynolds at his press conferences. These references indicated that McReynolds was a senior and trusted member of the White House staff, that Roosevelt was in close touch with him, and that McReynolds *indeed spoke for the president*. During a December 1942 press conference, FDR summarized his recent message to Congress on how to resolve some conflicting federal personnel policies (mostly statutory) on rates of pay, hours of work, and overtime. Then he said, "If you want more details on it, get hold of McReynolds. He will tell you all about it" (Roosevelt 1972, 20: 292).

In late 1943, the president explained at a press conference his (unchanged) wartime policy that federal employees would be expected to work on all holidays except Christmas. He told reporters that he had just "okayed a memorandum that Bill McReynolds wanted to send out" (Roosevelt 1972, 22: 215). The memo from McReynolds to the heads of executive branch agencies also stated that supervisors "may, in their discretion, permit offices or establishments to be closed not earlier than two hours in advance to the usual closing time on Christmas eve."[47] After Christmas, the head of the Federal Communications Commission wrote the president complaining that some offices—but not the FCC—had closed on Thanksgiving 1943, contrary to FDR's wartime holiday policy. In reaction, Roosevelt dictated a memo to McReynolds, stating that "if they did violate instructions, I think you and I should take them over our knee—and do the usual."[48] McReynolds had earlier notified the president that some agencies had closed one hour early on Thanksgiving. This created "an exceedingly bad morale situation in those agencies" that were complying with FDR's policy to work a full day on Thanksgiving.[49] But McReynolds did not identify any agencies closed for the whole day. In fact, these early-closing violations on Thanksgiving were precisely what had prompted McReynolds to recommend that FDR restate his policy with another memo in December 1943, before Christmas, as a reminder of the holiday policy for federal employees.

One of the ways that the president routinely kept in touch with McReynolds (and vice versa) during the war, albeit not in person, was in writing. This had been a common pattern of communication before Pearl Harbor (chap. 4) and continued through the war years. McReynolds periodically submitted memos and drafts of executive orders to FDR for guidance or approval. For example, in May 1942, he briefed the president in writing on his consultations with BOB, the CSC, and OEM's Coy on standardizing federal overtime pay at time and a half. Roosevelt wrote "OK F.D.R." on McReynolds's memo. As a result, the CSC submitted to Congress proposed legislation to resolve the problem.[50] The subject of overtime was not solved so easily. Six months later, in reaction to another memo on the subject from McReynolds, FDR asked BOB director Smith to arrange an appointment so that the three of them could meet and talk it over.[51]

Another issue merely required FDR's signature. Former congressman Maury Maverick (D-TX) was serving as chair of the Smaller War Plants Corporation. It was not clear if he had the authority to appoint dollar-a-year men (from business) to work for the corporation. McReynolds suggested resolving this personnel matter authoritatively. He submitted a draft to FDR that formally delegated to Maverick the HR power to do so. The president signed it.[52]

Sometimes, notwithstanding his best efforts, McReynolds could not resolve issues that came to him. When that happened, he had no choice but to refer them to the president. For example, Paul McNutt, a senior official in the economic mobilization effort, was concerned about the personnel impacts of the military draft (and that the consequent and inevitable impact on industrial output would become political complaints about *him*). McReynolds had a long talk with McNutt, but McReynolds was ultimately unable to resolve McNutt's concerns. So McReynolds wrote FDR that the president should probably meet with McNutt and give him "some direct advice and encouragement," implying more of a pep talk than making a commitment to any substantive change in policy.[53]

Also similar to prewar patterns, FDR frequently referred letters he received to McReynolds for answering. Sometimes the president wanted a draft that he would sign; sometimes he simply asked McReynolds to respond in his own name and handle it as he saw fit. For example, federal employee organizations were opposed to a War Department directive that all civilian employees have a social security number and provide it to their supervisor. They complained to Roosevelt, who asked McReynolds, "Will you be good enough to handle this?"[54] A few weeks later, BOB and CSC decided the directive was not necessary, and the issue became moot.[55]

Other referrals from the president to McReynolds included requests to assess a manpower plan proposed by a middle-ranking administration official (who was married to FDR's cousin),[56] to consider an appeal from Mayor LaGuardia to exempt several veterans employed by New York City from wartime regulations,[57] and to comment on a plan regarding utilization of scientific personnel submitted by Frederick Delano (the president's uncle), who was NRPB chair.[58] At least once, Roosevelt referred something his wife had brought up and asked McReynolds to deal with it. Mrs. Roosevelt was seeking a presidential reply to a letter from a woman acknowledging the availability of qualified women to serve the country in fields they were underrepresented in, such as international law and international relations. Mrs. Roosevelt then wanted to have the exchange of letters released to the press for publicity about opportunities for women and the White House's support for such efforts. McReynolds's office files only indicate that McReynolds was to talk to Mrs. Roosevelt, but do not indicate any further action.[59]

During the war, as LOPM head, McReynolds continued to be the representative of the president to the executive branch on policies relating to personnel. He routinely issued memos to the heads of all departments and agencies in the name of the administration with directives, requests, and explanations for HR and CSC matters. Examples included use of bulletin boards by employee organizations,[60] support for the "Government Girl" project (of female civil servants—mostly secretarial—raising funds for airplanes),[61] absenteeism policy,[62] time off to donate blood for the war effort,[63] time off to vote in Virginia's 1943 elections and in the 1944 presidential election,[64] and encouraging supervisors to support an employee recreation program with the National Symphony.[65] McReynolds's last executive branch-wide memo was on April 15, 1945 (three days after FDR's death), regarding how to handle time off requested by employees to observe Good Friday.[66]

The EOP agency that LOPM most frequently interacted with during the war was the Bureau of the Budget. This close working relationship reflected PCAM's view of budgeting and personnel as two of the three central managerial levers a president should use to oversee the executive branch. (The third was planning.) The trust and respect that McReynolds and Smith had for each other was a central factor, but the cooperative relationship was pervasive throughout their agencies (with BOB, of course, much bigger than LOPM). Turf was not a factor. Rather, there was a shared assumption that budgeting and personnel were related and intertwined, practically two sides of the same coin. In a letter to the GAO, McReynolds casually referred to working with "the Budget boys" on a personnel problem.[67] Some issues BOB and LOPM worked together on were channeling older military officers to vacant administrative positions in the civil service,[68] reduction of personnel by civil agencies and departments,[69] bailiffs in federal courts,[70] and a report on pay levels from the Customs Service.[71]

Probably the most impressive indication of the hand-in-glove cooperation between presidential budgeting and personnel management was a policy document to all executive agencies on how personnel management should be organized. Its premise was that "Management of human resources is inseparable from the administration of programs. At the same time there is a need within the line of command for complete and comprehensive unity embracing all aspects of management, including the fiscal and materiel as well as the personnel side" (BOB 1943, 4).

This circular (called a "specimen order") was released to all executive branch agencies by BOB's Division of Administrative Management.[72] It included a model directive and encouraged all departmental and agency heads to promulgate it as their formal HR policy. The circular publicly acknowledged the input from the CSC and CPA (3) but, tellingly, not from LOPM. This likely represented McReynolds's passion for anonymity and preference to give public credit to the agencies he oversaw. However, the contents perfectly reflected LOPM's view of the role of personnel management in public administration. In this policy statement, BOB and LOPM were jointly continuing to move toward implementing the goals of PCAM's personnel recommendations notwithstanding the ban on reorganizing the CSC.

McReynolds also interacted with other presidential staff and EOP agencies during the war. Once, McReynolds asked press secretary Stephen Early to conduct some publicity on the effort to professionalize the career track for lawyers in the federal government.[73] Another time, he analyzed some personnel administration problems in the office of the District of Columbia's municipal register of deeds. McReynolds recommended that the district's civil service system be expanded to cover the employees of that office.[74] For a delicate personnel matter that required the president's attention, he worked with fellow administrative assistant Jonathan Daniels.[75]

Liaising with the Council of Personnel Administration

It will be recalled that, a year before the US entered WWII, CPA lost its autonomy from the CSC because Congress cut off its separate funding (chap. 4). As a result, FDR had made it an entity within the CSC, making it eligible for CSC's appropriated funds. Reluctantly acknowledging it was no longer wholly independent, in 1942 CPA's letterhead changed, listing it as a sub-entity in the CSC, but still with its own letterhead, rather than using the regular CSC letterhead.[76] However, the concession to funding realities was as restrained as possible. A fact sheet on CPA's wartime work described the council as "an interdepartmental committee on Federal personnel matters," with no reference or link to the CSC. Issued in 1943, the summary stated that CPA's work "has been greatly stepped up by the huge expansion of Federal war activities," with emphasis on creating uniform executive branch–wide policies on such diverse personnel issues as "the growing labor shortage, overtime, work under pressure, loss of vacations, withdrawal of men for the armed forces, and the need for greater speed in personnel actions."[77]

The tensions between CPA and CSC surfaced regarding the issue of field personnel management (i.e., outside Washington, DC). In most major metropolitan areas, there was a federal personnel council, consisting of local CSC regional officials and the senior personnel officers of federal departments and agencies in that locality. The CSC argued that it oversaw these local personnel councils in part because the senior CSC officer in that city was usually the organizer and secretariat of each group. CPA claimed these local councils were part of CPA because they were mostly composed of non-CSC personnel officials. More specifically, the conflict was whether the local councils could communicate *directly* with CPA or if all contacts had to be *through* the CSC. Finally, McReynolds had to intervene. He attended the CPA meeting of July 6, 1944. In advance of the meeting, Davenport encouraged McReynolds to smooth over the problem "with your accustomed tact."[78] Archival records examined did not include McReynolds's comments at the meeting, but based on McReynolds's general orientation, he likely urged compromise and coordination by working especially with Flemming. Also based on his previous views, he probably tilted slightly in favor of the CPA as more reflective of a president-centric personnel management regime than the CSC (notwithstanding Flemming's positive impact). Kammerer did not cover this specific controversy, but hinted that after McReynolds's intervention, the regional councils maintained a closer association with CPA than the CSC proper, if only because she discussed the regional councils within her subchapter on CPA's wartime accomplishments (Kammerer 1951, 340).

McReynolds's support for CPA was also evidenced by his positive comments about CPA's accomplishments at a meeting of the Society for Personnel Administration[79] and a letter he drafted for FDR to send Davenport on CPA's fifth anniversary. In it, McReynolds/FDR congratulated Davenport for "a substantial contribution" to the war effort by "improving the management of personnel in the government service and advancing the concept of cooperative action in dealing with the many work-a-day problems that press for solution."[80] Another demonstration of his positive view of CPA's work was when McReynolds issued certificates "To Whom It May Concern" stating that Davenport's trips around the country to visit with local personnel councils were necessary for the war effort.[81] Had he thought poorly of Davenport's contributions, he could have declined to permit such travel. Davenport acknowledged publicly that CPA played a major role in the development of federal personnel policies largely because McReynolds, on behalf of the president, wanted CPA to do so (Davenport 1944, 11).

McReynolds did not always side with Davenport and CPA. When Davenport and the council wanted to insist on strict symmetry in the council's membership (i.e., the principle of one-agency-one-representative), McReynolds intervened to "suggest" an increase the representation from the military, so that each of the uniformed services would be on the council, as well as their civilian counterparts from the War and Navy Departments. McReynolds tried to soothe any opposition by suggesting the uniformed officers be non-voting members.[82] But, clearly, McReynolds expected that his intervention—however diplomatically worded—was to be viewed as final and authoritative.

BOB and LOPM sometimes worked jointly to review CPA recommendations on proposed policies. These included plans relating to increased employment of personnel with training in public administration (for future management positions),[83] night pay differentials,[84] and hours of work for field offices.[85] These examples of LOPM-BOB joint projects regarding CPA policy recommendations are also further demonstration of the implementation of PCAM's view that budgeting and personnel were both management tools for the president and were often inextricably linked, two elements of the same endeavor that should not be artificially separated.

While McReynolds occasionally interacted with the council, Moffett was much more involved in CPA's ongoing business as the president's representative. Moffett monitored and sometimes participated in CPA efforts to develop uniform personnel policies in such areas as management-labor relations (within federal agencies),[86] physical fitness,[87] absenteeism,[88] veteran reemployment rights,[89] training,[90] and appeals procedures for field personnel.[91]

During the last year of the war, the House Civil Service Committee issued a report assessing wartime personnel matters. It commended CPA for its contributions.[92] Van Riper concluded that during the war CPA "served an extraordinarily useful purpose," especially due to its "unique and constructive functions" (Van Riper 1958, 389–90). These are confirmation that CPA made a positive contribution to wartime personnel management under LOPM's gentle and unobtrusive oversight. The council continued professionalizing HR in the executive branch and promoting the development of uniform policies and procedures. All this even though CPA was now formally within the CSC and funded from its budget. As was more often the case than not, FDR got what he wanted for this component of a unitary federal personnel management system during the war. McReynolds and Moffett had helped guide CPA to accomplish these presidential HR goals.

Other Personnel Management Matters

LOPM, through McReynolds and Moffett, continued the prewar pattern of involvement in a potpourri of personnel policymaking and implementation throughout the executive branch, sometimes on a wholesale basis (i.e., applicable to all departments and agencies) and sometimes on a retail approach (i.e., agency-specific). Some of these subjects were continuations of prewar roles (chap. 4), such as draft deferment policies for federal employees in general[93] and, in a relatively typical case, a specific ruling about staff of the Federal Communications Commission

(Roop 1969, 66). Other issues were newer. This subchapter focuses on some examples of the latter.

The McKellar Amendment

McReynolds played a central presidential coordinating role in opposing a major threat to federal personnel management. Senator Kenneth McKellar (D-TN), a senior member of the Appropriations Committee,[94] was a patronage-obsessed politician who for years had been seeking to expand his influence over federal jobs through a variety of approaches and legislative vehicles (Lee 2007). In 1943, he introduced a bill requiring that all federal employees earning more than $4,500 a year be subject to Senate confirmation. The Senate Judiciary Committee recommended it, and the bill would be debated on the Senate floor (Harris 1968, 368–74). The bill would affect tens of thousands of federal employees. In effect, it would reverse FDR's post-PCAM expansion of the classified service, re-politicize major portions of federal employment, and give a virtual veto to senators over middle-ranking federal employees in their home states and regarding entire federal agencies that they had committee jurisdiction over. (McKellar particularly was seeking to control hiring by the TVA.) The bill was a major political threat to the administration and the presidency.

McReynolds took the lead in framing the president's rationale against the bill. His expertise helped present the problem posed by McKellar's idea as undermining modern public personnel management and undoing protections of the apolitical civil service. McReynolds was in the perfect position to depict the bill's negative impact on wartime manpower policies, rather than framing it as just another fight over mere partisan or political issues.[95] He urged FDR "to take a vigorous stand in opposition" to the bill by sending a public letter on the subject.[96] McReynolds met with FDR on February 18, 1943, and shared a draft of a letter with the intent that it would be released publicly. Cautiously, Roosevelt first checked with BOB's Smith to see if he agreed with McReynolds's recommendation and draft. Yes, replied Smith.[97]

Roosevelt then signed McReynolds's draft on February 19, 1943, and released it to the press after it was delivered to the Senate. In it, FDR/McReynolds argued that the bill confused the concept of salary levels with policymaking. Many federal employees had relatively high salaries, but they were not policymakers. Rather, they engaged in the routine "exercise of administrative discretion" after a policy had been determined within the agency. Power and pay were not necessarily related. Furthermore, many highly technical positions required trained scientists and specialists. While they might have salaries commensurate with their unusual or scarce specializations, they, too, were not policymakers. Finally, any position requiring Senate confirmation would have to be excluded from the merit-based classified service, thus narrowing the scope of the civil service system. This would "turn the clock back" on civil service reform and on an apolitical and merit-based employment system (Roosevelt 1969, 1943: 108–10).

McReynolds also encouraged the CSC to oppose the bill formally and similarly rallied the array of civil service reform organizations to testify against it.[98] In the end, the bill passed the Senate, but the House never took it up. It was referred to Ramspeck's Civil Service Committee and never heard from again.[99]

Hunting for Subversives in the Federal Service

Long before the McCarthyism of the early 1950s, fears of the Red Menace had been a potent political issue for the right for decades. Somewhat inconsistently, such fear-mongering continued through WWII even though the USSR was a wartime ally. The hunt for Communists and subversives was led by the House Un-American Activities Committee (HUAC), which held highly publicized hearings on the threat that Communists posed to America and its way of life. Some of the more brutal rhetoric from extreme Republican ideologues before (and during) the war equated socialism and even the New Deal with Communism. As such, the hunt for Reds was a tool used to bludgeon Democrats, including the implication Democrats were at least soft on Communism or, worse, were fellow travelers.[100]

One outcropping in the hunt for subversives was a routine rider attached to most appropriations bills during the war. It prohibited employing anyone "who advocates, or who is a member of an organization that advocates, the overthrow of the Government of the United States by force or violence."[101] This legal prohibition, in turn, required the CSC to conduct background checks on the loyalty of federal employees and applicants for federal positions. In the spring of 1944, Flemming reported that the CSC had, in four years, investigated 200,000 people and declared about a thousand to be ineligible for federal employment due to loyalty concerns.[102]

The CSC's investigative diligence then became fair game for partisans in Congress. Was the CSC truly vigorous in rooting out these traitors? Was FDR shielding disloyal Americans from the impact of the law? It had the potential to be an explosive and ongoing political attack. HUAC was seeking to keep this aspect of the issue alive by accessing and examining the CSC's investigative files. In early 1944, HUAC sent a subpoena to the CSC demanding all records "relating to the Commission's investigations of government employees and applicants for government positions."[103]

McReynolds was the point man on this. He was the White House official who would help craft the administration's policy on how to respond to such subpoenas. McReynolds sought to find the optimal stance to protect civil servants from HUAC rummaging through their HR files, while at the same time protecting FDR from accusations that he was soft on Communism in the government and deliberately undermining a vigorous investigative regime. McReynolds participated in drafting a letter for the president's signature. In it, he directed the CSC not to comply with the subpoena. The letter, signed by FDR on February 17, 1944, stated the administration's policy on such personnel files: "The disclosure of this confidential information would seriously prejudice the ability of the Commission to carry out investigations of this kind in the future and for that reason would not be in the public interest."[104] The commission's refusal to comply with the subpoena held, and these files remained inaccessible to HUAC during the rest of Roosevelt's presidency.[105]

From the other direction, interior secretary Harold Ickes complained to McReynolds about the conduct of the CSC's investigative staff. He characterized the investigations as "Star Chamber" proceedings that denied the investigated employee basic legal rights. Ickes further complained about the poor quality of the subsequent reports CSC investigators submitted to him as justification for firing an employee.[106] McReynolds replied sympathetically, saying that "this is a matter I have been giving consideration for some time and I appreciate your interest."[107] This suggested that he, too, was concerned about the methods used and quality of CSC investigations of the loyalty of federal civil servants. McReynolds's ongoing concerns had likely been a factor in an action the CSC took a few months earlier, when it released new guidelines for use by its field investigators and a training manual for new investigators.[108]

These relatively minor incidents foreshadowed the efforts by Democrats after WWII to prove they weren't soft on Communism and that their concern about civil liberties of federal employees did not make them disloyal to the country.

Promoting Personnel Management through Public Communication

While McReynolds kept a low public profile with the news media—as would be expected of a presidential administrative assistant "with a passion for anonymity"—he nonetheless understood the contribution that public communication could make to promote FDR's personnel management priorities. Before the war, he and Moffett (and Moffett's predecessor Belsley) had occasionally spoken at professional conferences (chap. 4). However, the quantity and range of their public speaking during the war seemed to increase, notwithstanding wartime limits on travel and gas rationing. A possible interpretation could be that, with the enormous expansion of the federal workforce during the war, they felt that public speaking was a kind of "force multiplier" to reach as many of their attentive audiences and relevant stakeholders as possible. And they had an underlying message that they probably felt could never be repeated too many times, namely preaching the gospel of the new dogma that HR was an integral element of management, rather than the past practice of independent CSCs as protectors of the merit system.

For example, during the war, McReynolds traveled to conferences of federal personnel officers in Cleveland[109] and San Francisco,[110] and addressed the annual convention of the National Federation of Federal Employees in Denver.[111] These were audiences intensely interested in the finer details of the administration's personnel management policies. In Washington, McReynolds addressed the public administration interns sponsored by Davenport's National Institute of Public Affairs on the "Need of Administrative Talent in the Federal Government" (Reining 1944, 12), spoke as a panelist at a federal conference on personnel appeal procedures,[112] and agreed to be one of three judges of the *Post*'s competition for money-saving ideas from federal employees (along with Smith and Ramspeck).[113]

Moffett similarly took advantage of public speaking opportunities to HR audiences directly or indirectly. He spoke to a conference on training agency staff to promote conservation of supplies and equipment,[114] encouraged the use of plain language in personnel policy documents at a public panel on red tape,[115] and was the after-dinner speaker at a conference of the Society for Personnel Administration in Washington.[116] In the published version of that speech, he said that the future orientation of personnel officers would likely shift to promoting a workplace culture of "cooperation" between managers and employees (Moffett 1943, 5). Impliedly, at least, he was criticizing the military's command and control model, as well as the traditional CSC model of tightly circumscribing employment practices with rules and regulations as the only way to protect the merit system. Moffett also participated in a conference in Manhattan in mid-1943 on "developing management personnel in the Federal service."[117] His role in the conference was part of a larger effort by public administrationists such as White, Brownlow, Gulick, and Smith to promote employment of trained public administration professionals in the executive branch in the post-PCAM era.

Generally, notwithstanding these public talks McReynolds and Moffett gave to specialized audiences, LOPM had a very low public profile during the war, reflecting McReynolds's pre-PCAM passion for anonymity and the eye-glazing (at least to White House reporters) nature of personnel issues that LOPM was involved in. Jerry Kluttz, columnist of the daily feature "Federal Diary" in the *Washington Post*, was one of the few who routinely covered McReynolds's personnel work because LOPM's policies directly affected the column's readership, federal civil servants. Otherwise, LOPM was rarely mentioned in news coverage and other general readership publications.

In some rare negative coverage, Drew Pearson's "Washington Merry-Go-Round" syndicated column took a shot at McReynolds for allegedly, after a party, wasting precious gasoline by driving some private citizens home to suburban Virginia and Maryland in his official car.[118] An even odder public attack came in an anonymous book published in early 1944. After criticizing the principle of executive order–only wartime agencies, it stated: "Fancy created them, fantasy keeps them churning, monstrosities are their principle output. What, for instance, are the duties of the Liaison Office for Personnel Management? Or the National War Labor Board? Some of the finest inquiring minds in the country have tried to discover—and they have failed. Even F.D.R. may not know exactly what they mean, what they are supposed to do, or why he set them in motion" (Man at the Microphone 1944, 115). The book then proceeded to list eighteen OEM agencies as "*under* this Liaison Office for Personnel Management" (emphasis added). This was a major factual error that even a minor amount of research (such as looking at the *US Government Manual* or the *Congressional Directory*) would have clarified.[119] The book, written by two semi-retired reporters (Wythe Williams and Frank L. Baer), was briefly the sensation of Washington, mostly for its arch and catty observations and the guessing game of the identity of the author(s).[120] The *Times* book review highlighted the sloppy reporting and frequent inaccurate facts in the book.[121] Therefore, it is probably fair to say that this characterization of LOPM did not represent a Washington consensus.[122]

Retail Personnel Management: One Agency at a Time

LOPM functioned as a definitive and authoritative venue where individual agencies went when they had problems with personnel management. Most were complicated and involved the minute details of federal laws and executive orders. McReynolds (and Moffett) were perfectly suited to deal with those complex personnel matters, given their long involvement in federal personnel policies. In particular, because of FDR's definition of LOPM's mission, McReynolds had the standing to approve or disapprove HR activities, especially those that were beyond the scope of the CSC's formal powers (mostly recruitment, examination, hiring, and appeals).

Early in 1942, the Office of Price Administration (OPA) decided that the field clerical employees it needed to staff its 9,000 local rationing boards *had* to be paid salaries no lower than personnel classification standards set in a 1923 law. McReynolds disagreed with that position, but OPA proceeded anyway. Later that year, OPA's chief Leon Henderson asked McReynolds to endorse a presidential executive order clarifying that these clerks and secretaries could be paid at prevailing rates of their localities, even if those rates were below federal classification levels. McReynolds refused. He reiterated that OPA could proceed to do exactly that without an executive order. He made a point of double-checking with GAO, as that agency had the final word on proper and improper expenditures of appropriated funds. GAO concurred with his view, based on a GAO precedent McReynolds remembered that related to the War Department. Being careful, McReynolds then made sure that his interpretation of the law was also that of the Justice Department. He even offered to draft a formal OPA request for a legal opinion.[123] A few years later, OPA's director of personnel, Wallace Sayre, consulted with Moffett on the policy he was developing dealing with releases and transfers of OPA staff. Moffett approved, saying, "I like both its content and spirit."[124]

In early 1944, the Treasury Department's personnel office was considering issuing a department-wide standard policy on rest times for employees. The draft recommended one or two breaks of about ten to fifteen minutes a day. The issue was somewhat complicated because of the heterogeneity of the department's component parts. The Bureau of Printing and Engraving was something like a private-sector factory with its printing presses, while many other bureaus were more conventional offices (like the IRS). Further complicating matters were the Secret Service and the Coast Guard, one a law-enforcement agency, the other a quasi-military one. However, any changes in working conditions for federal employees would interest the press (especially Kluttz of the *Post*). Also, given the wartime emergency, it could be politically embarrassing—reinforcing a stereotype of cushy federal jobs or of lack of uniform treatment of all civil servants. Charles Bell, Secretary Morgenthau's administrative assistant (McReynolds's pre-LOPM position), asked McReynolds for advice. In particular, he wondered, somewhat softly, if McReynolds wanted instead to issue a government-wide policy on the subject? McReynolds did not take the bait and declined to pursue the suggestion. He also was not as worried about potential negative press coverage. Instead, he replied to Bell, "I think this is O.K. for departmental issuance."[125]

Not all such LOPM interactions with agencies were reactive. For example, in mid-1944, McReynolds called and wrote Donald Nelson, chair of the War Production Board, about the administrative location of the board's personnel office. At one point early in the war, administrative responsibilities for the agency (including personnel) were under the board's secretary. Later in the war, the secretary was stripped of that role, and it was shifted to the deputy director. McReynolds told Nelson that, "I consider it desirable and would like to suggest that you reassign the administrative units involved to the Secretary's office so that they will report directly to you through your Executive Secretary." McReynolds said he was motivated to suggest the change because he thought it would help solve some "of the difficulties in connection with the functioning of your board."[126] While he did not state it explicitly, McReynolds was seeking to continue expanding the implementation of one of the personnel management principles of the PCAM and FDR, namely that personnel be viewed as an integral component of the management of federal agencies and, therefore, that personnel directors be placed directly under the agency's chief.

These examples of LOPM's role as the official and supreme federal personnel management agency reflected quite closely what PCAM and FDR were aiming for when advocating the creation of a presidential personnel agency directly accountable to the president. These examples of McReynolds's and Moffett's one-on-one dealings with federal agencies demonstrate the standing they had, notwithstanding Congress's 1939 prohibition on FDR using his reorganization powers to touch the CSC's role and powers.

March–April 1945

Just before FDR's death, two relatively modest activities by McReynolds in the spring of 1945 were symbolic of LOPM's origins and what it had emerged to be.

First, in terms of LOPM's origins, in March, Brownlow informed the White House that, having turned 65, he would soon be stepping down as director of the Public Administration Clearing House (PACH) in Chicago and retiring.[127] Of all the White House staff, McReynolds (and Smith) had probably worked the closest with Brownlow over the years. Brownlow had conferred frequently with McReynolds for advice as PCAM was developing its recommendations in 1936 (chap. 1), and McReynolds had sat in with Brownlow when FDR briefed the congressional leadership in early 1937 of his reorganization plans (chap. 2). In 1939, McReynolds's career embodied three aspects of FDR's implementation of the Brownlow Committee's recommendations. McReynolds became one of the six presidential administrative assistants "with a passion for anonymity," headed an agency in the new Executive Office of the President, and led the president's effort to make personnel management part of a president's integrated managerial oversight of the executive branch (chap. 3). Then, as head of LOPM, McReynolds continued being in touch with Brownlow, including asking his advice on reviving CPA and agreeing to be on a panel convened by Brownlow for a conference of the new American Society for Public Administration (chap. 4).

As a result of his close ties with Brownlow over the years, McReynolds volunteered to draft a letter for FDR to send to Brownlow on the occasion of his retirement. He began on a warm note: "For a long time I have been waiting for a suitable occasion to write you, and now comes news of your impending retirement as Director of [the] Public Administration Clearing House which presents that opportunity." Then, the letter praised Brownlow's overall record, noting, "Your advice has been realistic, objective and non-partisan, and at all times dedicated to the improvement of the public service of your country." The key focus of the letter was on the legacy of the Brownlow Committee: "Of course two of your outstanding contributions which I cannot, in justice, fail to cite are your work as chairman of my Committee on Administrative Management and the assistance you rendered me in establishing for the first time in our history an Executive Office of the President. I venture the prediction that future Presidents will be grateful to you as I have been for these monumental contributions to American public administration." In lieu of the conventional ending of letters, such as "Sincerely yours" or "Very truly yours," the draft ended with "Your old friend."[128] The letter was never sent. Roosevelt died before having a chance to sign it.

Second, McReynolds's last interaction with President Roosevelt was a fitting synecdoche of coordinated and centralized personnel management that FDR had sought and that LOPM had largely accomplished. In early spring 1945, Washington was anticipating V-E Day. The question already being raised for the federal workforce was would it be a day off, a celebration of the victory? The Navy Department had hinted to its civilian employees that it would be a *paid* day off. McReynolds thought otherwise. However, to be sure his thinking was in sync with the president's before enunciating it, McReynolds sent FDR a brief memo on the subject on March 26, 1945, including a draft of a memo LOPM would send to the executive branch stating a policy of V-E Day not being a day off. The next day, FDR dictated this response: "I do not think we should grant any non-work day. We have not sufficient information and the theoretical V-Day may occur over many days instead of on some special occasion."[129] Roosevelt dictated this response seventeen days before he died.

McReynolds followed through by issuing the memo that the president had approved. (For reasons that are not clear, it took him two weeks to do so.) On April 10, McReynolds signed and distributed to the executive branch the president's personnel policy for V-E Day. McReynolds wrote that he "could find no expression of thanksgiving more fitting than staying at our posts of duty and rededicating ourselves to the winning of the war against Japan. . . . Accordingly, officials and employees in all Federal departments and agencies will, I am sure, observe the spirit of teamplay [*sic*] so necessary for final victory by working together on V-E Day and on all the days to follow as long as our services are needed to achieve final victory."[130]

The *Post* reported on McReynolds's memo the next day, April 11, 1945.[131] Roosevelt died on April 12, the day after the story about his V-E Day personnel policy. This relatively minor issue just before his death captures the dominant role the president and LOPM played as the federal government's personnel manager and policymaker. This role was almost a full implementation of what PCAM had recommended, FDR had requested of Congress, and Congress had prohibited. Roosevelt and the public administration reformers had gotten their way. During the war, LOPM was a de facto presidential personnel management agency.

In summary, this chapter has documented LOPM's active role in personnel management during the war. Despite McReynolds's diminishing personal contacts with the president, he and Moffett were busy and engaged with the enormous scope and breadth of HR matters arising from the war. LOPM was involved in a multitude of issues, sometimes substantively, sometimes managerially. From the record documented here, it is clear that LOPM performed a *presidential* role of personnel management by clearing and revising policy—large and small—for the executive branch personnel system. The agency gave direction to personnel matters that reflected the president's priorities and values. Within the limits of the law banning reorganization of the CSC, LOPM can be seen as successfully projecting the president's power into ongoing HR issues. LOPM fulfilled its mandate and then some, probably more than the PCAM reformers had reason to expect after the enactment of the 1939 Reorganization Act.

In the first few years after the war, three textbooks gave modest yet positive appraisals to LOPM's wartime performance. Vieg preferred the ideal structure recommended by the Brownlow Committee of a federal personnel director reporting to the president. Yet, short of that, the "makeshift" structure FDR created "has not been unworkable" (Vieg 1946, 182). It was a mild, but distinct compliment, even if buried in the awkwardness of a double-negative. Patterson and Walker also preferred PCAM's approach. Given Congress's obstreperousness, they, too, had a tempered verdict on LOPM's record, noting that it "has not been so effective as was originally hoped and planned" (Patterson and Walker 1949, 286). Again, buried in the convoluted way academics tended to write, they were stating that LOPM had been somewhat effective, simply less that it could have been under the PCAM plan. These two rather pinched verdicts seem unnecessarily tepid. Pfiffner was a bit more complimentary. LOPM's record demonstrated that PCAM's stated HR goals "have been at least partially achieved and personnel administration given more emphasis in the management of governmental affairs" (Pfiffner 1946, 262).

The recounting in this chapter of LOPM's activities, scope, and accomplishments during WWII likely justifies a somewhat more full-throated and praiseworthy conclusion. For what essentially was two guys in an office, they did an awful lot, certainly moving the reality of day-to-day federal HR policy and administration discernibly closer to FDR's goal of centralized and presidentialized personnel management. LOPM moved the center of gravity of federal HR policymaking to the White House.

6
From the Liaison Office for Personnel Management to a Full-Fledged Presidential Personnel Agency, 1945–1979

Truman Fires McReynolds

FDR died on April 12, 1945. On Truman's first full day as president, the first executive order he signed related to personnel management (9538). It was the typical kind of eye-glazing, but important, matter that McReynolds had been overseeing for Roosevelt since 1939. In this case, with the end of the war in sight, the new order restored probationary status to candidates for civil service appointment who had entered the military while still in that probationary status. This HR policy put them at the front of the line when they were demobilized.[1] McReynolds had reviewed and approved it, then forwarded it to the president's inbox with a recommendation to sign it, but FDR died before being able to do so. (He died while in Warm Springs, Georgia, which meant that there was a greater time lag for paperwork to reach him.) This draft executive order from McReynolds was therefore on President Truman's desk that first full day he was in office. Two weeks after Roosevelt's death, Flemming testified at a Senate hearing on April 25 that the bill being heard had the approval of McReynolds (and BOB's Smith) as being "in accord with the program of the President of the United States," leaving ambiguous which president he was referring to (US Senate 1945, 6).

One of Truman's visitors that first day was Edward T. McKim, an Omaha insurance executive who had served as a private in Truman's WWI outfit. After the war they remained close friends. Almost immediately, McKim began working in a White House office as an unofficial assistant to Truman. Within a few days, rumors were circulating that McKim would become Truman's chief assistant (nowadays chief of staff).[2] Truman made it official on April 30.[3] McKim immediately began cleaning house to install a Truman White House staff. He began with the six administrative assistants. The next day, the United Press news service moved a story to the effect that McKim wanted to replace all the administrative assistants and that, while most had already offered their resignation, one had not.[4] That was likely a reference to McReynolds. One columnist speculated that McReynolds would stay because he did not function as a political aide, but rather was there for his knowledge of the highly technical area of personnel management.[5]

But McKim was insistent that McReynolds had to go as well. He demanded McReynolds's resignation immediately. McReynolds, of course, complied. On May 3, he submitted a handwritten letter:

> Dear Mr. President,
> Pursuant to your suggestion through your assistant Mr. McKim, I hereby submit my resignation, to be accepted at your pleasure, preferably on June 1 next.
> Respectfully,
> Wm. H. McReynolds[6]

A few days later, Truman replied with a terse acceptance:

> Dear Mr. McReynolds,
> Your letter of May third, 1945, tendering your resignation as Administrative Assistant to the President, effective June first, 1945, has been received. It is with regret that I accept it.
> I will appreciate it very much if between now and the date of your resignation you will cooperate with Mr. George J. Schoeneman.
> Sincerely yours,
> Harry S Truman[7]

In Washington parlance, accepting a resignation "with regret" signaled a firing. Phrases such as "with great regret" usually indicated when a resignation was wholly voluntary and that the person continued to have the high regard of the president. Truman's letter made no reference to McReynolds's long career in public service nor stated any appreciation for that service. The White House announced the resignation (and implicit retirement) the next day.[8] A conservative columnist charitably, but incorrectly, reported that McReynolds had "quit," implying his departure was at his own initiative.[9]

Why did Truman and McKim fire McReynolds, and why so brutally? There could be several relatively generic explanations. Perhaps it was simply to replace the FDR regime with Truman loyalists. Another explanation could be that McReynolds was now 65 and would be expected to retire around that age. One carryover White House aide, Jonathan Daniels, observed that by the end of the war McReynolds had appreciably slowed down and was showing his age. In Daniels's terms, McReynolds was already "on the vine."[10] Another related version was that McKim somehow misunderstood Truman's request that McReynolds be eased out, with McKim thinking he had been directed to fire McReynolds forthwith. According to White House press assistant Eben Ayers's oral history interview, Budget Director Smith intervened with Truman on McReynolds behalf. In response, Truman told Smith he "didn't want to hurt McReynolds any," would keep him on "for a while," and then would be "kicking him upstairs."[11] But that was not what went down.

These narratives don't get at the abruptness of the firing, including Truman's very terse letter of acceptance. There is some modest historical evidence suggesting two specific motivations for the firing, both relating to personnel management. The first relates to the charge of nepotism and the other to McReynolds ruffling the feathers of a Democratic mandarin.

Allegedly McReynolds engaged in nepotism while at the White House. His older daughter, Mrs. Margaret (Peggy) Holmead, was hired as a personnel officer at NDAC while McReynolds was simultaneously serving as LOPM director and FDR's liaison with NDAC from May 1940 to April 1941 (chap. 4). In their popular and gossipy syndicated column "Washington Merry-Go-Round," Drew Pearson and Robert Allen criticized this seemingly obvious case of nepotism and implied that she was incompetent—because congressmen complained she was not as pliant, prompt, or communicative as they desired regarding hiring their constituents (Lee 2012, 39–40). However, Holmead was retained at NDAC after McReynolds returned full-time to the White House, suggesting she performed at least creditably.[12] By July 1941, she was the chief of personnel at the Office for Production Management, the renamed NDAC.[13]

A few months after Pearl Harbor, Pearson and Allen resumed their criticism of McReynolds's nepotism. In this case, they noted that Holmead was not McReynolds's only relative employed by the federal government. By now Holmead had left federal employment, but four other of McReynolds's relatives now worked in federal agencies: his younger daughter, Mrs. Katherine Britt, was a secretary in LOPM; his son-in-law M. G. Britt worked for the War Production Board (the successor agency to OPM); Mrs. Holmead's husband, Henry Holmead Jr., worked in federal procurement; and Mrs. Holmead's father-in-law, Henry Holmead Sr., worked for the Farm Credit Administration.[14]

Their nepotism charge was still in the air three years later when Truman became president. Matthew Connelly, longtime Truman aide, recalled in an oral history interview:

> William McReynolds was the personnel officer for Roosevelt and shortly after we came into the White House we began to get a little

information about his activities, and he was not the type of man who would represent Mr. Truman's thinking about Government.

Q: Such as?

Well, number one, he was widely criticized for nepotism. I believe he had about nine relatives on the Federal payroll, which did not appeal very much to Mr. Truman. And shortly thereafter, he pulled a few indiscreet acts as director of personnel.

Q: What did he do?

This I don't recall; there were minor things, but they were important indications that he was not going to be Truman's man. So he had a short departure thereafter.[15]

How seriously should history take the nepotism charge against McReynolds? Certainly, it is impossible to imagine that—based on Connelly's reminiscences—McReynolds added *five more* family members to the federal payroll after the 1942 Pearson and Allen column. Two factors are probably important that would mitigate the accusation. First, in general, Washington was a one-industry town and, especially during the sharp expansion of government employment during WWII, most local residents inevitably worked for the federal government. Therefore, at least some of them may have obtained their employment on the merits. Second, McReynolds's two daughters grew up in Washington. It was their hometown. That they wanted to remain there, close to their parents and friends and for raising their families, is to be expected. If indeed they wanted to stay in DC and earn a living, then working for the federal government (or their husbands doing so) was largely their only choice.

Several other factors raise doubts about the nepotism accusation. Even though FDR did not like personally to fire people, he had an exquisite political antenna. If he had thought there was substance to the media's accusation of nepotism, he could have found a way to ease McReynolds out of his White House position. He did not do that. Also, it is probably significant that the allegation of four family members on the payroll was made in 1942, and yet three years later McReynolds was still running LOPM. Presumably, if the accusation of nepotism was valid and violated any federal law, it could have been investigated officially by other (relatively independent) legal authorities, such as the local US attorney or the FBI, and acted upon by then. It was not. Based on the laws at the time, his conduct does not appear to have been illegal. For example, in 1944, the *Post* noted five instances of daughters of high-ranking federal officials also working for the government, merely commenting that the women "have the reputations of their famous fathers to live up to." The column made no charge of illegality or unethical practice.[16] (McReynolds and *fille* were not in the list.) But no other mainstream newspaper picked up the nepotism charge as an ongoing news item. This suggests that the Pearson and Allen claim was somewhat exaggerated and not considered credible by other independent journalists.

The alternate specific explanation for McReynolds's firing relates to an influential Democratic politician. A conservative columnist told the story this way:

> A personnel dynasty had been built up within the government. It was headed by Mr. Roosevelt's administrative assistant, William H. McReynolds. He chose the heads of all the important bureaus, and the bureau chiefs whom he selected, in turn, carried out his will in selecting their subordinates.
>
> These were not political appointees (Democratic Party) as much as personal choices of various people around Mr. Roosevelt. He himself did not have much time for the matter, and left everything to McReynolds, who allowed himself full leeway in setting up a super-regime reaching into every government bureau.[17]

This story was fanciful and fictional in that it overstated McReynolds's role in hiring, as opposed to his involvement in abstract personnel policy or his casework regarding highly complicated individual civil service problems. He was not FDR's *appointments* director; rather, he was the personnel management guy. Someone else in the White House handled presidential appointments to the Cabinet, subcabinet, and other discretionary positions. McReynolds's office files do not indicate any major involvement in appointments unrelated to personnel directors and other senior HR professionals. Also, from his office files, he seemed to have little to no interest in power for its own sake or in doing things that FDR would not approve of. He was loyal to FDR, usually seeking more direct consultations or approvals during WWII than FDR thought necessary.

However, there appears to be a kernel of truth in the column (and in Connelly's fuzzy memory about something other than nepotism) that might get to the heart of the firing. This had to do with McReynolds's commitment to the merit system (with or without a CSC), his detailed knowledge of civil service laws, and his lack of active interest in politics. McReynolds described a 1944 incident in his oral history interview:

> The last contact he had with the President, McReynolds recalls, affected political affairs in Oklahoma during the 1944 campaign. Governor Kerr of Oklahoma had appointed the Democratic State Chairman as the head of the road service in that state. This service was supported by Federal funds, and thus the personnel who staffed it came under the Hatch Act [barring political roles]. Charges of violating the Hatch Act were submitted against

> the Democratic State Chairman who acknowledged them to be true. Thereupon, Governor Kerr and Robert Hannegan [chairman of the Democratic National Committee] called on McReynolds to intercede in the case. They asked that there be no prosecution. McReynolds said he replied, "I didn't write the Hatch Act. I don't intend to help anybody cover up. I'm going to give the go-ahead sign today to carry out the Hatch Act as it applies to this case." Governor Kerr and Hannegan left the office in a great huff. A month after the election they jointly wrote a letter to the President complaining about McReynolds' actions and suggesting that the latter be fired. Roosevelt called McReynolds over, handed him this letter and said to him, "You answer it." McReynolds did so. While the matter went no further during Roosevelt's lifetime, McReynolds inferred that after his death, the incident led to his retirement from the White House staff. (McReynolds 1949, 4)

McReynolds, as would be expected, got most of the details right. Indeed, in the fall of 1944, during the election campaign, the CSC ruled that France Paris, appointed by Governor Kerr to chair the state's highway commission, had violated the Hatch Act when he simultaneously served as state party chair. Paris resigned his party position, and, eventually, Kerr named him to a different post. Still the CSC ordered that, as a penalty, federal highway aid to Oklahoma should be reduced by an amount equal to twice Paris's annual salary.[18] Before the election, Kerr appealed the CSC decision to the local federal court.[19]

While the court case was pending, Kerr was looking for other ways to get even. He came from the old school of politics that operated based on the maxims "don't get mad, get even" and "never forgive, never forget." He used to boast, "They'll only beat me over my dead body—and I don't die easy" (Allen and Shannon 1950, 276). There was a strong political logic underlying this tough approach to politics. It was calculated to evoke fear of that politician by others, conveying to future opponents that, if you cross this guy, he will make you pay no matter how long he has to wait or how much it will take to do it. This modus operandi made people afraid of Kerr and helped him get his way more often than not. He was feared. Pooh-Bahs got what they wanted—or else. As Machiavelli observed, it was best for the Prince to be feared.[20]

In January 1945, Kerr wrote to FDR praising the work of Raymond Zimmerman, an Oklahoman who was a staffer at the CPA.[21] Kerr suggested FDR might want to consider promoting Zimmerman if, with the beginning of his new term, FDR "intends to make any changes in his top personnel staff." Given that Zimmerman's expertise was in personnel management, it was a not-very-veiled hint that Kerr was hoping FDR would ask McReynolds to retire as a belated punishment for McReynolds's handling of the Hatch Act case. Then, neatly, Zimmerman was available to take the newly vacant LOPM position. This would have been a two-fer for Kerr: only a few months after his showdown with McReynolds, he'd get his revenge by kicking McReynolds out of the White House and at the same time install in his place a political ally as the top personnel manager in the administration.

FDR didn't take the bait. He asked McReynolds to draft a bland and noncommittal thank you reply to Kerr. Cautiously, McReynolds first checked with Davenport, Zimmerman's boss at the CPA, about the possible origins of the letter, especially if Zimmerman had lobbied Kerr to write it. To Davenport, Zimmerman feigned complete ignorance of Kerr's letter, saying that it was not his idea and that he was somewhat abashed by it.[22]

When Truman became president in April, Kerr saw another way to get even with McReynolds. Kerr and Truman were from neighboring states, knew each other from Democratic politics, and were friendly. Kerr was a rising potentate of the national party, signaled by his selection as the keynote speaker at the 1944 Democratic National Convention. At that convention, he provided crucial support for Truman as the vice presidential nominee. That meant Truman owed him a favor (Ferrell 1994, 69, 88). Also, Truman was something of a party "regular" (i.e., linked to traditional courthouse political machines) who would possibly have been sympathetic to Kerr complaining that one of the holdovers from FDR had undermined the success of the Democratic Party. This claim would likely trigger a sympathetic reaction by Truman (especially if he was already thinking ahead to 1948).

Adding credibility to Kerr's role in the firing of McReynolds was the timing. Kerr visited with Truman on April 30, 1945 (Truman 1998, 111). McKim demanded McReynolds's resignation on May 3, just a few days later. This is also congruent with Connelly's recollection that, when Truman's team took over the White House, they already knew about the so-called nepotism charge against McReynolds, but only "shortly thereafter" they learned something else negative about him which justified a quick firing. This explanation that Kerr engineered McReynolds brutal firing by Truman rings true. It makes sense in terms of timing, rationale, political logic, Kerr's modus operandi, Truman's friendship with Kerr, and the available facts.[23]

McReynolds in Retirement

McReynolds retired effective May 31, 1945. The *Post*'s columnist on civil service matters called him "one of the outstanding career men in the Federal service" and said he had "a long and distinguished record." Furthermore, "he was no politician and he fought to keep politics out of the federal service."[24] Several former colleagues, including one from his Bureau of Efficiency days, organized a testimonial dinner for him.[25]

In retirement, McReynolds lived a quiet life. Van Riper interviewed him for a history of the CSC (Van Riper 1958, 302n41), and he did an oral history interview for the nascent FDR library (McReynolds 1949). He also served on an advisory committee to the First Hoover Commission. McReynolds died in 1951.[26] In a final tribute, *Post* columnist Kluttz described him as "a great public servant" who deserved credit for "most civil service reforms of the past generation."[27]

Truman's LOPM

On May 9, 1945, a few days after firing McReynolds, Truman named George J. Schoeneman as one of his administrative assistants with responsibilities including the Liaison Office for Personnel Management. Schoeneman had previously served as assistant commissioner of the IRS.[28] An example of his LOPM work occurred when he instructed all federal agencies to revert to prewar routines, including reducing the regular work week to forty hours and resuming observances of major holidays as days off (Truman 1961, 229). For reasons that are unclear, he ceased his LOPM role only a few months later, moved aside to be special executive assistant to the president (and then, in 1947, a promotion back to the IRS as its commissioner).

In September, Truman named in Schoeneman's place Raymond R. Zimmerman, the CPA staffer for whom Kerr was political patron.[29] This appointment would have been of great satisfaction to Kerr, McReynolds's enemy, who it will be recalled had recommended Zimmerman as McReynolds's replacement for FDR's fourth term (see preceding subchapter). Zimmerman had been active in the national Society for the Advancement of Management and was serving as its president at the time of his LOPM appointment (Truman 1961, 514–15). This indicated that he saw public sector HR as largely similar to business HR, the opposite of the Brownlow and ASPA crowd, who viewed all aspects of governmental management as qualitatively different from its practice in the for-profit sector.

Under Zimmerman, LOPM had no additional funding or staffing beyond what he had as a White House administrative assistant, such as FDR had done from a presidential discretionary spending fund (US House 1946, 51). In his HR activities, Zimmerman's work closely paralleled the template created by McReynolds. Zimmerman issued memos to heads of executive branch departments and agencies on personnel matters,[30] reviewed and recommended to the president proposed executive orders relating to the CSC,[31] worked with BOB on personnel policies,[32] promoted executive branch–wide policies on employee health and safety,[33] liaised with Capitol Hill as the president's spokesman on federal workforce policies,[34] gave talks to stakeholder audiences,[35] attended personnel conferences,[36] and wrote about federal personnel practices (Zimmerman 1947).

Zimmerman headed LOPM until March 1947, when he resigned. His departure was relatively abrupt and explained publicly as for "personal reasons."[37] A press release issued, oddly, by the Society for the Advancement of Management announced the resignation and stated that he would be taking a vacation "before making further plans."[38] Clearly, he did not leave for another governmental or private sector job. Truman accepted Zimmerman's resignation "with sincere regret," a formula usually used to indicate that he had not been fired or forced out due to his job performance.[39]

A few months after Zimmerman's departure, Truman named Donald S. Dawson as an administrative assistant and head of LOPM. Dawson, a Missouri native, had expertise in HR as the personnel director at the federal Reconstruction Finance Agency and, when in military service during WWII, as the chief of civilian personnel at the Air Transport Command.[40] Dawson was given two relatively unrelated personnel duties, serving as liaison officer for personnel management and overseeing presidential appointments. The latter, of course, was a highly political role.[41]

In his LOPM function, he, too, followed McReynolds's template. Dawson "coordinated planning and policy in the personnel and personnel management field for the executive branch." That included "almost daily contact" with the CSC and the review and approval of all CSC-proposed executive orders. As during McReynolds's time, the CSC almost never met with the president, conducting nearly all of its work through Dawson. He recalled only a handful of times that the commissioners formally requested a meeting with Truman (Dawson 1980). According to Hobbs, Truman gave Dawson "the right to make decisions on the spot in the President's name" regarding CSC business (Hobbs 1954, 91). Some of Dawson's other activities, also paralleling McReynolds, included liaising with Congress on personnel legislation, overseeing personnel policy for the District of Columbia municipal government, working with the Federal Personnel Council on executive branch–wide personnel policies, and speaking to federal employee groups.[42]

Truman, Personnel Management, and the First Hoover Commission

In mid-1947, President Truman appointed former president Hoover as head of a commission to study the organization and operations of the federal government. Known as the (First) Hoover Commission, its goal was to submit a report in time for use by the person elected president in November 1948 (hence removing partisan concerns about the commission's work). The scope of its remit included the president's general managerial role, as well as personnel management in the executive branch.

Several people with extensive knowledge of the organization (and politics) of federal personnel management participated in the work of the commission. Arthur Flemming, after WWII back full-time as CSC commissioner, was one of the four presidential appointees to the commission. He was the only member of the Hoover Commission then currently working in the executive branch. However, in mid-1948, Flemming resigned from the CSC to be president of Ohio Wesleyan University. So, by the time the commission issued its report in early 1949, Flemming was a private citizen. Hoover repeatedly tried to recruit Lyle Belsley to be the secretary to the commission. Hoover's public position on the role of the commission was that it would be nonpartisan and non-ideological and that he was interested only in recommending modern management principles. However, his interest in Belsley was precisely for the opposite reason, namely because Belsley—despite his many positions in the FDR administration during the war—was viewed as a Republican and not a New Dealer. Belsley declined (Arnold 1998, 130).[43] Instead, Francis P. Brassor, the head of the CSC's Administrative Services bureau was appointed commission secretary.[44] The Hoover Commission then appointed a Personnel Policy Committee, and one of its members was Leonard White. Another member was former congressman (and future CSC member) Robert Ramspeck. In turn, the committee appointed special advisory panel on position evaluation and pay practices, and McReynolds served on that group (Commission on Organization of the Executive Branch 1948, xii–xiii, 52).

These men were intimately familiar with the arguments about presidential personnel management, some of them going back to before PCAM. Therefore, it is understandable that during its final deliberations the Hoover Commission had to face and try to resolve the longtime fight over merit vs. management in the federal government. According to a leak to the *Post*, a majority preferred to abolish LOPM, retain the CSC as a commission, and make the CSC chair the personnel advisor to the president, as well as the sole administrator of the CSC staff. A minority of Hoover Commission members (three of the twelve) were still pushing for PCAM and FDR's preference: abolish the three-member CSC, replace it with a single administrator, and make that person the president's personnel adviser.[45] It was a seemingly subtle difference to outsiders unfamiliar with the long-simmering fight, but in Washington power came in the details. Was the CSC a presidential agency or not?

Trying to convey a (false) post-hoc unanimity, member Flemming wrote afterwards that the Hoover Commission supported the principle that "personnel aspects of administration were as important to the effective operations of the Federal Government as any other part of the total administrative process." That sounded like PCAM and FDR. But, for the Hoover Commission, where did the personnel management buck stop? The president? No. It was "the operating official responsible" for each federal agency (Commission 1949, 29). James Mitchell (a new CSC member appointed by Truman; no relation to CSC president Harry Mitchell) observed that the Hoover Commission tried to "reconcile" the two opposing approaches to federal personnel management (J. Mitchell 1950, 182). That was putting it politely. In fact, it was a muddled report, trying to straddle the un-straddle-able.

Issued in February 1949, the report of the Hoover Commission called for an Office of Personnel in EOP. Without saying so, this would convert LOPM into a presidential staff agency with full executive powers, comparable to BOB. It would be called the White House Office of Personnel and would be headed by a director of personnel. The CSC would be elevated into the "central personnel agency" for the executive branch. The three-person commission would remain, but its chair would have all administrative powers to run the agency. At one point in the report, he was called the "Administrator" of the CSC. That person would also, simultaneously, serve as the head of the White House Office of Personnel (Commission 1949, 10, 12, 18–19, 113, 132–33). In a very convoluted way, and without saying so explicitly (likely so as not to re-stoke the opposition to the PCAM recommendation by congressional conservatives and civil service reform traditionalists), this was implicitly and indirectly close to the PCAM report.

The commission's hazy recommendations never stated explicitly that LOPM would be re-created as a statutory agency (instead of its executive order status) and then be the nucleus for the presidential Office of Personnel. However, later that year, a congressional report on the implementation of the Hoover Commission recommendations noted that any effort to bring the personnel management recommendation into reality would "presumably" transform LOPM into the Office of Personnel (US Senate 1949, 50). Even though dozens of recommendations of the Hoover Commission were promptly enacted by Congress, no such legislation on LOPM was ever passed or even got beyond introduction. At least one of the likely reasons was that Truman quickly let it be known that, except for one, he generally agreed with the commission's personnel recommendations. Which one? He "rejected" the idea of making the CSC chair also the presidential personnel advisor. Instead, Truman wanted to keep the two positions separate. He "is more than satisfied" with that aspect of the status quo, the *Post* reported.[46] Dawson continued serving as LOPM head through to the end of Truman's presidency.

On the other hand, Truman was willing to use his reorganization powers to implement any other Hoover Commission recommendations in the area of personnel management that did not conflict with his desire to retain LOPM (or its equivalent) separate from the CSC.[47] In mid-1949, he submitted Reorganization Plan No. 5 to Congress to change the internal administrative structure of the CSC.[48] In his message to Congress, he said this plan "carries into effect *one* of the major recommendations" of the Hoover Commission in the area of personnel management (Truman 1964, 317, emphasis added). The plan tried to distinguish between the CSC's routine HR work versus its formal quasi-judicial and regulatory roles. For the former, Truman designated the chair of the CSC as (what would now be called) the CEO of the agency. To make clearer the lines of responsibility, the plan abolished the positions of commission secretary and chief examiner. In their place, Truman created an office of executive director who would be the commission's COO, accountable only to the commission chair. For the regulatory and judicial roles of the CSC, including recommending executive orders and regulations to the president, Truman assigned a personal assistant to each of the three commissioners to help them carry out those duties.

The literature generally approved the thrust of these Hoover Commission recommendations in the area of personnel and Truman's (partial) implementation of them. Binkley and Moos liked that "the trend in personnel management has been moving informally in the direction of a single director of personnel" (Binkley and Moos 1949, 379). However, opaquely, they also noted that "operating the personnel enterprise of the government cannot ever be made a simple matter by a shift in the command agency" (380). Graves also expressed support for Truman's actions "in the interests of a more comprehensive and better administered personnel program for the Federal government." But, he, too, qualified his endorsement with another hard-to-decipher comment: "It was also reported that extension of the authority of the Liaison Office for Personnel Management was planned" toward accomplishing that goal (Graves 1972, 24). Who reported it, who planned to do it, what the expanded powers of LOPM would be, and how it would be implemented were left unstated.

Eisenhower, Personnel Management, and the Second Hoover Commission

The first executive order President Eisenhower signed (10432) created an Advisory Committee on Government Organization (PACGO). It formalized the Special Advisory Committee President-elect Eisenhower had created during the interregnum. This was a very small committee of action-oriented men that the new president trusted: his brother Milton, Nelson Rockefeller, and the ubiquitous Arthur Flemming. PACGO quickly announced twenty reorganization recommendations (Arnold 1998, 162–65). One was to do away with LOPM as an EOP entity. This most certainly would have originated with Flemming who, based on his work on the Hoover Commission, supported having the CSC be "the President's staff agency" for all matters of personnel management (Flemming 1949, 29).

On May 1, 1953, Eisenhower signed Executive Order 10452 abolishing LOPM by revoking FDR's 1939 executive order that had created it. He transferred to the CSC chairman the centralizing presidential role that LOPM had played. This included advising the president regarding personnel management, assisting the president in planning executive branch–wide personnel policies and executive orders, and promoting improvement in personnel management throughout the federal government.[49] Under this arrangement, the CSC chair maintained a separate office in the Executive Office Building next to the White House, with a small staff to handle his presidential role (Patterson 1994, 293–94). The formal title of the new position was the President's Adviser on Personnel Management (Eisenhower 1958, 205).

Academician Somers endorsed Eisenhower's action, saying that LOPM was "not conspicuously successful" (Somers 1954, 135). However, there was less here than met the eye. While LOPM was formally abolished, Somers missed that the small personnel management staff unit in the White House was not. The CSC chair was their boss, but they functioned wholly separate from the CSC.

At this point the formal structure of federal personnel management looked awfully close to that recommended by FDR and PCAM. First, Truman's reorganization had effectively changed the CSC from an agency overseen by a multimember commission to an agency with a single administrative head. Second, based on Eisenhower's executive order, all personnel management responsibilities were under the purview of one person, functioning both as the CEO of the CSC and as presidential adviser on personnel management. He was now ostensibly the de facto federal personnel director, as urged by Roosevelt and PCAM.

However, there was one important distinction that meant this new arrangement was not what FDR and PCAM sought. The Truman and Eisenhower reforms had created a personnel structure with the CSC at its center. And the commission was, after all, an independent executive-branch agency with the primary mission of implementing and protecting *the merit system*. That was exactly the opposite of Roosevelt and PCAM's goal of having the personnel system within the presidential orbit and with the primary mission of personnel *management*. Their goal was a presidential personnel director who was comparable to the president's budget director, giving the president central managerial oversight of the executive branch through the levers of personnel and budgeting. Instead, the Truman and Eisenhower reforms shifted the center of gravity to the CSC and, inevitably, to the maintenance of the merit system rather than president-centric personnel management.

This organizational structure lasted 4½ years. Harris—hardly a neutral observer—wrote that Eisenhower's "plan attracted criticism," a reference to the Second Hoover Commission (Harris 1964, 172). That commission (1953–55) had been created by Congress at the beginning of the Eisenhower presidency (and with a distinct lack of enthusiasm by Eisenhower). Arthur Flemming was, again, a member. In turn, the commission created a Task Force on Personnel and Civil Service. It was chaired by political scientist Harold Dodds, with members including Leonard White (again!), Chester Barnard, and former congressman Robert Ramspeck. Of the commission's fourteen task forces, Arnold considered this one as the most distinguished, because it was "extremely professional" compared to the more ideological tilt of some of the other task forces. The personnel committee's 1955 report, he felt, was "a milestone in the development of the idea of an American public service" (Arnold 1998, 178).

One of the task force's recommendations called for re-separating the dual roles of the CSC chair. Instead, there was a need for "a full-time assignment within the Executive Office for the Presidential Adviser on Personnel Management." That person "should be a coordinator of personnel[,] attempting to get a more harmonious operation of the several separate merit systems within the Federal service. He should help the President to weigh the advice on personnel matters he receives from many sources" (Commission 1955, 146). In other words, revive a formal White House entity like LOPM, but without necessarily creating a new freestanding agency within the EOP.

In 1957, after the incumbent CSC chair Eisenhower had appointed in 1953 left office, the president decided to implement this recommendation and re-divide the two roles.[50] In Executive Order 10729, he repealed his 1953 executive order and superseded it with the position of Special Assistant to the President for Personnel Management. The duties of the new White House advisor were nearly identical to those that had been delegated to the CSC chair in 1953.

The special assistant's operations tracked quite closely to LOPM. To implement the mandate stated in the 1957 executive order, it had even *more* staff than McReynolds's LOPM. Rocco Siciliano, the first to hold the new position, supervised four professionals and five secretaries. For the Eisenhower White House, this was unusual. The personnel management office was one of only three White House entities with a staff (as opposed to separate EOP units like BOB), the other two being the national security advisor and the press secretary (Siciliano 2004, 134, 293). This indicates a relatively major commitment to a presidential role in overseeing and coordinating personnel management, policies, and activities throughout the executive branch. Siciliano resigned in 1959 to practice law in Washington. Eisenhower retained this structure, a kind of invisible LOPM, with Siciliano's successor, Eugene Lyons (Patterson 1994, 294).

Behind closed doors, during his second term, Eisenhower's PACGO recommended going further and doing something along the lines of the plans proposed by PCAM and the first Hoover Commission (Arnold 1998, 205). According to Siciliano, it sought to create an Executive Office of Personnel Management by merging the CSC and the president's special assistant's office.[51] This, by now, was *de rigueur* for personnel reorganizers, and it prompted the usual opposition from the CSC. BOB director Maurice Stans also opposed it, in part for turf reasons as well, with BOB having some personnel oversight powers that the proposed new presidential agency might impinge on.[52] Siciliano added a new twist to the long-standing idea. He insisted that the draft proposal contain no exclusions on the scope and breadth of the new agency, nor any exemptions of other agencies from its oversight. This triggered "heavy opposition" from other members of the administration in the departments and agencies that would be affected by this important detail. They claimed it would be "a jurisdictional nightmare" (Siciliano 2004, 173–174). Such in-house opposition would inevitably leak into congressional debates over the plan if Eisenhower were to issue a formal presidential Reorganization Plan subject to a legislative veto or propose a statutory change. He eventually decided not to bash that beehive so late in his presidency. If his successor wanted to, fine, that would be his decision to make.

Congressional Arguments about Merit vs. Management, 1956–1960

All this time, on Capitol Hill, the principled arguments about an independent merit system vs. presidential personnel management continued unabated (and without any knowledge of PACGO's draft plan). The House Committee on Post Office and Civil Service released a report in 1956 that, among other topics, strongly attacked the idea of presidential personnel management. The report emphasized that the CSC was equally accountable to Congress as to a president. Therefore, the CSC "should insist upon and practice complete independence of action" (US House 1956, 53). Why? "A strong and militant Civil Service Commission is the keystone of a healthy and efficient personnel structure in the Government" (6). It should be viewed as "the Central Government agency" for personnel matters (52).

Parts of the report even implied the CSC should be *more* accountable to Congress than the president (Harris 1964, 173). First, it complained about a recent record of inadequate advance consultation by the CSC with the committee prior to finalizing new personnel policies. The CSC "should reexamine and strengthen its policy and practice with respect to its appearances before and dealings with Congress" (US House 1956, 55). Second, the report criticized the extant structure of the CSC chair also serving as the president's adviser on personnel management. This was "a deterrent to the effective discharge of the full responsibility of the Commission. In the judgment of the committee the disadvantages of the dual role far outweigh the advantages." In particular, it feared that the added presidential role "may subject him to pressures and special concerns of individual administrative officials" (5). Such pressures "are above and beyond those normally found in the relationship of the head of an independent agency to the Chief Executive" (53). In other words, the president's desire to manage the executive branch was antithetical to an autonomous merit protection agency.

On the other hand, beginning in the 85th Congress (1957–58), Senator Joseph Clark (D-PA) persistently pushed for legislation to create a personnel agency in EOP comparable to BOB. All of the CSC's operating functions would be transferred to that White House agency and led by a single administrator accountable directly to the president. In 1958, as chair of a small special subcommittee appointed to examine his plan, he held several public hearings (US Senate 1958a). It didn't pass (US Senate 1958b, 8). In 1959, during the 86th Congress, he arranged for the committee's (formal) Subcommittee on Civil Service to hold further hearings on his (reintroduced) bill. Louis Brownlow, then in his eighties and blind, testified in favor. Recounting the rationale of the PCAM report, he argued "that this particular department or office of personnel management should be directly under the President, but I think that is true also in other governmental jurisdictions. The personnel officer ought to be directly connected with the executive head" (US Senate 1959, 73). Just as they had toward a similar idea suggested by PACGO within the White House, spokesmen for the CSC and BOB opposed the bill at the congressional hearings.[53]

In June 1960, the full committee voted in favor of a slightly revised version of the bill on a party-line vote. As with earlier proposals going back to PCAM, it would create an Office of Personnel Management as an EOP agency. Its head, called the director of personnel, would be nominated by the president to the Senate for confirmation, as would the agency's deputy director. They would serve at the pleasure of the president, with no fixed terms. The CSC would continue, with commissioners appointed for nine-year terms, with the roles of administering quasi-judicial hearings on appeals and as a watchdog to protect the merit system.[54] The three Republican members of the committee filed a minority report opposing the bill as unnecessary (US Senate 1960). Coming out of committee in the summer of a presidential election, Majority Leader Lyndon Johnson kept deferring floor consideration of the bill through to the end of the floor sessions of the 86th Congress (Harris 1964, 174–75).[55]

Carter Creates the Office of Personnel Management, 1978–1979

From 1960, when Congress failed to act on reorganizing the CSC into a presidential management system, until Jimmy Carter's election in 1976, the interest in civil service reform persisted in the academic, professional, and reformist literature

(Rosen 1975; Rosenbloom 1971; Sayre 1965; Shafritz 1975; Vaughn and Brewer, 1975). However, the attention to grand reorganization to attain presidential personnel management seemed to fade from primary attention. Instead, the literature and political developments focused much more on specific and detailed matters relevant to the smoother operation of the current merit system. Some of the subjects attracting attention and commentary included, for example, expanding the classified service, equal rights, collective bargaining, the ban on political participation, a senior executive corps, and discharge (e.g., Beaumont 1974; Frug 1976; Spero 1962). The Library of Congress's Congressional Research Service summary of important civil service reform events and reports between 1960 and 1976 referred to over a dozen significant developments, including new laws and presidential executive orders (US House 1976).

The return to a bigger picture of federal HR management occurred with the election of Jimmy Carter. He was committed to government reform in general and intent on using his presidency to accomplish it. One of the most thankless political jobs he voluntarily tackled was a major structural reform the federal personnel system. He appointed Alan "Scotty" Campbell as CSC chair with the mandate to pass civil service reform.[56] Campbell immediately acknowledged the difficulty of the task: "It's a good-government issue, and although we have broad support, it's thin support."[57] Salience was all on the other side: entrenched bureaucrats who did not want their ox gored, employee labor groups opposing anything that did not give them additional economic and political gains, traditionalists who clung to the Progressive-era template of an autonomous CSC, and just plain political opponents hoping to deprive Carter of a win. Reorganization, Seidman emphasized, is not driven by supposedly apolitical, technocratic, and efficiency reasons. Rather, it is a political process reflecting power and conflict (Seidman 1998).[58] Nonetheless, and nearly miraculously, Carter's plan passed Congress, with political credit substantially going to Campbell.

Often forgotten, Carter's civil service reform entailed two separate initiatives. The most well-known was the legislation to make major changes in civil service laws. He submitted it in March 1978 and signed it half a year later, in October. Separately, using presidential reorganization powers, in May 1978, he submitted to Congress his Reorganization Plan No. 2 that would abolish the Civil Service Commission and replace it with the Office of Personnel Management (OPM) and a small Merit Systems Protection Board (Carter 1979, 953–959). Though this plan was subject to a legislative veto, Congress did not exercise it. Carter then arranged for the reorganization plan and the Civil Service Reform Act to go into effect within days of each other in early January 1979.

Carter's OPM only differed slightly from what FDR and PCAM had sought. The agency would indeed be headed by a single administrator, not a commission. Similarly, the agency head would be nominated by the president and subject to Senate confirmation, and then serve at the president's pleasure. (To appease political opponents, the final version of PCAM suggested the appointment be made through a civil service process, but that was simply a preemptive concession.) However, OPM was not an agency within EOP; rather, it was "an independent establishment in the Executive Branch" (Carter 1979, 954). Two reasons for keeping it out of the EOP were the size of the CSC's staff (which would have dwarfed the rest of the EOP's other agencies) and that some of its functions were "relatively routine and are not appropriate for the Executive Office" (NAPA 1980, 11).[59] Nonetheless, OPM was viewed as the personnel counterpart to the Office of Management and Budget (OMB).[60] Helping make this point clear to Washington power watchers, OPM's director would be at the same executive rank as the OMB director—one rank higher than that of the CSC chair.[61] Campbell described the mission of the proposed new HR agency as a management arm of the president. It would be "the same with people as the Office of Management and Budget is with budgets. . . . It will treat people the same way OMB treats dollars—putting them to the best use possible."[62]

The US Civil Service Commission officially closed its doors on December 31, 1978. A formal presidential personnel agency came into existence on January 1, 1979, forty-two years after FDR and Brownlow proposed it. Carter named Campbell as its first director. At the beginning of 1980, in a report on OPM's record in its first year, Campbell characterized OPM as one of the four "central management agencies" of the federal government, precisely what FDR and PCAM had envisioned (Campbell 1980, 20).[63]

Conclusion

What conclusion can be drawn from this history of the conflict between the ideas of merit vs. management, as well as from the history of LOPM as the agency born of those 1930s arguments? Based on the recounting in the preceding chapters, such judgments are presented here by focusing separately on the end result of the clash of ideas, on FDR's efforts to implement the idea of management over merit notwithstanding the congressional ban on using his reorganization powers to touch the CSC, and on LOPM's substantive record.

Evaluating History's Verdict: The Idea of Management over Merit

The supposition that an autonomous civil service commission was an absolute necessity for a merit system died hard. Supporters of that perspective, especially congressional conservatives, were still echoing Meriam's 1937 critique of PCAM and succeeded in keeping the CSC as is through the 1950s and 1960s (chap. 6).

Probably the most significant defection from their ranks occurred in 1970, when the National Civil Service League released the sixth version of its model law. This one wholly abandoned the orthodoxy of a CSC as essential to a merit system or even as one of several acceptable options for public sector HR. The title of the league's new model law said it all. Instead of the five preceding versions of a *Model* ***Civil Service*** *Law*, this was a *Model Public* ***Personnel Administration*** *Law* (NCSL 1970, emphasis added). The league concluded unequivocally that CSCs "have outlived their usefulness and their continuation is incompatible with sound administrative concepts." The claim that a merit system would be undermined if autonomous CSCs were abolished was "often unfounded." From the league's new perspective, management was now more important than merit. CSCs should be replaced by a personnel department headed by a personnel director who would be accountable and responsive to the chief elected executive official. Personnel policy should be viewed largely as a management issue because "the chief executive must be able to determine the personnel needs of the jurisdiction and, under merit principles, to meet those needs" (5). One could practically hear the metaphorical concrete cracking. In fact, traditionalists viewed this new model law as an apostasy, so heretical to the long-standing orthodoxy that they withdrew their support and brought down the league (Henry 2006, 907). It dissolved in 1980, abandoned by its traditional supporters (Lee 2012b, 223).

It was a long tortuous path from the first discussion in 1913 of the idea that, in the public sector, HR management was more important than merit (chap. 1) to its enactment by Congress in 1978 and the replacement of the CSC with OPM in 1979 (chap. 6). The idea of the primacy of management considerations over merit persisted and eventually won out in part because the basic elements of a merit system had become such a deeply established institution and value that it could not be easily erased, certainly not endangered by an executive-centric personnel agency. The concept that the permanent workforce of any governmental unit be merit-based had seeped deeply into the DNA of American political culture. Nonetheless, American society and values increasingly came to defer to the wisdom and imperatives of *management*, whether those senior managers were in the private or public sectors. Management should not be second-guessed, or, at least, not be provided with an easy alibi or able to pin failure on someone or something else. There could be no blame game (darn those untouchable civil servants!) when an elected chief executive failed. Eliminating autonomous CSCs took away any such facile excuse for a president, governor, or mayor.

Evaluating the Presidential Imperative for Personnel Management

In May 1936, just seven weeks after FDR had formed PCAM, Floyd Reeves submitted to the three committee members a tentative plan for his assignment to study federal personnel management. Putting the cart before the horse, he listed his expected recommendations, including:

- "There should be a Central Personnel Agency established in the President's office [to] coordinate with other service agencies" involved with management of the executive branch.
- It should be headed by "an assistant to the President [who] should serve as a liaison officer" for all federal personnel activities.
- The liaison officer "should be selected in the same manner as a member of the Cabinet since he will serve as one of the political, policy-forming heads of the administration."
- "The establishment of this Central Personnel Agency does not involve necessarily the abolition of the Civil Service Commission."
- The president should "instruct the Civil Service Commission to report to the

President through him," in other words through the new White House official overseeing personnel management.

- Given potential opposition to the suggested new central personnel agency, PCAM requests for changes in federal laws "should be held to a minimum. . . . It might be possible, for example, without any further legislation, to select a head for a Central Personnel office, [and] place him in office as one of the President's secretaries, or as an Assistant to the President."
- The presidential personnel office should have "a small staff," especially "an assistant to the liaison officer" with a strong background and experience in personnel policy
- The president's assistant for personnel management could be funded "from available appropriations" for presidential operations
- The assistant to the president would "be responsible for preparing recommendations for further legislative and organization steps" in personnel matters.[1]

It is uncanny how closely FDR's eventual actions unfolded as Reeves had outlined so quickly and early in the planning process. The president appointed McReynolds as one of his administrative assistants and then designated him as the liaison officer for personnel management. This entailed no new legislation, as LOPM was created by executive order. McReynolds oversaw the CSC, meeting with it weekly. All commission reports and requests to the president went through him. LOPM was largely funded from general presidential appropriations, had a small staff, and McReynolds's primary assistants (Belsley and Moffett) had significant previous experience in public sector personnel and civil service policy before their appointments. Finally, McReynolds also was responsible for personnel-related legislation.

Using Reeves's principles for constructing an effective central presidential human capital agency, Roosevelt accomplished just about everything Reeves felt was necessary for such a mission. PCAM largely endorsed Reeves's construct. After a fierce three-year argument on Capitol Hill, Congress absolutely refused to permit creating a presidential personnel management agency (chap. 2). Yet FDR found ways to implement Reeves's principles notwithstanding the legal ban on using his reorganization powers to touch the CSC in any way (chap. 3).

LOPM as a presidential institution had surprising, but unnoticed, durability (chap. 6). Truman kept it, and then Eisenhower seemingly abolished it within months of becoming president. In 1953, when Eisenhower transferred the responsibility for presidential personnel management to the chair of the CSC, he apparently disbanded LOPM. What many histories have missed was that the Eisenhower executive order merely transferred *who* served as liaison officer for personnel management, but did not disband the small presidential agency. The presidential-centric personnel management staff continued working in the Executive Office Building as employees of the presidency, distinctly separate from the CSC staff. The CSC chair divided his time between his presidential office and his CSC office. So, the de facto LOPM continued within the presidency.

Further missed by history was that this arrangement did not work out to Eisenhower's satisfaction. That's why, in 1957, Eisenhower repealed his 1953 executive order and re-established a more formal presidential office for personnel management separate from the CSC chair's responsibilities. The position was called "Special Assistant to the President for Personnel Management" and had a small staff. Based on the 1957 executive order, the unit largely had the same duties as LOPM performed during FDR's presidency. This post-FDR record demonstrates that the need for presidential personnel management and coordination had become a permanent element of the managerial presidency.

Evaluating the Performance of FDR's LOPM, 1939–1945

Reeves's prescience also provides something of a measurement formula for assessing what FDR accomplished with his personnel reforms relative to the status quo of his first term. Historians have long called PCAM's personnel recommendations a failure because Congress prohibited presidents from using their reorganization power to affect the CSC. The historical verdict for LOPM has flowed from that 1939 statutory ban on reorganizing the CSC. The literature has assumed, therefore, that LOPM was largely a political fig leaf that permitted FDR to claim a symbolic win and little more. It will be recalled (as described in the Introduction) that in 1954, Somers concluded LOPM was "not conspicuously successful" (Somers 1954, 135). Arnold's assessment 40+ years later confirmed how much this conventional wisdom had hardened in the literature, namely that LOPM was merely "a ghost of the Brownlow Committee's original intention" because, in part, it was limited to "a one-person office lacking formal authority" (Arnold 1997, 416).

Wrong, wrong, wrong. Based on LOPM's documented record (chaps. 4–5), the agency performed as a de facto central personnel agency, especially considering the constraints of staffing. It performed all the major functions that PCAM and FDR sought: overseeing and directing all civilian personnel-related matters throughout the executive branch (including, especially, the CSC), promoting the work of the Council of Personnel Administration, and controlling all major personnel policy decisions that either needed the president's personal approval or could be decided by McReynolds in the president's name. FDR may have lost the fight with Congress over personnel reorganization on a de jure basis, but the wily maneuverer got just about everything he wanted anyway. And most historians have missed it.

Beyond that general point, how can one systematically and disinterestedly develop a conclusion on the success or failure of the actual performance of LOPM? I present four methods: Somers's generic criteria for presidential coordinating offices; the success or failure of LOPM exercising power over the CSC notwithstanding the congressional ban on reorganizing the CSC; a public statement from FDR of his mission for the agency; and McReynolds's HR policy–specific criteria of good personnel management.

First, one way to evaluate the record of LOPM as a presidential coordinating body was suggested by Somers when he developed a generic framework for assessing the success or failure of the presidential Office of War Mobilization and Reconversion (OWMR). He suggested seven generic principles for evaluating White House coordinating agencies:

1. "institutional status in the president's office"
2. "jurisdiction over all agencies"
3. "restriction of functions to top policy and program issues"
4. "non-involvement in normal functions of individual departments"
5. "maintenance of reasonable control"
6. "qualifications of the program coordinator"
7. "small high-level staff" (Somers 1969 [1950], 224–30)[2]

Oddly, even though Somers dismissed LOPM's importance in a separate piece (Somers 1954, 135), LOPM met practically all of the evaluative criteria that he used in 1950 when he judged OWMR as a valuable contribution to the presidency. Following his checklist:

1. LOPM had institutional status in the president's office based on an executive order that created it as one of five agencies in the new Executive Office of the President. (Late in WWII, OWMR received statutory status.)
2. Based on the executive order defining its mission, LOPM had no legal line jurisdiction over all relevant agencies; rather, it was to function in a liaison and coordinating role for the entire executive branch.

3–4. McReynolds kept LOPM focused on major policy issues, opting not to micromanage the CSC's routine work and rulings.

5. McReynolds exercised informal powers to assure the implementation of his decisions. For example, all requests by the CSC for the president to promulgate new regulations with an executive order went through McReynolds. FDR would only consider and approve them if they had McReynolds's positive recommendation. Also, he largely interposed himself between the CSC

and the president. In-person meetings between FDR and the CSC virtually ceased after LOPM's creation.

6. McReynolds had the background, characteristics, and standing to be the head of LOPM. He worked with FDR in World War I, when FDR was assistant secretary of the Navy, and then received presidential assignments from FDR during his first term in office (i.e., before PCAM and LOPM). During PCAM's deliberations, Brownlow and the committee staff frequently consulted with McReynolds for information and advice. McReynolds also had standing with members of Congress interested in personnel issues, dating back to his work at the Post Office, Bureau of Efficiency, Personnel Classification Board, Farm Credit Administration, and Treasury Department.
7. LOPM had a small senior-level staff of about six people including secretaries, with Belsley and Moffett as high-level staffers.

Summarizing LOPM from the perspective of Somers's evaluative criteria, LOPM should probably be judged as fully attaining five of his seven criteria and partially the other two. The two partial ones relate to LOPM's non-statutory basis and not having formal line jurisdiction over all relevant agencies. Therefore, notwithstanding Somers's poor opinion of LOPM, the agency met nearly all of his generic criteria needed by a presidential coordinating office for success.

A second way to evaluate LOPM is based on its success or failure in overseeing and subordinating the CSC, theoretically untouchable due to Congress exempting the commission from the president's 1939 reorganization powers. The question is if, after the 1939 reorganization, the CSC continued acting as an autonomous and independent body. A way to assess this is suggested by a 1940 incident unrelated to the CSC and LOPM. FDR was meeting with a senior management executive from the private sector who he was naming to the new National Defense Advisory Commission (NDAC). The appointee asked the president the bald but obvious question: "Who's my boss?" "I guess I am," answered FDR (Lee 2012, 27). The same question can be put to the historical record of the CSC *vis-à-vis* LOPM. Did the CSC recognize that LOPM/McReynolds was its boss? Generally yes. Before the 1939 reorganization, the CSC had routine face-to-face meetings with the president. After the reorganization (and especially after Pearl Harbor) the commission ceased having such meetings. Instead the commissioners (or the president of the commission) met frequently with McReynolds. In particular, the appointment of Flemming to the commission was done in a way to designate him as a kind of super-commissioner. He fully recognized that McReynolds was his boss and spoke for the president (chaps. 4–5). It will be recalled that commission president Harry Mitchell's memoir omitted any reference to LOPM and claimed that his wartime White House contact person was FDR's son. I have interpreted this odd omission as reflecting Mitchell's unhappiness at having a new "boss" other than the president (two actually, McReynolds and Flemming). Therefore, based on the criterion of LOPM operating as the CSC's boss, then, yes, LOPM was successful. It overcame the 1939 congressional ban on the president using his reorganization powers to affect the CSC in any way. Roosevelt deftly found another way to accomplish his goal.

In 1946, McDiarmid also concluded that LOPM indeed had played an important and constructive role *vis-à-vis* the CSC. With McReynolds's direct access to the president and his collegial working relationships with other EOP agencies, LOPM "has dredged the channel of communication and influence in so far as the human side of personnel management is concerned" (McDiarmid 1946, 1072). In particular, LOPM contributed to reshaping the CSC from an autonomous, lumbering, and independent body to "a staff advisor to the Chief Executive" (1079).

A third way to assess LOPM is based on the president's public declaration of LOPM's goals before it had time to develop a record (apart from his 1939 executive order creating it, which, by necessity, had to use careful and restrained legalistic language [chap. 3]). In the fall of 1939, only a few months after FDR had created LOPM, he sent a message of greetings to the annual conference of the Civil Service Assembly of the United States and Canada. In that statement, FDR reported with pride on his creation of LOPM and his expectations for the new agency: "through which I shall be able to keep in closer touch with the problems in the field of personnel administration."[3] Using this formulation as the agency's prospective mission and its measure of performance, then LOPM must surely be considered to have had some distinct degree of success. McReynolds not only kept the president (and the institutionalized presidency in EOP) abreast of personnel management issues, but he also helped guide final decisions to reflect the president's preferences in each particular area.

Finally, a more policy-specific way to evaluate LOPM's record in personnel management can be based on McReynolds's overview of LOPM's role. In mid-1943, he gave the after-dinner talk at the Federal Personnel Management Conference in Cleveland.[4] In it, he crystallized his experiences at LOPM as a reflection of the management philosophy propounded by PCAM and FDR. He detailed how it applied to modern personnel management. In particular, he said that HR "is a major part of the job of over-all management" and criticized earlier approaches viewing it "as a separate authority acting independently." The earlier philosophy seemed to him to "enthrone the personnel man as a sort of super-expert." This criticism was a not-so-subtle knock on the paradigm of an independent and autonomous CSC. Instead, personnel management needed to be "a staff officer" oriented to help the chief administrator accomplish his management goals. In all cases, the activities of a personnel manager "would be thought of as acting merely as the agent of the chief" executive officer. If engaging in an historical verdict of LOPM, then based on the standards that McReynolds had crystallized after four years on the job, one can creditably view LOPM as successful.

Evaluating the Future: The Office of Personnel Management

It is beyond the scope of this inquiry to suggest conclusions about the subsequent record of OPM and if its outcomes justify the claims made by the advocates for a presidential personnel agency. Given that the daily work of public administration is about managing people, one can't expect that an organizational change would wholly *eliminate* problems. Further, as is usually the case in public sector history, the absence of a counter-factual scenario makes it nearly impossible to judge how different the substantive results of the new OPM would have otherwise been if Congress had defeated the Civil Service Reform Act of 1978 and insisted on maintaining the CSC as an autonomous agency tasked with protecting the merit system.

Any comprehensive evaluation of OPM's past, current, and future performance should likely assess at least one important lesson from this history of LOPM. Certainly, drawing immutable lessons from the past is a dangerous approach that is often wrong. Nonetheless, if history is any kind of guide, then one of the factors contributing to whatever successes LOPM had would be its close working relationship with BOB (chaps. 4–5). As the Brownlow Committee repeatedly emphasized, a president's three key managerial tools were budgeting, personnel, and planning. Indeed, these three elements of management blend into each other. They cannot be artificially separated and demarcated—nor should they be. For an example unrelated to LOPM, BOB employed several economists to provide economic forecasting for the purposes of the planning premises for a presidential budget. This book noted many examples of the overlap between personnel management and budgeting, such as BOB having several personnel specialists on its staff who worked in tandem with McReynolds on the budgetary implementation of personnel management matters. In general, the archival record shows a close working relationship between the two agencies, including LOPM's input to BOB's decision-making when preparing a draft of the president's budget proposal to Congress for the next fiscal year, BOB support for expanding LOPM's budget and staffing during WWII, multiple meetings with the president attended by both Smith and McReynolds, and FDR's requests for a joint recommendation from the two on a pending issue. There was a general sense that both agencies reflected the president's managerial oversight of the executive branch and that a cooperative and consensus-based relationship was a key to operationalizing it.

Without prejudging conclusions that historians of OPM will come to, there is a general perception that OPM's record does not appear to include a significantly close relationship with the president, the White House, or the Executive Office of the President. In part, this can be explained formally by OPM not being an EOP agency, in contrast to LOPM. It is possible that OPM is so large an agency that it is impractical to bring it into the EOP. In size, it would dwarf all the other EOP entities and, politically, it would look as though the president's official family had suddenly grown in size. This would then be a tempting target for criticism by the party not in control of the White House. Charges of an imperial presidency gone out of control would be catnip to reporters. So, perhaps, OPM *must* remain outside EOP.

Perhaps this history of LOPM and of Eisenhower's second-term approach (chap. 6) suggests a way around some of the current unsatisfactory manifestations of the status quo. Perhaps a future president should create a small office for personnel management *policy* within EOP. The head of that office would be much more of the president's intimate agent than OPM's director is now generally seen to be. Furthermore, the head of the policy office within EOP would be the peer of the OMB director, an important relationship from the history of LOPM and BOB that needs to be nurtured. However, this approach contains a major conceptual and intellectual flaw. It is premised on being able to separate personnel management *policy* from the routine operations of personnel management *implementation*. Public administration has long pointed out the impossibility of such a generic bifurcation of policy and administration. However, setting aside the reflexive academic critique of this suggestion, perhaps the real world of the federal government could very roughly identify the distinction between HR policy and routine personnel operations. Politics is much more pragmatic than the academy. It may be possible to operationalize a small presidential HR policy office in the institutional White House that would work, of course, in close relationship with OPM's more routine activities. Precedents for this exist. EOP currently has an Office of Science and Technology *Policy*.[5] Similarly, the White House Domestic Council has an Office of National AIDS *Policy*.[6] These examples indicate that real world of government is able to concentrate policy in one organizational box and line programs in another.

As for the current status of personnel management in government, sometimes it seems that the concept of "civil service reform" is so embedded in the political and academic culture that it lives on indefinitely, regardless of already-implemented improvements. It's as though civil service can never be reformed *enough*. Plans and proposals for improving the federal personnel system are ongoing, practically a perennial cottage industry. In 2000, a book assessed CSRA after twenty years and explored "the future of merit" as unfinished business (Pfiffner and Brook 2000). Seven years later, two academics called for "radical reform" of the merit system (Bowman and West 2007). In 2008, prominent political scientist Paul Light characterized American government as "ill executed" and presented "an agenda for reform" (Light, 2008, 124). A year later, the revised edition of a textbook on public sector HR identified six major problems in government personnel management that needed to be addressed: affirmative action and diversity, gender and workplace issues, IT, ethics, labor relations, and outsourcing (Hays, Kearnye and Coggburn 2009, chaps. 14–19). In 2013, an academic review of the state of personnel management in the United States identified several ongoing issues that needed attention and reform, including decentralization and compensation (Llorens 2013). The next year, another textbook presented a postmortem on all the problems caused by or not solved by the CSRA in 1978 (Naff, Riccucci and Freyss 2014, 19–32).

Generally such reform ideas and suggestions are process reforms that need to be distinguished from organizational and structural ones. For example, a report from the Brookings Institution in 2013 focused on the specific problems of the current merit-based pay system.[7] Most prominent of the ongoing reform initiatives have been from the Partnership for Public Service, a coalition of business, academe, practitioners, and other reformers.[8] In 2014, it published a comprehensive report on the need for *A New Civil Service Framework*.[9] Significantly, in relation to the focus of this book, the plan did not propose radical changes in the organization or structure of federal personnel management. This suggests that OPM is here to stay, at least for the foreseeable future, and that reformers do not see the need for any tectonic structural or organizational redesign. That personnel management policies and the operations of OPM can be improved are a given. That OPM needs to be reorganized into a wholly different managerial relationship with the president is practically never heard nowadays.

Hence, notwithstanding the continuing flow of suggestions for improving federal human capital management since OPM's creation, it is important to note the absence of one reform idea from these lists and agenda. Despite the voluminous and seemingly endless proposals for modernizing federal personnel management, *none* that I could locate have suggested that a crucial and needed reform would be to *go back* to an autonomous, multi-member, bipartisan CSC. For example, Newland criticized "the partisan politicization of OPM" and Kettl called for a stronger HR professional to lead OPM, but neither called for reverting to the *status quo ante* (Newland 2015, 58; Kettl 2015, 22). Here is a case of a dog not barking, an idea that HR reform experts have no interest in resurrecting. There is not a revisionist literature in public administration arguing that Carter and Congress got it wrong in 1978 as relates to the organization of presidential personnel management and that their decision needs to be reversed. If anything, the one constant in all the reform ideas is to further improve personnel management without the need for major organizational change. As such, management has won over merit—although with the strong caveat that merit is alive and well, despite being within an institutional structure oriented to personnel *management*.

Democratic principles underlie public administration. In government, as in other aspects of life, ideas matter. The long fight by good government reformers from Theodore to Franklin Roosevelt to create a merit system for America's public sector was an important and valid one. And it succeeded. It is inconceivable in the twenty-first century that elected institutions could defy public opinion and wholly eliminate a merit-based HR system. The wholesale firing of *all* public employees after an election will not recur. Americans expect an apolitical, neutral, and merit-based public sector workforce.

On the other hand, the long view will likely conclude that the results of what the goo-goos accomplished went a bit too far. CSCs began being viewed as too bureaucratic, too focused on process, paperwork, rules, and regulations. They embodied the principle of merit, especially in their autonomy from the chief executive. It was PCAM's argument that the voters had a right to expect a president to have the management tools to accomplish the policy goals he (or, in the future, she) campaigned for. Ensconced bureaucrats should not be able to sabotage what a president, governor, or mayor was trying to accomplish—assuming the acquiescence of the legislative branch as a check and balance to the executive.

The longstanding argument instead focuses on tidying up the borders between executive appointees and the classified service. How deep or shallow should a president be able to go with appointments in a federal agency? There never will be a final, one right answer to that question. Instead, the dynamics of American history are at play and will likely re-answer the question based on the times. Kaufman theorized that American governmental history reflected a constant swinging of a pendulum among the antithetical values of neutral competence, executive leadership, and representativeness (Kaufman 1956). Neutral competence held sway for most of the twentieth century. While reformers like PCAM and FDR sought to elevate executive leadership in the area of personnel management over neutral competence in the 1930s, their views did not prevail until the passage of the Civil Service Reform Act of 1978.

These battles are never over. That the priority of values changes is inherent in American politics and society. This will continue into the future, for the rest of the twenty-first century and even beyond. Yet any stasis that emerges during a given political era is likely to be merely a minor redefining of the line separating civil servants and politicians. Americans, it turns out, want merit *and* management. Both are right, important, and contributions to democracy. FDR's fight for a presidential personnel agency redefined the framework of the argument as first presented by the civil service reform movement in the late nineteenth century. At the time of writing (2015), history's verdict has been that FDR's recommendation on federal personnel management was more right than wrong. HR is a management tool, just as budgeting is. It simply took four decades for his views to be enshrined into formal law instead of the informal subterfuge of presidential practice.

Notes

Introduction

1. The motivation of the good government reformers—especially those in the WASP elite—also had a tinge of nativism and anti-Catholic prejudice. A recent revisionist history of the Tammany Hall machine in Manhattan suggests that anti-Irish bigotry was one of the primary motivations of good government reformers, at least in New York city and state (Golway 2014).

2. Kaufman also identified a third value, representativeness.

3. She favored the latter.

Chapter 1

1. Theodore Roosevelt was impatient with the other two commissioners and "much preferred to proceed unilaterally" (Goodwin 2013, 140). In that respect, one could lightheartedly view him as the first of the good government reformers to demonstrate the advantages of having a (de facto) one-person CSC over the (de jure) three-member structure.

2. Later in his career, Moses was the construction czar of New York city and state.

3. "Program of the Better Government League: As to the Federal Service," *The Public Business* 1, 1 (June 1926): n.p. (informally, p. 4).

4. In his Foreword, Feldman expressed appreciation to those who helped him in his research. It was a foretelling of a kind of *Who's Who* of the next fifteen years in federal personnel management: William McReynolds, Lewis Meriam, G. Lyle Belsley, and Guy Moffett (US House 1931, iv). That these four continued to play major roles in the 1930s and 1940s indicates how small the network of so-called "experts" in personnel policy and management really was.

5. The committee is more familiar in American history by its later name, the Government Operations Committee.

6. The hearing was also dominated by the committee chair's political war on the Bureau of Efficiency and his use of Hoover's proposal as an excuse to try to kill the bureau.

7. Even sans any of the major contentious personnel reorganization proposals, Congress nonetheless exercised its legislative veto and rejected all of his proposed reorganization *executive orders* (the format for reorganization plans required under the reorganization powers delegated to Hoover in the 1932 Economy Act). The Democratic Congress would not give the lame-duck Republican president any last political wins or boasting rights. It also did not want to tie the hands of President-elect Roosevelt's potential reorganization and economy measures.

8. Elliot H. Goodwin, Secretary, Civil Service Reform Association, to FDR, November 21, 1908; Harry W. Marsh, Secretary, National Civil Service Reform League, to FDR, November 13, 1924; FDR to Richard Henry Dana, Cambridge, MA, September 4, 1925; and FDR to Thomas W. Swan, President, National Civil Service Reform League, November 12, 1926, all in Civil Service Reform file, FDR Family, Business, and Personal [Records], Franklin D. Roosevelt Presidential Library, Hyde Park, NY (hereafter cited as FDRL).

9. *Public Personnel Studies* 6, 1 (January 1928): inside front cover.

10. Public administration literature has largely erased White's partisan affiliation. It rarely mentions that, when FDR named White to the CSC, it was for the Republican slot on the three-member bipartisan commission.

11. Correspondence between Richard Crane and FDR, November 1933, Government & Municipal Civil Service Employees file, President's Personal File (PPF) 807, FDRL. Indeed, in January, the War Department contacted the White House regarding a request it had received from the commission for information and asked if it was accurate that the president supported the survey? Should the department cooperate? Yes, White House Executive Clerk Rudolph Forster replied, confirming the president's support and desire that the department cooperate.

12. Associated Press (AP), "New Employee Survey to Open," *Los Angeles Times*, December 11, 1933, 5.

13. "Spelman Grants $807,748 in 1933," *NYT*, December 15, 1934, 10.

14. Besides publishing the hearings, McGraw-Hill, a major commercial and reputable publishing house, issued six other volumes from the commission. It strains credulity that some of the publications, on quite obscure topics, were financially viable to a for-profit publisher. It is possible that the commission (i.e., the Rockefellers) subsidized the publication of the series as a way to publicize and promote public opinion support for the commission's effort to create a new incarnation of civil service reform. According to Brownlow, the report was out of print "within less than a year" and then was republished in paperback for 25¢, and it also sold out quickly (Brownlow 1958, 297).

15. "Civil Service as a Career" (editorial), *NYHT*, July 14, 1934, 10; "Experts See Aid to Government in Merit System," *CT*, October 5, 1934, 7; "U.S. Public Service Quiz Group Meets," *Oakland [CA] Tribune*, November 12, 1934, 1; "Greatest Needs of U.S. Voiced at Service Inquiry," *Berkeley [CA] Daily Gazette*, November 15, 1934, 1–2.

16. "Public Service Inquiry," *Wall Street Journal*, December 22, 1933, 9; "Studying Methods of Improving the Public Service" (photo), *NYHT*, December 31, 1933, 8; "Wide

Scope Urged for Career Plan," *NYT*, January 7, 1935, 8; AP, "Career System Urged as Plan to Kill 'Spoils,'" *WP*, January 7, 1935, 3.

17. As an indication of its secondary status, the subject was not mentioned among the suggestions to the commission from the American Political Science Association (Ogg 1934).

18. At the time, Beyer headed the Philadelphia Bureau of Municipal Research, putting him in the category of a professional good government advocate, like Brownlow and other non-academic public administration professionalizers. Later, with a PhD, Beyer capped his career as a professor at the University of Pennsylvania.

19. "A Career Postmaster" (editorial), *NYT*, January 8, 1935, 20.

20. "Building Up a Civil Service" (editorial), *CSM*, January 9, 1935, 14.

21. Years later, Joseph Harris complimented the work of the commission, describing it as "a distinguished private body" (1964, 169). Harris was no neutral observer. He had been the research director of the Rockefeller-funded Committee on Public Administration of the Social Science Research Council and then the staff director of FDR's Brownlow Committee, the de facto second act of activists like Brownlow and Gulick.

22. Ordway Tead, "Civil Service Reform" (review of *Better Government Personnel*), *NYHT*, June 9, 1935, G12.

23. Charles W. Kliet II, "Notes - Re Conference with the President," February 20, 1936, 1, File A-II-5, Box I, President's Committee on Administrative Management (hereafter cited as PCAM), FDRL. See also Merriam to Brownlow, February 20, 1936, File A-II-6, Box 1, PCAM. The filing style of PCAM records often titled a file with the same title as the key document it contained. To avoid redundancy, in those cases, I have omitted the title of the file and only listed the file number.

24. Even that caution did not prevent the accusation from being made. When debating the PCAM bill on the floor of the Senate, James Davis (R-PA) said "certain groups of study clubs, highly respected in the past, have allowed themselves to be subsidized for an attack on the Civil Service Commission by private endowments, with more money than public interest to support them" (*CR*, March 9, 1938, 3093). This was evidently a reference to the Commission of Inquiry and perhaps other Rockefeller-funded good government activities, such as Brownlow's Public Administration Clearing House (PACH).

25. Instead, FDR had PCAM located at and supported by the National Emergency Council (PCAM 1937, viii). The council's own fate was subsequently affected by the PCAM-inspired reorganization in 1939. It became the Office of Government Reports, one of the original five agencies of the newly created Executive Office of the President (Lee 2005a, chaps. 2–3).

26. Brownlow does not specifically identify *when* FDR made those comments. It is possible he made them later in the process. But the quote is consistent with Merriam's summary of the meeting. Even if FDR had made this comment later, the sentiment he expressed is consistent with his thinking all along, through to the showdown vote in the House in April 1938.

27. Kliet, "Notes - Re Conference with the President," February 20, 1936, 3.

28. Merriam to Brownlow, February 20, 1936, File A-II-6: Rough Notes, Box 1, PCAM.

29. Merriam, "Fragmentary Memoranda on Administrative Management: Observations of a Layman to my Professional Colleagues," n.d. (probably March 1936), File A-II-14: Minutes of the Meeting of the Committee, April 11, 1936, Box 1, PCAM.

30. For biographical information on Reeves's professional career before and after PCAM, see Floyd W. Reeves, "Essentials of a Modern Personnel System," *Annals of the American Academy of Political and Social Science* 189 (1937): 141; Richard O. Niehoff, *Floyd W. Reeves: Innovative Educator and Distinguished Practitioner of Public Administration* (Lanham, MD: University Press of America, 1991).

31. "Franklin D. Roosevelt: Day by Day," FDRL website, accessed July 6, 2015, http://www.fdrlibrary.marist.edu/daybyday/ (hereafter cited as Franklin D. Roosevelt: Day by Day, online).

32. "Preliminary Outline of an Inquiry into Administrative Management of the Federal Government, Confidential," n.d. (probably about April 28, 1936), 17–18, File A-II-17, Box 1, PCAM.

33. Reeves, Memorandum to the Committee, Subject: Memorandum on Personnel Administration, May 28, 1936, Part I: Principles of Federal Personnel Administration, File E-II: Tentative Draft of Personnel Report, Box 11, PCAM.

34. Part III, section 4, ibid.

35. Part III, section 17a, ibid.

36. Part III, section 5d, ibid.

37. Harris, "Progress Report on Staff Activities Covering the Period from June 22 to August 15," 78–79, File A-II-31, Box 1, PCAM.

38. For more biographical information on David, see Stephanie P. Newbold and Larry D. Terry, "The President's Committee on Administrative Management: The Untold Story and the Federalist Connection," *Administration & Society* 38 (2006): 527. Somewhat artificially, PCAM elevated David's role to that of a co-author of Reeves's study when PCAM published it in 1937. None of the other PCAM staffers who later participated in revising the original Reeves submission were so credited.

39. Miller had been on the staff of the Commission of Inquiry and had written a report for it on veterans' preference points (Miller 1935). As a PCAM staffer, he was assigned to write a staff study on "The Federal Personnel System" covering personnel policies and workforce statistics ("List of Special Studies," n.a., n.d., File A-II-47, Box 2, PCAM). It is unclear what happened to Miller's assignment because it was not mimeographed for internal circulation and not published in 1937 as a standalone study (PCAM, 1937). It is possible that some material from Miller's report was folded into the final and published version of the Reeves study, given that Miller had a hand in revising it.

40. Harris, "Progress Report on Staff Activities Covering the Period from June 22 to August 15," 78, File A-II-31, Box 1, PCAM. This is a somewhat odd circumlocution to describe the role of other PCAM staffers involved in revising and rewriting Reeves's submission. Indicating deliberateness, Brownlow used the same verb during his congressional testimony: he said that Reeves "was assisted by various other people" (US Congress 1937, 141).

41. Herbert Emmerich, "Revised Memorandum for the organization of a Central Per-

sonnel Agency; Written in accordance with suggestions made at the conference of October 30," October 31, 1936, File E-VII-2, Box 11, PCAM.

42. Earlier that day, FDR had met with the CSC commissioners, a relatively unusual event in his presidency. I was unable to determine the content of the meeting from the records at the FDRL. While that might be due to gaps in archival collections, it more likely reflects FDR's dislike of written summaries of meetings (Kaiser 2014, 49). It is possible that rumors about a potential PCAM recommendation to reorganize the commission prompted the request for the meeting. By scheduling this appointment before his meeting with Brownlow, FDR could have credibly and evasively been able to respond that he did not yet know what exactly PCAM would recommend in the personnel area. That FDR promptly sent a mildly apologetic letter along with copy of the report to the CSC's president on the same day he sent it to Congress suggests that FDR had made a soft commitment at the November meeting to keep the commission informed (FDR to Harry B. Mitchell, CSC President, January 12, 1937, File Jan [*sic*]–May, Box 2, [President's] Official File 2: CSC, FDRL [hereafter cited as OF 2]).

43. Belsley had been a personnel officer at the Farm Credit Administration at the same time that William McReynolds (later head of LOPM) was there as administrative assistant to FCA head Henry Morgenthau. Before and after Belsley's work with PCAM, he was the executive director of the Civil Service Assembly of the US and Canada, which was based at Brownlow's PACH in Chicago.

44. Emmerich and Belsley, "Personnel Management, December 10, 1936," 44, File E-VII: Emmerich-Belsley Initial Draft, Box 11, PCAM.

45. Handwritten note on the back of p. 8, "Tentative Short Summary Report of the President's Committee on Administrative Management, December 18, 1936," File A-II-40a, Box 2, PCAM.

46. "Tentative Draft of the Report of the President's Committee on Administrative Management, December 22, 1936," 33, File A-II-41, Box 2, PCAM.

47. Draft of "Report On Administrative Management In the Government of the United States, January 5, [1937]," 35; and paper-clipped insert as substitute for section c, both in File A-II-42, Box 2, PCAM. (The cover page has a typo, listing the year as 1936. To avoid unnecessary confusion, I have corrected it in brackets in the formal reference to the archival document.)

Chapter 2

1. This last assertion was debatable. It was based on the theory behind FDR's effort in 1933 to discharge William Humphrey without cause from the Federal Trade Commission before the end of Humphrey's term.

2. FDR to Mitchell, CSC President, January 12, 1937, File Jan–May, Box 2, OF 2.

3. Franklin Waltman, "Hostility Flares on Capitol Hill within an Hour," *WP*, January 13, 1937, 6.

4. Arthur Sears Henning, "Congress Split by Roosevelt Shakeup Plans," *CT*, January 13, 1937, 4.

5. "Defeating a Noble Ideal" (editorial), *NYHT*, January 16, 1937, 14.

6. "Backs Reorganization," *NYT*, January 25, 1937, 15.

7. White's confidential advice to PCAM in 1936 described his alternative of shifting the CSC's powers to a new central executive staff serving under the Council of Personnel Administration ("Memorandum," n.d., 6, File E-XII-4: Memorandum by Leonard White, Box 11, PCAM).

8. *CR*, March 4, 1938, 2813.

9. "U.S. Shake-Up Hit by Former Head of Civil Service," *Washington Star*, January 20, 1937; and copy forwarded to PCAM by the Division of Press Intelligence of the National Emergency Council (later OGR), File E-XV-7, Box 12, PCAM.

10. Telegram from Thomas Campbell to Brownlow, February 23, 1937, File E-XV-6: Campbell Statement, Box 12, PCAM.

11. "Should All Government Employees be Under Civil Service?" *America's Town Meeting of the Air* (transcript) 2, 9 (January 14, 1937): 26.

12. "Reorganization Bill Opposed by C. I. Stengle," *WP*, June 27, 1937, 7.

13. "Should All Government Employees be Under Civil Service?," 18.

14. Ibid., 20–21. At one point in the radio broadcast, the moderator introduced her as "Mrs. Eugene Meyer of *The Washington Post*," suggesting she had a formal link to the paper (5). It is possible that she held a corporate position, such as on the board of directors. The *Post* placed a wire service story of the radio debate on its front page (AP, "Broadening of Civil Service is Discussed in Radio Forum," *WP*, January 15, 1937, 1, 4). The story identified her as "Mrs. Eugene Meyer, of Washington, DC." A month later, Mrs. Meyer gave a talk to a women's group and again expressed support for the civil service reform aspects of the Brownlow report and urged her audience to notify their members of Congress of their support ("Civil Service Reforms Urged by Mrs. Meyer," *WP*, February 14, 1937, 5).

15. At the time, the title used for the commissioner chosen by the commissioners to chair their official meetings was president. This derived from the major task of the commissioner who was so designated, namely to preside at commission meetings. In modern usage, however, a title of president generally suggests an *executive* role, including holding and exercising certain top management powers on one's own. For historical accuracy, I have retained using the term of CSC president even though it is somewhat misleading in what powers it conveys. During WWII, McReynolds suggested superseding the office of CSC president with that of CSC *chairman*, who would be designated by the president, not the commissioners. Confusingly, at least in relation to modern usage, in McReynolds's scheme the CSC chairman would have executive powers, tantamount to being the CEO of the commission's permanent staff, as well as chairing official meetings of the commission (chap. 5).

16. This latter category was probably a hint at the role the Brookings Institution would be playing in the reorganization legislation, given that it had been hired by Senator Byrd to provide a kind of counter-PCAM report from an expected conservative perspective.

17. Mitchell to FDR, February 11, 1937, File Jan–May 1937, Box 2, OF 2.

18. Memo from FDR to Brownlow, February 13, 1937, ibid.

19. Brownlow to FDR, with draft reply to Mitchell, February 22, 1937, ibid.

20. Draft on White House stationery with handwritten markings and dictated inserts, February 23, 1937, ibid.

21. FDR to Mitchell, February 26, 1937, ibid.

22. "Competitive Selection of the Civil Service Administrator," n.a., n.d., File E-XV-3; and Frederick J. Lawton, "Civil Service Administrator," n.d., File E-XV-5, both in Box 12, PCAM. Lawton was a rising star in BOB when the Senate's Select Committee on Government Organization, somewhat oddly, asked BOB to detail to it a specialist to provide staff expertise while it was considering the Brownlow plan. Lawton then briefly served as the "Consultant and Advisor" to the Senate committee (US Congress 1937, ii). As Lawton's memo is undated, it is unclear if he wrote it while working for the Senate or, later, back at BOB, trying to assist the president in getting the bill passed.

23. Joseph Alsop Jr., "Reorganization Bill Gives Rights to Roosevelt," *NYHT*, February 26, 1937, 9. It is possible that "appanage" was a typo, intended to be "appendage." More likely, Alsop deliberately chose the unusual and rarely-used term (sometimes spelled "apanage"), which means the possession of a ruler or for the ruler to do with as he wished. In the 1950s and 1960s, Alsop was an influential Washington pundit, co-authoring a regular and widely-syndicated column with his brother Stuart.

24. Robert C. Albright, "Reorganization Plan Is Revived, Split Into Four," *WP*, May 16, 1937, 1, 5.

25. For reasons that are unclear, the bill omitted the plan for a seven-member Civil Service Board. The fifteen-year term was likely intended to look familiar on Capitol Hill, because the (politically independent) comptroller general of GAO also had a very long term.

26. "7-Man Board Proposed for Civil Service," *WP*, June 28, 1937, 3; "Roosevelt Body Asks Expansion of Merit System," *NYHT*, June 28, 1937, 6.

27. AP, "Publicity Pay of Half Million By U.S. Listed," *WP*, June 14, 1937, 2.

28. Albert L. Warner, "Reorganization Battle Pushed by Coalition," *NYHT*, June 7, 1937, 32.

29. Now the Government Accountability Office.

30. "Asks Wider Staff for Civil Service," *NYT*, June 22, 1937, 4; "New Plea is Made for Extension of U.S. Civil Service," *CSM*, June 22, 1937, 1, 4.

31. Kaplan later simplified the position of the National Civil Service Reform League by flatly endorsing the personnel-related sections of the version of the reorganization bill submitted to the House by its Select Committee on Government Organization (*CR*, April 8, 1938, 5110).

32. FDR later named Byrnes to the Supreme Court. During WWII, Byrnes resigned from the court to become the White House economic czar, a position so powerful he was sometimes called the "assistant president." Byrnes then was Truman's Secretary of State (after George Marshall and before Dean Acheson). After serving as South Carolina's governor during the court battles over desegregation, he endorsed Nixon for president in 1968. His action was one of the earliest indications of the shift of southern white conservative voters from the Democratic to the Republican Party in reaction to the 1964 Civil Rights Act and 1965 Voting Rights Act.

33. "Hoover Sees Blow At Civil Service: Roosevelt Reorganization Bill Would Substitute One-Man Political Rule, He Says," *NYT*, November 13, 1937, 6.

34. For a brief period, Brookings granted graduate degrees. However, there is at least the appearance of awkwardness about Meriam receiving a PhD from his employer, especially because Brookings did not have a significant-sized, independent, and permanent faculty as would traditionally be expected for an institution of higher education granting graduate degrees. Generally, by modern standards, one would expect overt evidence of faculty tenure, autonomy, academic freedom, and absence of ethical conflicts of interest—and the *appearance* of such—when the faculty of an institution recommended awarding a doctorate. That Meriam was an employee of Brookings (for twenty years at that point) when it granted him a PhD muddies the academic waters. To clarify the chronology of the entity that awarded him the doctorate: Meriam had been hired in 1916, during the first year of operation of the Institute for Government Research, which was founded and funded by businessman Robert Brookings. In 1922, Brookings founded and funded an Institute of Economics and in 1924 a graduate school. The three organizations merged in 1927 to become the Brookings Institution. Hence, Meriam's 1936 PhD was from his employer.

35. For more details on his biography and qualifications, see Lewis Meriam, *The Problem of Indian Administration: Report of a Survey made at the request of Honorable Hubert Work, Secretary of the Interior, and submitted to him, February 21, 1928* (Baltimore, MD: Johns Hopkins Press, 1928), 79–80, and *Who's Who in America, 1942–1943* (Chicago, IL: A. N. Marquis Co., 1942), 1533. He died in 1972 ("Retired Brookings Official," *WP*, November 1, 1972, B6). Despite the similar sounding family names and close spelling, Meriam, of course, was not related to PCAM member Charles E. Merriam.

36. In 1934, Meriam's major assignment at Brookings was to "undertake in the immediate future the preparation of a study of personnel problems of public administration, also preparing as a by-product a study on classification of personnel" (Entry for March 22, 1934, Folder 6, Box 1, Brownlow Diaries, University of Chicago Library [hereafter cited as Brownlow Diaries]).

37. While Mitchell included a long excerpt from Meriam's report in his memoirs, he provided no citation of the original document. I was not able to locate it and, therefore, could not determine its date, length, or whether it was paid for or provided *gratis* by Brookings.

38. December 21, 1933; January 15–16, 1934; and February 22, 1934, entries, Box 1, Brownlow Diaries.

39. Sources for this paragraph were Meriam, Lewis, Office Files 1928–39; and the 1934 annual report by Brookings's president to the Board of Trustees, May 18, 1934, in Brookings Institution Board of Trustees, Minutes, p. 286, both located in the archives of the Brookings Institution, Washington, DC (hereafter cited as Brookings Archives).

40. Memo from Meriam to Harold G. Moulton, President, Brookings Institution, January 13, 1934, Meriam's office file, 1928–39, Brookings Archives.

41. Meriam's statement was evidently unpublished. Oddly, Feldman, an academic familiar with the standards of referencing sources (especially long quotations), provided no citation of a published version of this statement nor any other sourcing information.

Chronologically, this would have been a different Meriam document from the 1933 report to Harry Mitchell, the new Democratic president of the CSC.

42. October 13 and December 20, 1934, entries, Box 1, Brownlow Diaries.

43. The stridency of Meriam's attack on the PCAM's effort to promote a new conventional wisdom of public personnel administration could be explained by the nonmonolithic views of the recognized "experts" in public administration (Roberts 1995; 1996), but also perhaps by underlying political values and/or personal animus. Based on an interview with Meriam's son-in-law in 1976, Critchlow characterized Meriam as "an avid anti-New Dealer" who ultimately felt compelled to change his party registration from Democratic to Republican. In part, the son-in-law said, Meriam's hostility was motivated by the "financial losses he suffered during the Depression" (Critchlow 1981, 329n2). This allegation about one of the prime motivations for his critical views seems simplistic and, at least, exaggerated in its importance. Also, Critchlow mistakenly identified a 1938 book by Meriam as his "first criticism" of the New Deal, overlooking this 1937 pamphlet.

44. James D. Secrest, "Report Rejects One-Man Rule of Civil Service," *WP*, December 2, 1937, 1, 6; AP, "Brookings Institution Vetoes Civil Service Plan," *Hartford [CT] Courant*, December 2, 1937, 7; Arthur Sears Henning, "Rap Roosevelt Plans for Rule in Civil Service," *CT*, December 2, 1937, 4.

45. For example, *CR*, March 9, 1938, 3092–93.

46. AP, "Reorganizing Plan Altered," *Los Angeles Times*, January 28, 1938, 20.

47. "State Chamber Opposes Bill on Reorganization," *NYHT*, February 2, 1938, 18.

48. "Defense Society Protests on Reorganization Bill," *NYHT*, March 17, 1938, 6.

49. "Ordway Attacks Civil Service Plan," *NYT*, February 25, 1938, 6.

50. Fred Brenckman, Washington Representative, National Grange, to all senators, March 23, 1938, reprinted in *CR*, March 28, 1938, 4194.

51. "Protest 'One-Man' For Civil Service Director," *Chicago Defender*, March 12, 1938, 3.

52. Albert L. Warner, "Democrats Join Senate War on Reorganization," *NYHT*, February 25, 1938, 6.

53. "Babcock Raps 1-Man Rule of Civil Service," *WP*, March 1, 1938, X15. In those days, the common spelling for employee was with one "e": employe.

54. Ibid.

55. *CR*, March 8, 1938, 3010.

56. *CR*, April 8, 1938, 5108.

57. Arthur Krock, "Basis of Attack on the Reorganizing Bill" (In the Nation column), *NYT*, March 10, 1938, 20.

58. Franklyn Waltman, "Constitution—Not President's Inclinations—Held Issue in Reorganization Fight" (Politics and People column), *WP*, April 2, 1938, X2.

59. "Efficiency in Government" (editorial), *NYHT*, March 2, 1938, 18.

60. "Opposing Reorganization" (editorial), *Washington Star*, March 22, 1938; reprinted in *CR*, March 23, 1938, 3934.

61. *CR*, April 7, 1938, 4988.

62. Walter Lippmann, "The Attack on the Civil Service Proposal" (Today and Tomorrow column), *NYHT*, April 7, 1938, 21.

63. "Reorganization Bill Gets Test in Senate Today," *NYHT*, March 15, 1938, 10.

64. "A Bold Grab for More Power" (editorial), reprinted in *CR*, March 2, 1938, 2685. The insertion in the *Record* did not identify the name of the newspaper.

65. *CR*, March 4, 1938, 2808; March 14, 1938, 3298–99.

66. *CR*, March 14, 1938, 3301.

67. *CR*, March 9, 1938, 3093–94.

68. *CR*, March 14, 1938, 3304.

69. "Reorganization Bill Gets Test in Senate Today," *NYHT*, March 15, 1938, 10.

70. *CR*, March 14, 1938, 3308. Before becoming an independent, Norris had been elected to the Senate as a Republican from the progressive wing of the party.

71. "Senate Votes 1-Man Rule of Civil Service," *CSM*, March 15, 1938, 1.

72. *CR*, March 15, 1938, 3373. The *Post* had quite a different quote: "the greatest step forward in the merit system since the Civil Service was established in 1883" (Robert C. Albright, "Senators Vote 1-Man Rule of Civil Service," *WP*, March 16, 1938, 7). It is unclear why the two quotes are at such variance. Explanations could include the reporter mishearing or misremembering the floor statement, taking poor notes, or post-delivery revisions by La Follette to the final published text in the *Congressional Record*.

73. For example, *CR*, March 14, 1938, 3310.

74. *CR*, March 4, 1938, 2813, 2817; "Opens New Attack on Reorganization: Vandenberg Calls It Symbol of 'New Deal's March to a Totalitarian State,'" *NYT*, March 5, 1938, 4.

75. *CR*, March 14, 1938, 3303, 3308.

76. Albright, "Senate Votes."

77. *CR*, March 15, 1938, 3379.

78. Albright, "Senate Votes."

79. "Senate Votes 1-Man Rule of Civil Service," *CSM*, March 15, 1938, 1.

80. "Senate Metes Death to Civil Service Board: Foes of Dictatorship Bill Lose, 50 to 38," *CT*, March 16, 1938, 8.

81. For example, *CR*, March 21, 1938, 3727–29; March 23, 1938, 3933–34; and March 28, 1938, 4193–94.

82. Robert C. Albright, "Reorganization Voted by Senate, But Error Returns Bill to House," *WP*, March 29, 1938, 1, 5, 8 (photo).

83. There was a slight overlap between the end of the Senate debate and the beginning of the House's. For clarity purposes, I have separated the discussion of how each house treated the personnel reorganization idea.

84. "'Dutch is Up': F.D.R. vs. Congress" (news analysis), *NYT*, News of the Week in Review (Sunday section), April 3, 1938, E1 (including three photos).

85. "Civil Service Rule by One Head Scored: Rep. Ramspeck Attacks Change Proposed in Reorganization Bill," *WP*, February 18, 1938, X13.

86. Robert C. Albright, "Ground Yielded by New Deal on Reorganization," *WP*, April 3, 1938, 9.

87. *CR*, April 5, 1938, 4799; April 8, 1938, 5105. These views did not inhibit Ramspeck from taking the opposite position during WWII. His Civil Service Committee issued a report denouncing "uncoordinated" personnel efforts and called for "over-all, centralized

authority with powers of management control" (AP, "Inexperience in Top Federal Personnel Jobs Hampers War Effort, House Group Charges," *Wall Street Journal*, October 14, 1943, 4). He suggested the executive branch should have a "super Federal agency" to enforce personnel policies on hiring and staffing (Jerry Kluttz, "Frank Oliver Wins *Post* September Award" [Federal Diary daily column], *WP*, October 18, 1943, B1).

88. *CR*, April 1, 1938, 4614–15.

89. John C. O'Brien, "Leaders Beg, Bargain, Use Whip in Vain," *NYHT*, April 9, 1938, 1A.

90. *CR*, March 31, 1938, 4493.

91. Ibid., 4496.

92. *CR*, April 2, 1938, 4639.

93. *CR*, April 1, 1938, 4582.

94. Ibid., 4604.

95. Ibid., 4613.

96. *CR*, April 8, 1938, 5107.

97. *CR*, April 1, 1938, 4615.

98. *CSM*, April 8, 1938, 2.

99. AP, "Bureau Bill Foes Keep Debate Open," *Hartford [CT] Courant*, April 6, 1938, 1.

100. "House Nears Merger Vote," *CSM*, April 6, 1938, 2.

101. AP, "Leaders in Congress Left Free to Pursue Bureau Bill Changes," *Hartford [CT] Courant*, April 4, 1938, 1.

102. "House Nears Merger Vote."

103. AP, "Bureau Bill Foes Keep Debate Open."

104. Robert C. Albright, "Foes of Reorganization Win Fight for Majority Curb on Merger Orders," *WP*, April 3, 1938, 1.

105. In fact, a PCAM staff member, John Miller, had written a strong critique of veterans' preference points in his report to the Commission of Inquiry (Miller 1935). But the subject was not addressed by the PCAM bill, even though almost all civil service reformers agreed with Miller. It was simply too hot politically, giving the appearance of being anti-veteran.

106. *CR*, April 8, 1938, 5102.

107. Ibid., 5105–06.

108. Ibid., 5112.

109. Robert C. Albright, "House Kills Reorganization Bill, 204–196," *WP*, April 9, 1938, 1.

110. "Public, Leaders Hail Defeat of Reorganization," *WP*, April 9, 1938, 15.

111. "Women Voters Plan Civil Service Drive," *NYT*, July 4, 1938, 2.

112. Scott Hart, "Constitutional Merit System League Goal," *WP*, October 18, 1938, 16 (including photo).

113. "Universities Warned by Expert on Training for Public Service," *CSM*, September 6, 1938, 1.

114. "Hails Death of Bill for Reorganization," *NYT*, September 13, 1938, 9.

115. "Merit System in Peril, Warns Senator Walsh," *CT*, September 15, 1938, 10.

116. Robert C. Albright, "Senate to Reject Donald Smith, Green Predicts," *WP*, December 21, 1938, 12.

117. "Roosevelt Acts to Revive His Reorganization Plan," *NYT*, December 9, 1938, 1, 4; Chesly Manley, "New Roosevelt Dictator Bill Plans Hit Snag," *CT*, December 9, 1938, 1, 6.

118. John Miller, "Reorganization Fallacies," January 1939, p. 6, File A-II-56: Reorganization General Message, John Miller Memo, Box 2, PCAM.

119. Arthur Krock, "Reorganization Shaped for a Better Reception," *NYT*, December 11, 1938, E3.

120. Delbert Clark, "Reorganization Up for a New Debate," *NYT*, December 18, 1938, E6.

121. Robert C. Albright, "Substitute Reorganizing Bill Drawn," *WP*, January 19, 1939, 1, 9.

122. *CR*, March 8, 1939, 2494–95.

Chapter 3

1. Nowadays, it is more common to refer to that differentiation in roles as operational vs. functional duties.

2. 53 Stat. 1423.

3. 53 Stat. 1431.

4. Entry for May 12, 1939, 4, File Conferences with President Roosevelt, 1939, Box 3, Harold Smith Papers, FDRL (hereafter cited as Smith Papers). Smith routinely disregarded FDR's preference that notes not be taken of meetings with him (Kaiser, 2014, 49) because he wanted to be able to pass on all of FDR's instructions as accurately and detailed as possible to the appropriate BOB staffers for implementation.

5. Alfred Friendly, "Ordway to Leave Civil Service Post," *WP*, May 29, 1939, 1, 4.

6. Entry for May 12, 1939.

7. Mitchell ended up serving as CSC president until 1951.

8. There was also a partisan problem. Davenport would be appointed as the *Republican* member of the three-person CSC. It would be politically awkward for the minority party member to be the president of the commission, making him supposedly more important than the two Democratic members.

9. Entry for May 23, 1939, 2, File Daily Memoranda, April–June 1939, Box 1, Smith Papers.

10. Entry for May 13, 1939, File Daily Memoranda, April–June 1939, Box 1, Smith Papers. Flemming was sometimes described as a faculty member at AU and called "Dr." or "Professor." He did not have a PhD and was not a faculty member in the traditional sense of being on a tenure track or having tenure. The "Dr." title derived from having a JD (A. Flemming 1942, 15; B. Flemming 1991, 92.) Flemming went on to a major career in federal public service, including serving as a Cabinet member for President Eisenhower and as the head of several universities. His last public office was as chairman of the US Civil Rights Commission, and President Reagan fired him for critical comments on the administration's civil rights record.

11. Entry for May 31, 1939, 1, File Conferences with President Roosevelt, 1939, Box 3, Smith Papers.

12. Entry for June 2, 1939, 2, File Daily Memoranda, April–June 1939, Box 1, Smith Papers.

13. Entry for June 6, 1939, 2, ibid.

14. Memo from Smith to FDR, June 16, 1939, n.t., File White House Memoranda, 1939–40, Box 4, Smith Papers.

15. Entry for June 18, 1939, 2, File Conferences with President Roosevelt, 1939, Box 3, Smith Papers.

16. Entry for June 19, 1939, ibid.

17. Reporters picked up rumors that FDR was considering Dykstra for an appointment to a senior position, but were unable to pin it down to the CSC: "John Carmody Added to List for Works Job," *WP*, June 20, 1939, 3; "Navy, FSA Posts Reported Offered McNutt," *NYT*, July 10, 1939, 1.

18. Entry for June 26, 1939, 3–4, File Daily Memoranda, April–June 1939, Box 1, Smith Papers. About a year later, Dykstra finally felt he could step down from the University of Wisconsin and accepted a presidential appointment. In the fall of 1940, FDR named him the first director of the draft, called the Selective Service System. It was a very controversial position and program because it began before Pearl Harbor (i.e., it was a peacetime draft, the first in American history). Later in the war, Dykstra chaired the National Defense Mediation Board. After the war, he returned to academic administration as provost of UCLA.

19. "Arthur S. Flemming Named to Civil Service Commission," *WP*, June 24, 1939, 2.

20. There was also the same political problem of Flemming *ever* becoming CSC president, as had been the case with Davenport, because Flemming was appointed as the Republican member of the commission.

21. Entry for September 16, 1939, File Daily Memoranda July–September 1939, Box 1, Smith Papers. Other indications of Flemming's stand-out role in the CSC, despite not being its president, were the roles he accepted in addition to his commissionership. In the production mobilization before the US involvement in WWII (1940–41), Flemming simultaneously served as chief of the Labor Supply Division of the Office of Production Management. After the US entered the war, he was a member of the War Manpower Commission and chaired its Management-Labor Policy Committee. He also served on the Navy's Manpower Survey Board (B. Flemming 1991, 110–17). CSC president Mitchell played no such dual roles.

22. Rodney Dutcher, "Behind the Scenes in Washington" (syndicated column), *[Biloxi, MS] Daily Herald*, October 27, 1937, 4.

23. For such a precise person, McReynolds was unusually vague about how much public schooling he had. The biography he submitted to *Who's Who in America, 1944–1945* alluded merely to his education as "public schools, Topeka, Kan." (p. 1432). In a biography he submitted to Treasury Secretary Morgenthau (who wanted FDR to nominate him for GAO comptroller general), McReynolds described his education as limited to "brief periods of schooling." Later in the same document, he expanded on that, writing that "my formal education is limited to high school." The phrasing seems to be deliberately am-

biguous, implying he was a high school graduate, but clearly not stating so. Therefore, this was probably not the case (McReynolds to Morgenthau, July 29, 1936, File McReynolds, W. H. 1935–36–39, Box 199, Henry Morgenthau Jr. Papers, FDRL [hereafter cited as Morgenthau Papers]).

24. Philleo Nash, oral history interview, August 19, 1966, items 172–73, Truman Library, accessed July 6, 2015, http://www.trumanlibrary.org/oralhist/nash4.htm.

25. "Caddie Titlist Wins Medal by 5 Shots," *WP*, August 22, 1933, 17.

26. Transcript of Secretary's staff meeting, May 14, 1940, Morgenthau Diaries 262: 198 (microfilm), Morgenthau Papers; Grace Tully, Executive Secretary, FDR Memorial Foundation, to McReynolds, November 13, 1947, File IV.A.4: McReynolds, William H., Box 23, Records of the FDR Memorial Foundation, FDRL.

27. Oscar S. Cox, Office of the General Counsel, Treasury Department, to McReynolds, March 26, 1940, File Library of Congress, Box 19, William H. McReynolds Papers, FDRL (hereafter cited as McRP); "Men Who Arm America: William H. McReynolds," *Beatrice [NE] Daily Sun*, January 31, 1941, 3; Jerry Kluttz, "Food Prices, Wages to be Increased in Federal Cafeterias" (Federal Diary daily column), *WP*, January 19, 1951, B1.

28. Mitchell to McReynolds, October 21, 1943, File CSC—1943, Box 1, McRP. This may have been merely a stenographic error, if Mitchell had dictated the letter and to the stenographer "Mac" sounded like "Mack." That would mean Mitchell did not carefully review the final typed letter before signing it.

29. Memo from McReynolds to Heads of Departments and Establishments, May 17, 1940, n.t., File CSC—1939–40, Box 2, McRP. His middle name was Henry, but he always used an initial.

30. For a contemporaneous description of the Personnel Classification Board when it existed, see Paul V. Betters, *The Personnel Classification Board: Its History, Activities and Organization*, No. 64, Service Monographs of the United States Government, Institute for Government Research, Brookings Institution (1931; repr., New York: AMS Press, 1974).

31. "Discrimination Denied by Personnel Board," *WP*, June 20, 1926, 2; "Classifying Board Qualifies Union Ban," *WP*, July 17, 1927, 14; "Promotion Snarl Settled by Board," *WP*, October 19, 1930, R4.

32. "125,000 U.S. Field Employes [*sic*] to Get Salary Increases," *WP*, July 20, 1925, 1.

33. "Most New U.S. Pay Scales Will Stand, M'Reynolds Thinks," *WP*, November 4, 1923, 8.

34. Steil claimed that Morgenthau had "limited smarts" and "was not of particularly nimble mind" (Steil 2013, 5, 32), apparently as an explanation of why Morgenthau hired a staff of such high caliber. Regardless of the reason, Morgenthau deserves recognition for surrounding himself with high quality staff, including McReynolds, a phenomenon that is not always the case in Washington.

35. The incumbent, William H. Woodin, resigned due to ill health.

36. For text of Morgenthau's Order No. 1, see "Press Protests Treasury Ban on 'Loose Talk,'" *NYHT*, November 22, 1933, 2.

37. "M'Carl Looses a 2d Blast at New Deal Costs," *CT*, July 2, 1936, 12.

38. Macmahon and Millett were both staff members of PCAM, and Macmahon authored the published PCAM study on departmental management (PCAM 1937, 245–70).

However, their book (originally published in 1939) was an outgrowth their PCAM work, not a staff study prepared under PCAM's auspices (Macmahon and Millett 1967, viii).

39. Drew Pearson and Robert S. Allen, "General Wavell Wanted British to Quit Mediterranean—Churchill Said No" (Washington Merry-Go-Round syndicated column), *Hagerstown [MD] Daily Mail*, July 7, 1941, 4.

40. Alfred Friendly, "Civil Service, on 57th Birthday, Entering Period of Transition," *WP*, January 14, 1940, B7. When Congressman Ramspeck quoted from it, he mistakenly attributed it to the *Post*'s fierce competitor, the afternoon *Washington Star* (*CR*, January 17, 1940, 424).

41. "American University Commencement; 85 Awards A. B. Degrees," *WP*, June 6, 1939, II-1. McReynolds may have been something of a workaholic, but he also was an avid golfer and took long summer vacations with his wife (Henry Litchfield West, "From Tee to Green" [column], *WP*, October 7, 1928, 22; Dave Herman, "Men's Event Slated for Hillendale," *WP*, March 8, 1936, X3; "Washington" [social news feature], *NYHT*, September 18, 1938, A7; Entry for September 5, 1939, File Daily Memoranda July–September 1939, Box 1, Smith Papers). McReynolds also apparently enjoyed gambling. When his appointment was first announced, he was ribbed at the next secretary's senior staff meeting. Daniel Bell said Harry Dexter White (Treasury's senior economist) predicted McReynolds would "have them shooting craps in the White House before very long" (Entry for July 13, 1939, Morgenthau Diaries 203: 11 [microfilm], Morgenthau Papers). White was John Maynard Keynes's protagonist when designing the post-WWII monetary system at the Bretton Woods conference. White was later exposed as more than a leftist fellow traveler. As a sympathizer of Communist economic system of the USSR, he passed confidential information and documents to Russian spies in the US (Steil 2013).

42. Entry for May 22, 1940, File Conferences with President Roosevelt 1940, Box 3, Smith Papers.

43. Of the other three, two were PCAM staffers (Harris and Emmerich) and the third was Clinton Hester, Treasury's assistant general counsel, who helped with legal issues regarding the plan.

44. "'Dark Horse' Forecast for Ordway's Job: None of the Prominent Possibilities Believed Willing to Accept," *WP*, May 30, 1939, 2. This was the same situation as Daniel Bell had been in. As a Treasury civil servant, he declined FDR's offer to be BOB director. Instead, Bell served for about five years as BOB acting director. When Smith was appointed, Bell returned to Treasury.

45. Entry for May 31, 1939, 1, File Conferences with President Roosevelt 1939, Box 3, Smith Papers.

46. Entry for June 2, 1939, 2, File Daily Memoranda, April–June 1939, Box 1, Smith Papers.

47. Entry for June 6, 1939, 2, ibid.

48. Entry for May 31, 1939, 1, File Conferences with the President Roosevelt 1939, Box 3, Smith Papers.

49. Entry for June 6, 1939, 2, File Daily Memoranda, April–June 1939, Box 1, Smith Papers.

50. Not *everyone* thought well of McReynolds. Congressman John Taber (R-NY),

a highly partisan and conservative member of the Appropriations Committee, said in mid-1940 that, at his pre–White House appearances at congressional hearings, McReynolds "has been repeatedly characterized as the most incompetent man ever to appear before congressional committees representing a government department" (Willard Edwards, "House Boosts Defense Funds Over 5 Billions," *CT*, June 13, 1940, 11). The quote caused much hilarity at Secretary Morgenthau's daily staff meeting. The secretary followed up after reading the quote out loud with the (somewhat patronizing or, at least, grandiose) observation, "Poor old Mac. I don't know whether he can take it. When he was over here, you see, I always protected him. I don't know who is going to protect him now" (Transcript of Secretary's staff meeting, June 12, 1940, Morgenthau Diaries 272: 13–14 [microfilm], Morgenthau Papers).

51. One of the benefits of choosing July 1 was that it was also the first day of the new fiscal year, FY 1940 (as fiscal years are named by the year they end in). In the 1970s, Congress bumped the federal fiscal year forward by a quarter, to start on October 1, to give it more time to adopt a budget resolution and then pass the dozen or so appropriations bills funding the executive branch for the upcoming fiscal year.

52. Harlan Miller, "Over the Coffee" (column), *WP*, May 21, 1939, 2.

53. Memo from FDR to Rudolph Forster, July 12, 1939, File McReynolds, William H., Official File 3745, FDRL (hereafter cited as OF 3745). Forster was a longtime civil servant in the White House (first appointed during the McKinley presidency) who handled official and formal paperwork.

54. AP, "Aides Named by President," *Los Angeles Times*, July 13, 1939, 2; Felix Cotten, "Roosevelt Names 3 of 6 Assistants," *WP*, July 13, 1939, 1. Amusingly, reporters had trouble deciding where McReynolds was *from*. One said he was "a westerner" (because of his Kansas birthplace); another that he was "of Michigan" ("President Picks Three of His Six New Assistants," *CT*, July 13, 1939, 7; "Roosevelt Picks With 'a Passion,'" *NYHT*, July 13, 1939, 7).

55. "3 New Aids [*sic*] to Roosevelt Bring Varied Backgrounds to Job," *NYHT*, July 30, 1939, A1.

56. Oddly, earlier in 1939, a Washington newspaper story said McReynolds was a highly partisan Republican who was active in a Republican cabal—including Frederick Davenport and Leonard White—trying to take control of the CSC and thereby the classified service. The reporter claimed McReynolds was "regarded as a close friend of former Republican Senator Reed Smoot" (George D. Riley, "Control of Public Service Again Shifts More Tightly into Hold of Minority Politico-Professor Group," *Washington Herald-Times*, February 20, 1939, reprinted in *CR*, February 23, 1939, 1848). Smoot was a longtime patron of the Bureau of Efficiency, so it would be no surprise if McReynolds had had some direct contact with him (Lee 2006). But there seems to be little basis to document that this studiously apolitical and professional civil servant had a partisan ideology or agenda that colored his work. If anything, due to his work for Morgenthau and then FDR, one could perhaps expect more logically an attack that McReynolds was a closet Democrat, rather than a closet Republican.

57. Presidential appointees were generally not considered permanent federal employ-

ees within the civil service retirement program. McReynolds's salary was slightly lower than the other presidential administrative assistants as an offset to his continuing eligibility for a pension.

58. Even after Social Security began, McReynolds would not have been eligible for it. In its initial stages, the scope of Social Security was very limited. Two of the categories it did not cover were federal civil servants and congressional staff. They neither paid payroll taxes to fund Social Security nor qualified for benefits upon retirement. For the latter category, this was still the case in 1975–76, when I worked as legislative assistant to a member of Congress.

59. "3 New Aids [*sic*] to Roosevelt Bring Varied Backgrounds to the Job."

60. Roosevelt would have had an above average familiarity with the building because his office was there when he was assistant secretary of the Navy in the Wilson administration. The building later came to be called the Executive Office Building, then the Old Executive Office Building, and now (2015) the Eisenhower Executive Office Building (by act of Congress).

61. In the initial phase of moving into the building, space was so tight that only part of the National Resources Planning Board could be housed there (Roosevelt 1969, 1939: 496). Even though the new Office of Government Reports (the former National Emergency Council) was one of the original five EOP agencies, it was—correctly—not viewed as a central *management* agency. Therefore, it did not need to be so close to the White House.

62. "Roosevelt Finds Ample Quarters for 6 New Aids [*sic*]," *CT*, July 23, 1939, 10. The building of the Pentagon during WWII made things awkward for the War Department. It had just moved into its new building. If only to justify the cost of the new building, some argued that the War Department should stay there even after the Pentagon opened. But Secretary of War Stimson made the simple decision that the department and the Army needed to be located together and insisted on the move. In office-starved Washington, it was easy to fill the now-former War Department building with other federal agencies. It is often forgotten that several federal civilian agencies with little link to the war effort were forced to move their central headquarters offices out of Washington to other cities (many in the Midwest) for the duration.

63. Entry for July 25, 1939, File Conferences with President Roosevelt 1939, Box 3, Smith Papers. This incident was not out of the ordinary. Roosevelt relished getting involved in details and seemed to be well informed about all aspects of federal operations (Kaiser 2014, 298, 320). After an extensive meeting with FDR earlier in 1939, Smith observed that "the knowledge of the details of the Federal establishment on the part of the President impressed me during this conference as being nothing short of amazing" (Entry for April 26, 1939, File Conferences with President Roosevelt 1939, Box 3, Smith Papers).

64. A few years later, the State Department moved into a new building in Foggy Bottom and totally vacated the old building.

65. Perhaps partly due to the delay of moving from the Treasury building to the State, War, and Navy building, McReynolds stayed on the payroll of the Treasury Department for the first quarter of FY 1940. On November 1, 1939, he transferred to the White House

salary line (Morgenthau to McReynolds, November 10, 1939, File McReynolds, William H. 1935–36–39, Box 199, Morgenthau Papers).

66. Entry for September 5, 1939, File Daily Memoranda July–September 1939, Box 1, Smith Papers.

67. It is often forgotten that Germany's invasion was timed in coordination with its new ally, the USSR. A few weeks later, the Soviet Army invaded Poland from the east and took over the eastern half of the country.

68. The executive order also unobtrusively created a sixth standby agency, the Office for Emergency Management (OEM). Almost everyone missed that detail because the title of the agency was not capitalized in the executive order (Lee 2012a, 28).

69. McReynolds also had a small amount of non-personnel related responsibilities in his portfolio. For example, he was the president's representative on the Mount Rushmore Commission (McReynolds to Smith, July 9, 1941, file BOB, Box 24, McRP). The monument was completed and opened during FDR's presidency.

70. Roosevelt signed the executive order on a Saturday, and the press release announcing his action was embargoed until the Sunday papers (Morstein Marx 1947, 17). Given the high circulation of the Sunday edition, the executive order dominated the news coverage and reached a larger audience.

71. The explanatory notes and commentary after each major entry in the published series of FDR's papers and addresses was written by his longtime aide and speechwriter, Samuel I. Rosenman. The volume for 1939 was published in 1941, so the perspective on LOPM was only two years after it had been created. For the volumes of FDR's papers and addresses that were published after he died, Rosenman was identified as the author of the commentaries.

72. Oddly, in 1964 Harris flubbed McReynolds's title and the name of the EOP's personnel agency. He wrote that Roosevelt "created the position of Special Assistant on Personnel Administration in his Executive Office" (Harris 1964, 172). It should have been an administrative assistant as the liaison officer for personnel management in the Executive Office of the President. One would expect Harris, as former PCAM staff director, as well as a respected political scientist, to be more accurate about something that evolved out of PCAM's recommendations.

73. Entry for September 16, 1939, File Daily Memoranda July–September 1939, Box 1, Smith Papers.

Chapter 4

1. However, Congress's power of the purse also includes the right to curb a president's discretionary allocation of appropriated funds. For example, a few years later, Congress limited how much he could transfer to OGR (Lee 2005a, 133–34), and it banned *any* transfers to NRPB (Clawson 1981, 219).

2. Another reason was the implication of closeness to the president in the former title vs. the latter. In Washington, proximity is usually a measure of power. Being in the White House office and with "president" in his title would likely confer more respect and deference for McReynolds than his LOPM title.

3. *CR*, May 16, 1941, 4155.

4. Postmaster General James Farley to McReynolds, March 1, 1940, File Post Office Department 1940–44, Box 8, McRP.

5. McReynolds to Roy Hendrickson, Director of Personnel, USDA, June 7, 1940, File CSC 1939–40, Box 2, McRP.

6. Strictly speaking, NDAC was created by the statutory Council of National Defense, a Cabinet-level group established by act of Congress late in WWI. The body, of course, stopped functioning after the war, but Congress never repealed the law. FDR arranged for the statutory membership of the council to meet once, create NDAC, and then adjourn, never to meet again (Lee 2012a, 27–28).

7. "Personnel Changes," *Personnel Administration* 2, 10 (June 1940): 23.

8. Jerry Kluttz, "Navy May Cut Out Vacations This Year" (Federal Diary daily column), *WP*, May 18, 1941, B1.

9. "G. Lyle Belsley Dies at 88; Federal Official," *WP*, April 17, 1993, D7. For a brief period in the 1920s and 1930s, Brookings also functioned as a graduate school that awarded advanced degrees, including to Meriam (chap. 2).

10. Ward Stewart, "SPA [Society for Personnel Administration] Discussion Sections End Year's Work," *Personnel Administration* 3, 8 (April 1941): 14.

11. Belsley to Maxwell Devoe, Director of Personnel, Rhode Island State Civil Service Department, October 12, 1940; and Belsley to Don K. Price, Society for Public Administration, January 9, 1941, both in File G. Lyle Belsley, Box 23, McRP. McReynolds's papers at the FDRL relate almost wholly to his LOPM activities (and non-personnel assignments) and contain very little relating to his NDAC assignment. The fact that Belsley's correspondence files are within the McReynolds Papers also ties him closely to LOPM. The NDAC archival files at the National Archives II likely include Belsley's NDAC-related paperwork. Belsley's letter to Devoe provided feedback on an early draft of an article Devoe was writing. It was eventually published as "Administrative Relationships of Public Personnel Agencies," *Public Personnel Review* 2, 1 (January 1941): 18–27.

12. "News of the Society," *Public Administration Review* 1, 3 (Spring 1941): 316; Belsley to Charles Ascher, Secretary, Committee on Public Administration, Social Science Research Council, March 27, 1941, File Committee on Public Administration, Box 14, McRP. The letter is marked "not sent" because, according to the notation, the arrangements were "taken care of by telephone."

13. "Mitchell Appointed Director of CSA [Civil Service Assembly] Headquarters Office to Succeed Belsley," *Civil Service Assembly of the United States and Canada News Letter* 7, 7 (July 1941): 1. Note: Later, during WWII, the Assembly changed the formal title of its publication from *News Letter* to *Newsletter*.

14. Winston B. Stephens, CSC Coordinator and Director of Training, to Belsley, January 3, 1941, File G. Lyle Belsley, Box 23, McRP.

15. McReynolds to George Hulverson, Assistant Director of Personnel, Home Owners' Loan Corporation, May 14, 1941, File White House—LOPM, Box 21, McRP.

16. Within two months, the reporter for the *Post* who wrote a daily column on personnel matters of interest to federal employees referred to Coy as "OEM chief," an informal and journalistic shorthand term that conveyed Coy's role as being more substan-

tial than McReynolds's (Jerry Kluttz, "G.A.O. to Crack Down on Lawyers on the Side," *WP*, June 12, 1941, 17).

17. Kluttz, "The Federal Diary" (no headline for that day's column), *WP*, June 22, 1941, B1.

18. For example, he *knew* he had no expertise in public relations. So, up front, he announced that he would not hire or oversee any PR staff serving the commission (Lee 2012a, 29).

19. Summary of a note from FDR to McReynolds, April 23, 1941, File McReynolds, William H., President's Personal File (PPF) 7367, FDRL.

20. Authorization letter from FDR to the Secretary of the Treasury, September 11, 1941, File Liaison Office for Personnel Management, Official File 3780, FDRL (hereafter cited as OF 3780).

21. Memo from McReynolds to FDR, n.t., September 25, 1941, File White House—LOPM, Box 21, McRP.

22. Letter of appointment from FDR to Guy Moffett, September 25, 1941, File OF 3780, FDRL.

23. "Biographical Sketch: Guy Moffett," n.d. (apparently originally prepared in 1941 and then updated in 1944), File Mr. Moffett, Box 23, McRP.

24. Sam Stavisky, "Guy Moffett is the Rare Kind of Official Who Makes Red Tape and Makes Friends, Too" (People in the News column), *WP*, October 8, 1948, 2.

25. FDR to Moffett, May 3, 1918, Box 1, FDR Papers, University of Virginia; Kluttz, "Heads are Falling at Export Control," *WP*, September 24, 1941, 21.

26. "Committee Approves State Separation Plan," *WP*, June 16, 1926, 10.

27. Brownlow's diaries are replete with references to Moffett as Brownlow's funding partner in professionalizing public administration. For example, in 1934, Moffett appears in entries for January 7 and 26, February 22, March 6 and 10, October 31, and November 1 (Box 1, Brownlow Diaries).

28. Entry for July 7, 1939, File Daily Memoranda July–September 1939; and entry for December 28, 1939, File Daily Memoranda, October–December 1939, both in Box 1, Smith Papers.

29. Memo from Smith to FDR, September 12, 1940, n.t., File White House Memoranda 1939–1940, Box 4, Smith Papers.

30. "$1,218,500 Given By Spelman Fund," *NYT*, May 17, 1942, 39.

31. Transcript of Secretary's staff meeting, May 14, 1940, Morgenthau Diaries 262: 252 (microfilm), Morgenthau Papers; Charles S. Bell, Treasury Department, to McReynolds, October 13, 1941, File Treasury Department, Box 9, McRP. Brownlow slightly exaggerated when he wrote the meetings were "once or twice a week" (Brownlow 1958, 421).

32. For example, Mitchell to McReynolds, September 18, 1939; and reply by McReynolds, September 21, 1939, both in File CSC 1939–40, Box 2, McRP. In this case, the draft became Executive Order 8257, issued on September 23, 1939.

33. Memo from McReynolds to the CSC, October 5, 1939, n.t., File CSC 1939–40, Box 2, McRP.

34. Invitation to McReynolds to speak at CSC district managers' conference, October 20, 1939, File CSC 1939–40, Box 2, McRP.

35. McReynolds to Mitchell, April 22, 1941, File CSC 1941–42, Box 2, McRP.

36. Memo from McReynolds to Lawson A. Moyer, March 27, 1940, n.t., File CSC 1939–40, Box 2, McRP.

37. Winston B. Stephens, CSC Coordinator and Director of Training, to Belsley, January 3, 1941, File G. Lyle Belsley, Box 23, McRP; Stephens to Belsley, February 14, 1941, File CSC 1941–42, Box 2, McRP; Stephens to Belsley, May 24, 1941, File (CSC-CPA) Training Committee 1941–44, Box 6, McRP.

38. Memo from McReynolds to Smith, February 29, 1940, n.t., File BOB, Box 24, McRP. The only way to get around the CSC, McReynolds concluded, was a presidential executive order. FDR signed Executive Order 8370 on March 8, 1940.

39. Memo from McReynolds to Smith, November 16, 1939, n.t., File CSC 1939–40, Box 2, McRP.

40. McReynolds to Professor J. Alton Burdine, University of Texas, May 25, 1941, File American Society for Public Administration 1941–42, Box 14, McRP.

41. Memo from FDR to General Watson, February 5, 1940, File Ramspeck Act and Related Executive Orders 1941–43, Box 1, McRP. Edwin "Pa" Watson was the White House aide who handled FDR's scheduling (hereafter cited as Watson).

42. Memo from FDR to Watson, April 11, 1941, ibid.

43. President's Schedule for 1939, meetings with McReynolds June 21, October 4, and December 12, Franklin D. Roosevelt: Day by Day, online.

44. President's Schedule for 1940, meetings with McReynolds February 7 (with Smith), May 17, June 17 (with Smith), August 3, and August 24 (with Smith), ibid.

45. President's Schedule for 1941, meetings with McReynolds February 3 and April 15 (with Rowe), ibid. McReynolds was a meticulous note-taker. He knew shorthand and used it frequently during phone conversations to write notes of the conversation. However, his office records do not include any formal "memo for the files" summarizing meetings with the president. This likely reflected FDR's express preference that notes not be kept of meetings with him (Kaiser 2014, 49). He preferred to convey oral instructions (which sometimes conflicted, depending on who he was meeting with) and not to be bound by previous commitments.

46. Transcript of Secretary's staff meeting, May 14, 1940, Morgenthau Diaries 262: 252 (microfilm), Morgenthau Papers.

47. Entry for November 20, 1939, 3, File Conferences with President Roosevelt 1939, Box 3, Smith Papers.

48. Memo from Smith to McReynolds, January 3, 1940, Subject: Hours of Duty Report, File Bureau of the Budget, Box 24, McRP.

49. Memo from McReynolds to Edgar Young, BOB, November 13, 1941, n.t., File Bureau of the Budget, Box 24, McRP. An indication how deeply BOB was involved in personnel policy was the work of its management consultant, Eric A. Nicol. In 1940, he spoke at the annual conference of the Civil Service Assembly on "The Role of the Personnel Director in Management" (Nicol 1940). A year later, he wrote an article on his involvement in the CSC's management training program for rising executives (Nicol 1941).

50. Memo from Watson to FDR, June 17, 1940, regarding La Follette amendment on overtime policy for civilian employees of the military, File OF 3780.

51. For example, Jacob Baker, United Federal Workers of America, to FDR, June 17, 1940, referred to McReynolds, ibid.

52. For example, Memo from Rudolph Forster to McReynolds, November 21, 1939, attaching letter from Ada Price to FDR with FDR's handwritten notation of November 17, 1939: "See if you can do anything about," File OF 3745; McReynolds to James Baity, Assistant to the Comptroller General, July 21, 1941, regarding letter from Brady Warner to FDR, File Confidential File, Box 24, McRP; Memo from FDR to McReynolds, November 21, 1941, regarding letter from Hugh Miller, November 10, 1941, File OF 3780.

53. Memos from McReynolds to Heads of Departments and Establishments, May 17, 1940, n.t.; and to Heads of Departments and Independent Establishments, May 22, 1940, n.t., both in File CSC 1939–40, Box 2, McRP.

54. Executive Order 7916, June 24, 1938.

55. Executive Order 8046, February 11, 1939.

56. Memo from McReynolds to FDR, August 4, 1939, n.t., [unnamed file], Box 22, McRP.

57. 53 Stat. 1303.

58. *CR*, January 17, 1940, 439.

59. AP, "Another Agency Refused Funds: House Kills $25,040 Item for Council of Personnel Directors," *Los Angeles Times*, January 18, 1940, 5.

60. United Press, "Senate Refuses to Slash C.A.A. by $1,000,000," *NYHT*, February 8, 1940, 2; FDR to former CSC member Samuel Ordway (drafted by McReynolds), March 9, 1940, File CPA—I, 1939–43, Box 5, McRP.

61. Memo from McReynolds to Congressman [Clifton A.] Woodrum [D-VA], February 19, 1940, File CPA—I, 1939–43, Box 5, McRP.

62. Memo from McReynolds to FDR, April 4, 1940, n.t., File CPA—I, 1939–43, Box 5, McRP. For reasons that could not be determined from the archival record examined for this inquiry, the transfer of Davenport's salary to LOPM's budget did not occur. A possible concern may have been to keep LOPM's staffing and budget numbers as low as possible, so as not to trigger congressional attention.

63. Edward Ryan, "U.S. Personnel Council Rises Like Phoenix: Agency Reborn with All Old Members, and Some New Ones" (Federal Diary column), *WP*, July 4, 1940, 9.

64. For example, Davenport to McReynolds, July 10, 1941, File CPA—I, 1939–43, Box 5, McRP.

65. For a photo and list of CPA members after its funding was transferred to the CSC, see "Federal Council of Personnel Management," *Civil Service Assembly News Letter* 7, 4 (April 1941): 4. The participation of the regulatory agencies in CPA was a major accomplishment for FDR. PCAM had recommended these commissions be brought more closely into the president's orbit and supervision. Congressional opposition was fierce, partly based on the principle that these commissions exercised regulatory powers delegated them by Congress and that they were intended to operate in a neutral and quasi-judicial manner. The opposition was also, of course, strongly stimulated by the special interest groups regulated by those commissions, who did not want FDR influencing the policies the commissions adopted and enforced, possibly to their detriment.

66. Draft of presidential response prepared by McReynolds to letter from League of Women Voters, April 2, 1941, File OF 3780. Also, White to McReynolds, March 19, 1941, File Veterans' Preference 1940–45, Box 9, McRP.

67. McReynolds to Eliot Kaplan, Executive Secretary, NCSRL, April 8, 1941, File Veterans' Preference 1940–45, Box 9, McRP.

68. Winston Stephens, CSC Coordinator and Director of Training, to Belsley, April 19, 1941, File CSC 1941–42, Box 2, McRP; draft of presidential response prepared by McReynolds to letter from Fred Catlett, Federal Home Loan Bank Board, to FDR, February 10, 1941, File OF 3780.

69. Memo from Evelyn M. Crowell, US Information Service, OGR, to Belsley, May 20, 1941, n.t.; and memo reply from Belsley to Crowell, May 24, 1941, n.t., both in File (OEM) Office of War Information 1942–44, Box 7, McRP.

70. Note in file on McReynolds calling NAACP's Arthur Spingarn to discuss the subject, [unnamed file], Box 22, McRP.

71. Davenport to Belsley, May 23, 1941, File CPA—I, 1939–43, Box 5, McRP.

72. Davenport to McReynolds, August 20, 1941, ibid.

73. Memo from McReynolds to FDR, August 21, 1941, n.t., File Minority Groups, Box 17, McRP.

74. Memo from FDR to Heads of All Departments and Independent Establishments, September 3, 1941, n.t., File Minority Groups, Box 17, McRP.

75. "President Orders Race Bars Lifted," *NYT*, September 7, 1941, 38; United Press, "Roosevelt Orders Inquiry into Racial Discrimination," *WP*, September 7, 1941, 1, 5; "FD Orders U.S. to Stop Job Discrimination," *Chicago Defender*, September 13, 1941, 1, 4.

76. Memo from McReynolds to Heads of Departments, Establishments, and Agencies of the Federal Government, October 17, 1940, n.t., File Selective Service System—I, 1940–42, Box 8, McRP.

77. Letter of greetings from FDR to the Civil Service Assembly of the United States and Canada, October 13, 1939; September 27, 1940; and October 23, 1941, File Civil Service Assembly of the United States and Canada, President's Personal File 4080, FDRL (hereafter cited as PPF 4080).

78. Charles S. Ascher, Secretary, Committee on Public Administration, Social Science Research Council, to McReynolds, December 15, 1939 and January 12, 1940; and Belsley to Professor Pendleton Herring, Graduate School of Public Administration, Harvard University, October 19, 1940, all in File Committee on Public Administration, Box 14, McRP; Gulick telegram to McReynolds, August 12, 1940; and Gulick to McReynolds, March 24, 1941, both in File Institute of Public Administration, Box 15, McRP. My impression from reading the files was that McReynolds usually declined, begged off, or found other reasons to avoid active assistance or participation. However, it is possible that predictable gaps in the archival record (such as unrecorded phone calls, meetings without follow-up summaries or confirmations, and informal luncheons and dinners) could lead to a misimpression.

79. The yearly edition of FDR's papers and speeches for 1939 was first published by Macmillan in 1941.

80. "Personnel Administration in National Defense is Keynote of Successful Assembly Meeting," *Civil Service Assembly News Letter* 7, 11 (November 1941): 1–2.

81. McReynolds to Professor J. Alton Burdine, University of Texas, May 25, 1941, File American Society for Public Administration 1941–42, Box 14, McRP.

82. Millett had been a staff member of PCAM.

Chapter 5

1. An oft-forgotten detail is that, even though FDR viewed Nazi Germany as the greater threat and was assisting the UK in every way possible (legal and otherwise), on December 8 he asked for a congressional declaration of war only on Japan. A few days later, Hitler—in solidarity with ally Japan (although not required to do so by the treaty between the two countries)—declared war on the US. This then permitted FDR, anti-climactically, to ask Congress to reciprocate by expanding its declaration of war to include Germany.

2. The private secretary was L. Haag (note from McReynolds to John Dirks, December 6, 1944, file White House—LOPM, Box 21, McRP), and the two secretaries were Miss Edna G. Miller and Miss Lenora Green (January 28, 1942, File OF 3780).

3. Miss Dorothy E. Gleason (McReynolds to Commissioner of Internal Revenue, November 17, 1944, File White House—LOPM, Box 21, McRP).

4. Robert C. Albright, "Senate Measure Cracks Down on TVA, Score More Agencies," *WP*, March 10, 1944, 3.

5. Robert C. Albright, "Senate Unit Votes to Delete TVA Curbs," *WP*, March 24, 1944, 2.

6. AP, "Authority of FDR to be Challenged," *[Hagerstown, MD] Morning Herald*, February 28, 1944, 8.

7. International News Service, "Anti-Bureaucrat Amendments Sent to Conference," *Tipton [IN] Daily Tribune*, March 27, 1944, 4.

8. C. P. Trussell, "House Votes Bill with FEPC Funds," *NYT*, May 27, 1944, 8; *CR*, June 1, 1944, 5185.

9. "Two McKellar Riders Lose in Conference," *WP*, May 25, 1944, 1–2; *CR*, June 1, 1944, 5170.

10. *CR*, June 1, 1944, 5183–85.

11. Robert C. Albright, "House Passes Death Sentence for Agencies," *WP*, June 2, 1944, 1–2.

12. 58 Stat. 387.

13. 58 Stat. 599. Besides benefiting from the careful wording of the provision in the Deficiency bill (practically a reverse legislative veto), FDR had also legally protected LOPM and the other executive order–only agencies in another way. By signing the Deficiency bill into law a day *after* signing the Independent Offices bill, he was relying on the judicial approach to statutory construction, which deems a later enactment as impliedly repealing any earlier one it contradicted. The tactic of the sequence of when FDR signed the bills protected LOPM's (and other like agencies') funding, but was not automatically necessary. Another rule of statutory construction puts great emphasis on trying to harmonize

seemingly contradictory enactments, because having a court declare a law impliedly repealed was to be avoided as much as possible (Lee 2005b). In this case, the Independent Offices Act only affected spending money that it appropriated. Given that the source of funding in the Deficiency Act was wholly different (the president's emergency fund), it could have been argued that the two provisions were not automatically in conflict.

14. "Agency Bill Voted With FEPC Funds," *NYT*, June 21, 1944, 20; International News Service, "House May Leave FEPC Fate to Senate," *WP*, July 5, 1945, 4.

15. Moffett to McReynolds, August 14, 1944, File Mr. Moffett, Box 23, McRP.

16. Jerry Kluttz, "U.S. Pay Raise Hearings Shelved as Recess Nears" (Federal Diary daily column), *WP*, August 31, 1944, 7.

17. McReynolds to Moffett, August 15, 1944, File Mr. Moffett, Box 23, McRP. Moffett remained engaged after his retirement from LOPM. Van Riper interviewed him in 1947 for his history of the CSC (Van Riper 1958, 254n11). A month before the 1948 presidential elections, Truman called Moffett out of retirement to chair the CSC's Fair Employment Board, assigned to deal with racial discrimination complaints by federal civil servants (AP, "Moffett Made FEPB Chairman," *NYT*, October 8, 1948, 28). This was one of Truman's many public signals to the coalition he was trying to put together to win the election he was expected to lose. In this case, it was a (modest) concrete demonstration of his concern about prejudice against African Americans. Moffett served only a year as head of the FEPB before resigning due to a heart attack (Kluttz, "Compromise Suggested by Truman on Measure to Raise Executive Pay," *WP*, October 6, 1949, B1). He died in 1963 at age 81 ("Moffett, Guy" [paid death notice], *WP*, February 16, 1963, C3). Despite his service to the Rockefellers and in the federal government, neither the *New York Times* nor the *Washington Post* noted his death with obituaries. The University of Virginia Library's Small Special Collections has his papers, consisting of twelve boxes. None relate to LOPM because that material was part of McReynolds's office files.

18. Edward T. Folliard, "Fourth Term Letter Hits at Argument of Dewey," *WP*, July 12, 1944, 2.

19. Mitchell to Robert A. Nathan, January 11, 1945, File CSC—1945, Box 1, McRP. Emphasis added.

20. The CSC issued a press release to explain the significance of this executive order (February 17, 1942, File CSC—1941–42, Box 2, McRP).

21. The White House press office issued a press release with a statement by FDR on the significance of this executive order (December 21, 1944, File CSC—1944, Box 1, McRP). McReynolds, Flemming, and BOB were involved in an extensive and detailed review of the CSC draft before recommending their approved version to the president (handwritten note from McReynolds to Flemming, November 24, 1944; note from McReynolds to BOB's Ed Young, November 30, 1944; and note from McReynolds to Maurice C. Latta [presidential executive clerk], all in File CSC—1944, Box 1, McRP). See also "Executive Order Modifies Classified Status Rule," *Civil Service Assembly Newsletter* 11, 1 (January 1945): 4.

22. "President Orders Classification of Field Jobs," *Civil Service Assembly Newsletter* 11, 2 (February 1945): 13.

23. Mitchell to McReynolds, December 7, 1944, File CSC—1944, Box 1, McRP. At

the bottom of the filed letter, McReynolds's secretary typed an addendum of McReynolds's reply on December 8, 1944: "Here is the final draft of the CSC annual report duly cleared. McR." Roosevelt formally sent the report to Congress on December 11, 1944 (File OF 3745).

24. "U.S. Commission Recommends New Legislation in Annual Report," *Civil Service Assembly Newsletter* 11, 1 (January 1945): 1, 5.

25. Arthur S. Flemming, oral history interview, June 19, 1989, items 13–14, Truman Library, accessed July 7, 2015, http://www.trumanlibrary.org/oralhist/flemming.htm.

26. McReynolds to Lawson A. Moyer, CSC Executive Director and Chief Examiner, February 13, 1942, File CSC—1941–42, Box 2, McRP.

27. C. Rogers Arundell, Member, Board of Tax Appeals, to McReynolds, March 7, 1942, ibid.

28. Mitchell to McReynolds, October 15, 1943, File Proposed Plan to Show Deductions on Salary Checks, 1943, Box 3, McRP.

29. Mitchell to McReynolds, October 21, 1943, File CSC—1943, Box 1, McRP. A reminder that the District of Columbia did not have home rule powers nor an elected municipal government at that time. For all intents and purposes, Congress was the legislative branch of the district's government (akin to a city's common council), and the federal CSC therefore was somewhat linked the district's civil service system.

30. CSC to McReynolds, March 6, 1944, File CSC—1944, Box 1, McRP.

31. Memo from Flemming to McReynolds, October 31, 1944, n.t., ibid.

32. Francis P. Brassor, Chief of CSC Administrative Services, to Moffett, September 9, 1943, File CSC—1943, Box 1, McRP.

33. Mitchell to Moffett, July 27, 1943, ibid.

34. CSC to Moffett, August 24, 1943, ibid.

35. J. H. Weiss, Chief of CSC Field Operations, to Moffett, July 18, 1944, File CSC—1944, Box 1, McRP.

36. Memo from Moffett to McReynolds on Allocation Standards Legislation, January 20, 1945, File CSC—1945, Box 1, McRP.

37. Memo from McReynolds to FDR on executive order strengthening the organization of the Civil Service Commission, November 9, 1944, File CSC—1944, Box 1, McRP.

38. Ibid.

39. Memo from McReynolds to Watson, February 3, 1943, File OF 3745.

40. Ibid.

41. Memo from McReynolds to FDR, February 22, 1943, File OF 3780.

42. Ibid., pencil notation on this document: "Not sent."

43. By now, Reeves was back at the University of Chicago (Reeves 1944, 327). However, he continued accepting subsequent assignments within FDR's administration before and during WWII.

44. At the beginning of the war, White was more temperate regarding the CSC's already obvious efforts to adjust to the wartime conditions. He suggested this would be a subject worthy of study by academic researchers. White also recommended research into LOPM and CPA's "effectiveness in solving the problems of adequate overall organization for a large jurisdiction" (White 1942, 10).

45. In 1942, January 29, October 10 (with Smith), December 4 (with Smith), 9 (possibly cancelled), and 15. In 1943, February 18. Franklin D. Roosevelt: Day by Day, online.

46. For example, FDR sometimes had "appointments off the record" (Hassett 1980, 67).

47. Memo from McReynolds to Heads of Executive Departments and Agencies, December 17, 1943, n.t., File OF 3745.

48. Memo from FDR to McReynolds, December 28, 1943, n.t., File OF 3780.

49. Memo from McReynolds to FDR, December 9, 1943, n.t., File OF 3745.

50. Memo from McReynolds to FDR, May 18, 1942, n.t., File OF 3780. McReynolds testified several times at congressional hearings on this subject to try to help untangle the complicated and sometimes contradictory policies then in effect (US House 1942, 3–7; US Senate 1943, 2–11). Interestingly, his testimony as a White House administrative assistant was treated as a routine matter at these hearings. Years later, the concept of executive privilege was advanced as a supposedly longstanding practice that White House staff never testified on Capitol Hill because of their intimate and advisory roles *vis-à-vis* a president.

51. Memo from FDR to the Director of the Budget, October 6, 1942, File OF 3780. After the meeting, McReynolds wrote a rare memorandum for the files to have a record of what FDR's decisions had been. He cc'd it to Smith (McReynolds, Memo for the Files, October 12, 1942, File Conferences with the President, 1942, Box 3, Smith Papers).

52. Memo from McReynolds to FDR, January 12, 1944, n.t., File OF 3780.

53. Memo from McReynolds to FDR, April 4, 1944, n.t., File OF 3745.

54. Memo from FDR to McReynolds, July 29, 1943, n.t., File OF 3780.

55. Flemming to McReynolds, August 9, 1943, File CSC—1943, Box 1, McRP.

56. Memo from Marvin McIntyre to McReynolds, December 15, 1941; and memo from FDR to Smith, February 16, 1942, both in File OF 3780.

57. McReynolds follow-up to phone call and telegram from Mayor LaGuardia to FDR, December 15, 1941, File OF 3780.

58. Memo from FDR to Smith, December 29, 1941, File OF 3780.

59. Memo from FDR to Stephen Early (White House press secretary), January 11, 1945, File OF 3780.

60. Memo from McReynolds to the Heads of Executive Departments and Agencies, April 16, 1943, n.t., File Library of Congress, Box 19, McRP.

61. Memo from McReynolds to the Heads of All Departments, Establishments and Agencies of the Federal Government, March 29, 1943, n.t.; and President's Message to Federal Employees on the Occasion of the Dedication of the "Government Girl" Planes, May 7, 1943, both in File Government Girls, Box 21, McRP; Kluttz, "Government Girl Plane Drive Starts Today in U.S. Agencies," *WP*, April 7, 1943, [A]1, B1.

62. "Federal Government Changes Rules on Annual Leave," *Civil Service Assembly News Letter* 9, 8 (August 1943): 60.

63. Kluttz, "Henderson's Handling of Personnel Criticized," *WP*, March 12, 1943, B1.

64. Kluttz, "Lovett, Job Abolished, Back on U.S. Payroll," *WP*, October 28, 1943, B1; Memo from McReynolds to Executive Departments and Agencies, October 12, 1944, n.t., File OF 3745.

65. Memo from McReynolds to the Heads of Executive Departments and Agencies, January 26, 1944, n.t., File CSC—1944, Box 1, McRP.

66. Memo from McReynolds to the Heads of Executive Departments and Agencies, March 15, 1945, n.t., File General—Extra Copies of General Letters, Box 17, McRP.

67. McReynolds to Frank Yates, GAO, January 27, 1943, File CSC—1943, Box 1, McRP.

68. Donald Stone, BOB Assistant Director, to Flemming, March 13, 1944, File CSC—1944, Box 1, McRP.

69. McReynolds to Mitchell, May 20, 1943, File CSC—1943, Box 1, McRP.

70. Memo from John Blandford Jr., BOB Assistant Director, to McReynolds, December 16, 1941, n.t., File CSC—1941–42, Box 1, McRP.

71. McReynolds to Mitchell, September 15, 1944, File CSC—1944, Box 1, McRP.

72. It was headed by Donald Stone, who thought well of McReynolds (Stone 1983, 31–32; 1990, 7).

73. Memo from McReynolds to Stephen Early, September 15, 1942, File Board of Legal Examiners, Box 2, McRP.

74. Memo from McReynolds to Marvin McIntyre, July 12, 1943, n.t., File 1942–43, Box 8, Official File 51-C: Recorder of Deeds [District of Columbia], FDRL. See also prewar memo on the same subject from McReynolds to FDR, April 14, 1941, n.t., File CSC—1941–42, Box 2, McRP. The issue was touchy politically because of race. The Recorder of Deeds was African American, while most of municipal government was directed by whites by virtue of Congress's direct control over Washington's local government. Congress, of course, was dominated by southerners, who were usually in control of committees and legislation due to their seniority. With the growing proportion of District residents who were African American, these southerners were that much more focused on preventing any home rule or elections for the capital's municipal government.

75. Memo from Jonathan Daniels to McReynolds, February 3, 1944, n.t., File Confidential File, Box 24, McRP.

76. For an example of new CSC-linked letterhead, see Henry F. Hubbard, CPA Staff Assistant, to Moffett, October 30, 1942, File CPA—I, 1939–43, Box 5, McRP.

77. CPA, "What It Is and How It Works," February 20, 1943, File CPA—III, 1940–45, Box 5, McRP.

78. Davenport to McReynolds, June 27 and 30, 1944, File CPA—II, 1944, Box 5, McRP.

79. Davenport delivered a speech at the meeting, and the text was later published as an article (Davenport 1944). A box titled "Panel Praises Council" was inserted on the first page of the article (p. 5). It stated that McReynolds (and the other panelists) commented "favorably" on CPA's wartime work after Davenport's speech.

80. FDR (drafted by McReynolds) to Davenport, March 29, 1944, File OF 3780.

81. January 16, 1943, File CPA—I, 1939–43; March 22, 1944, File CPA—II, 1944; and March 1, 1945, File CPA—III, 1940–45, all located in Box 5, McRP. During the war, there were restrictions on travel by federal employees, partly to save money, but mostly due to the gas rationing and heavy use of the transportation system by military personnel and for materiel. The wording of the letters conveys McReynolds's standing to issue such approvals. The 1943 letter stated that Davenport's official duties required his presence outside of

Washington and that these duties "cannot effectively be performed or carried on without travel by automobile. . . . [It] will amount to approximately three hundred miles per month" above and beyond commuting to his office. The 1944 letter certified that Davenport "is traveling by rail to various parts of the country on government business which necessitates his arriving at certain cities on a definite schedule" (i.e., that he should not be bumped to a later train).

82. McReynolds to Davenport, February 17, 1944, File CPA—II, 1944, Box 5, McRP.

83. Memo from McReynolds to FDR, March 16, 1943, File CPA—I, 1939–43, Box 5, McRP.

84. Davenport to McReynolds, December 2, 1943, ibid.

85. Davenport to McReynolds, December 6, 1944, File CPA—II, 1944, Box 5, McRP.

86. Henry F. Hubbard, CPA Staff Assistant, to Moffett, October 20, 1942, File CPA—I, 1939–43, Box 5, McRP.

87. R. R. Zimmerman, CPA Executive Assistant, to Moffett, January 30, 1943, ibid.

88. Memo from CPA Committee on Absence to Moffett regarding Extent and Causes of Absence and Experience in Reducing Undesirable Absence, May 11, 1943, ibid. For a more general discussion of this problem, see Frank Kelley, "Survey Studies Absenteeism in Agencies of U. S.," *NYHT*, March 19, 1943, 9.

89. Copy for Mr. Moffett; and memo from E. R. Ballinger, Chairman, CPA Committee on Post War Problems, to committee members, February 3, 1944, File CPA—II, 1944, Box 5, McRP.

90. Richard O. Niehoff, Chairman, CPA Training Committee, to Moffett, May 11, 1944, ibid.

91. Note from Arthur B. McLean, Chairman, CPA Efficiency Rating Committee (and Director of Personnel, Federal Security Agency) to Moffett, December 8, 1944, ibid.

92. "Ramspeck Investigating Committee Issues Report," *Civil Service Assembly Newsletter* 11, 1 (January 1945): 2.

93. Kluttz, "U.S. Agencies Advised on Deferment Requests," *WP*, February 8, 1943, B1.

94. During this period, McKellar was the acting chairman of the Appropriations Committee due to ill health of Chairman Carter Glass (D-VA).

95. Moffett also contributed by flagging for McReynolds an 1820 letter from former president Thomas Jefferson to former president James Madison criticizing the expansion of the number of presidential appointments subject to Senate confirmation. "Sounds like the McKellar Bill," note from Moffett to McReynolds, 1943, n.d., File CSC—1943, Box 1, McRP.

96. Memo from McReynolds to FDR, February 17, 1943, n.t., File Congressional Civil Service Committees, Box 1, McRP.

97. Notation in written summary of the president's actions on McReynolds's recommendation and draft, February 19, 1943, File OF 3780.

98. "Civil Service Forces Hit McKellar's Exemptions," *CSM*, February 1, 1943, 3; Robert W. Harvey, "McKellar Plan Draws Fire of Civil Service," *WP*, February 12, 1943, 1.

99. S. 575 bill history, Index for 78th Cong., 1st sess., *CR* 89:13, 647. Later in 1943, McKellar added his $4,500 rider to two bills, the FY 1944 Labor Department-Federal

Security Agency Appropriation Bill and the War Agencies funding bill, but in four consecutive showdown votes on conference committee reports, the House refused to accept it ("Differences Over Crop Insurance and $4,500 Jobs Delay Congress," *NYT*, July 8, 1943, 14; Edward Ryan, "Congress Passes Final Supply Bills: House Kills Senate Job-Confirmation Rider Attached to 4.3-Billion Measures," *WP*, July 9, 1941, 1,8; C. P. Trussell, "Corn Ceiling Lost: House Stands Pat and Beats Senate's Plan to Confirm Employes [*sic*]," *NYT*, July 9, 1943, 13). The next year, McKellar tried again with similar language attached to the Independent Offices Appropriation Bill. It got caught up in the fight over the Russell amendment defunding executive order–only agencies. The inter-house compromise was to delete McKellar's riders and retain Russell's (see earlier subchapter on LOPM funding and staffing).

100. It was true that the USSR engaged in spying in the United States during the war, such as stealing the secret of the atomic bomb. When such spying efforts were initially aided by American Communists, the Russians usually tried to get those individuals to disengage completely from the party. Therefore, HUAC's (and the FBI's) obsessive attention to the formal American Communist Party was unlikely to uncover many authentic spies. As for Russian spies who worked for the federal government in Washington, this turned out to be true in a handful of cases, such as Alger Hiss and Harry Dexter White (Steil 2014), but was nowhere near as widespread as Republicans implied, and did not warrant the commensurate energy they invested to root it out. However, it was a potent political issue that probably helped Republicans win some elections when they made it an issue.

101. For example, 57 Stat. 194, from the Independent Offices Appropriation Act for FY 1944, enacted on June 26, 1943.

102. Arthur L. Flemming, "Flemming Decries Federal 'Witch Hunts'" (guest column in Federal Diary daily feature), *WP*, April 25, 1944, 3; "U.S. Civil Service Weeds Out Axis-Communist Sympathizers," *CSM*, April 25, 1944, 1, 11.

103. FDR to Mitchell, February 17, 1944, File CSC—1944, Box 1, McRP.

104. Ibid.

105. Kluttz, "Washington's Birthday Used to be a U.S. Day Off," *WP*, February 22, 1944, 3.

106. Ickes to McReynolds, March 3, 1944, Confidential File, Box 24, McRP. Ickes's reaction may have been triggered in part by a recent critical magazine article on the subject (Henry F. Pringle, "Snooping on the Potomac," *Saturday Evening Post*, January 15, 1944, 19, 93–94).

107. Reply from McReynolds to Ickes, March 6, 1944, ibid.

108. CSC, December 22, 1943, n.t., File CSC—1943, Box 1, McRP. A handwritten note at the top of the document, "Confidential," was likely made by McReynolds.

109. "Relation of Personnel Management to Over-All Management," text of speech delivered to Federal Personnel Management Conference, Cleveland, June 10, 1943, File Federal Personnel Management Conference, Box 17, McRP. For a summary of his talk, see the Conclusion.

110. Thank you letter from Everett Van Every, Executive Secretary of the Federal Personnel Council of San Francisco, to McReynolds, n.d., File CSC—1943, Box 1, McRP.

Given that the letter was in the 1943 CSC folder, it is likely a reference to the August 20–24, 1943, conference.

111. Kluttz, "Redistribution Division First Casualty at WPB," *WP*, September 7, 1944, 6.

112. Kluttz, "Agencies Get Authority to Lop Off War Employes [*sic*]," *WP*, June 19, 1944, 3.

113. Kluttz, "Judges Chosen for the *Post*'s $100 Federal Workers' Contest," *WP*, September 20, 1942, 1, 6.

114. Thank you letter from F. X. A. Eble, Treasury Department Conservation Liaison Officer, to Moffett, April 17, 1943, File Treasury Department, Box 9, McRP.

115. Kluttz, "OPA Ration Division Facing Reorganization," *WP*, January 13, 1944, B1.

116. Flier for Dinner Meeting of the Society for Personnel Administration, Washington, DC, June 7, 1943, File Society for Personnel Administration, Box 15, McRP. Notwithstanding the generic title of the organization, it focused only on HR in the public sector.

117. George D. Riley, "New York Personnel Fest," *Washington Times-Herald*, August 31, 1943, located in File New York Conference, August 26, 27, 28, 1943, Box 3, McRP. Riley's column was the competitor to Kluttz of the *Post*.

118. Drew Pearson, "Feud with Wall St.-Backed Cuban Sugar Interests," *WP*, January 15, 1943, B4.

119. Another mistake that easily could have been avoided was listing McReynolds's title as special assistant to the president, instead of administrative assistant to the president (Man at the Microphone 1944, 49).

120. Hope Ridings Miller, "'Broadcast' Exposed: It was a 2-Man Job," *WP*, March 16, 1944, 9.

121. John H. Crider, "Some Careless Needling," *NYT Book Review* Sunday section, April 9, 1944, BR10.

122. For what little it's worth, the book also described the CSC as a "dead duck" (5), apparently because so much wartime hiring was outside the regular CSC recruiting and examination process and the new employees were not within the permanent classified service.

123. Leon Henderson, OPA Administrator, to McReynolds, April 17, 1942; and McReynolds to Oscar Cox, Assistant Solicitor General, Department of Justice, April 21, 1942, both in File Office of Temporary Control (Formerly OPA)—NWA, 1941–44, Box 7, McRP.

124. Moffett to Sayre, August 11, 1944, ibid.

125. Bell to McReynolds, May 12, 1944; and McReynolds response, May 30, 1944, both in File Treasury Department, Box 9, McRP.

126. Memo from McReynolds to Don Nelson, August 1944, n.t., handwritten note "Confidential," File Office of Temporary Control (Formerly OPA)—NWA, 1941–44, Box 7, McRP. Nelson responded in a warm ("Dear Mac") but noncommittal note on August 21. The War Production Board was the current incarnation of what had started out in 1940 as the National Defense Advisory Commission (NDAC). McReynolds had served as the president's liaison officer to the commission (chap. 4).

127. He made his decision public a few weeks later: AP, "Louis Brownlow to Retire

as Director of Research Unit," *WP*, April 30, 1945, 3. In a nice touch reflecting continuity, Brownlow's successor was Herbert Emmerich, who had been a PCAM staff member and then senior federal public administrator during WWII.

128. Draft of FDR letter to Brownlow, April 1945, File Public Administration Clearing House, Box 15, McRP.

129. Memo from FDR to McReynolds, March 27, 1945, File OF 3745.

130. Memo from McReynolds to the Heads of Executive Departments and Agencies, April 10, 1945, n.t., File General—Extra Copies of General Letters, Box 17, McRP.

131. Kluttz, "Hutson, Vinson's Advisor, Will Succeed Jones," *WP*, April 11, 1945, 3.

Chapter 6

1. "First Truman Order Gives Job Priority to Veterans for the U.S. Civil Service," *NYT*, April 15, 1945, 6; "Veterans are Eligible for Permanent Appointments," *Civil Service Assembly Newsletter* 11, 5 (May 1945): 34.

2. Jerry Kluttz, "Navy Reduces Enlisted Personnel in Office Jobs" (Federal Diary daily column), *WP*, April 18, 1945, 3.

3. James E. Chinn, "Truman Picks War Buddy as His Chief Aide," *WP*, May 1, 1945, 1–2.

4. United Press, "Truman Picks E. D. McKim as Chief Aide," *[Valparaiso, IN] Vidette-Messenger*, May 1, 1945, 2.

5. Bascom N. Timmons, "Wartime Washington" (opinion column), *Wichita [Falls, TX] Daily Times*, May 6, 1945, 10.

6. McReynolds to Truman, May 3, 1945, File Resignations, Official File 1210, Box 1752, Harry S Truman Presidential Library, Independence, MO (hereafter cited as Truman Library).

7. Reply from Truman to McReynolds, May 8, 1945, ibid.

8. Kluttz, "Senate Committee Approves 15.8% Basic U.S. Pay Boost," *WP*, May 10, 1945, 3.

9. Ray Tucker, "The National Whirligig: 'News Behind the News'" (syndicated column), *Ironwood [MI] Daily Globe*, May 19, 1945, 10.

10. Jonathan Daniels, oral history interview, October 4–5, 1963, item 50, Truman Library, accessed July 7, 2015, http://www.trumanlibrary.org/oralhist/danielsj.htm.

11. Eben A. Ayers, oral history interview, August 15, 1969, items 314–15, Truman Library, accessed July 7, 2015, http://www.trumanlibrary.org/oralhist/ayers.htm.

12. For example, in mid-1941 (a few months after McReynolds's role with NDAC had ceased), a Texas newspaper published a profile of a local woman who was now working in Holmead's office. This kind of profile could easily serve as a platform for the native hometown innocent to complain about the awful bureaucracy in the capital. Not in this case. The woman described how busy the personnel department was, how much hiring it was doing, and how Holmead usually accepted the woman's hiring recommendations. While there was no explicit praise or criticism of Holmead, the Texas native's description

of her work in Holmead's office suggested she thought well of Holmead (L. T. Easley, AP, "Cooper Girl Has Important Personnel Position in OPM," *Paris [TX] News*, July 14, 1941, 1, 7). Similarly, one senior NDAC official was chided by Holmead for sloppy paperwork. Known for his temper and undiplomatic tirades, he did not respond by attacking her supposed red-tape overzealousness, but instead grudgingly complied with her requests (Lee 2012, 52, 219n130).

13. As LOPM head, McReynolds routinely served as intermediary between some agency personnel directors and the CSC regarding complicated or sensitive matters (chaps. 4–5). Humorously, in one case that role related to Holmead's agency. He addressed her formally "Dear Mrs. Holmead," explained how he tried to untangle the problem, and made suggestions for follow-up (McReynolds to Holmead, July 1, 1941, File Office of Temporary Control [Formerly OPA], OEM 1941–45, Box 7, McRP).

14. Drew Pearson and Robert S. Allen, "Japs Exploit Caste System" (Washington Merry-Go-Round syndicated column), *Tucson [AZ] Daily Citizen*, March 12, 1942, 10.

15. Matthew J. Connelly, oral history interview, November 30, 1967, items 186–87, Truman Library, accessed July 8, 2015, http://www.trumanlibrary.org/oralhist/connly.htm.

16. Kluttz, "WPB Labor Divisions Facing Personnel Cut," *WP*, September 16, 1944, 3.

17. Paul Mallon, "Full Shakeup of Cabinet is Forecast" (syndicated column), *Hartford [CT] Courant*, May 24, 1945, 3.

18. AP, "France Paris is Cited for Hatch Act Violations," *Miami [OK] Daily News-Record*, September 11, 1944, 1.

19. AP, "Petition Says Hatch Act Unconstitutional," *Miami [OK] Daily News-Record*, September 22, 1944, 1.

20. Long after the showdown with McReynolds during the 1944 campaign, Kerr futilely kept fighting the CSC's decision. Federal judges ruled against him at the trial and appellate level. The US Supreme Court accepted the case and in February 1947 ruled 5–2 against Kerr. It was a landmark decision defining the application of the Hatch Act to local governments accepting federal funding (Rosenthal 1987, 1144ff; Heady 1947, 695–96).

21. McReynolds and Zimmermann knew each other from the small network of federal personnel specialists who worked towards FDR's goal of executive-centered personnel management. McReynolds was, of course, at a much more senior level than Zimmerman. In 1940, Zimmerman sent McReynolds a copy of a paper he had presented on personnel management at a conference of the American Management Association. In a fawning cover letter that hinted at his ambition, Zimmerman asked if McReynolds would read it, "make some marginal notations and then let me come over and get the benefit of your thinking" (Zimmerman to McReynolds, March 4, 1940, File CPA—I, 1939–43, Box 5, McRP).

22. Kerr to FDR, January 9, 1945; and memo from FDR to McReynolds, January 16, 1945, both in File OF 3780. McReynolds's reply to Kerr's letter to FDR was dated January 25. Davenport belatedly answered McReynolds's query about Zimmerman only after McReynolds had already written to Kerr (Davenport to McReynolds, January 29, 1945; and reply memo from McReynolds's secretary to Davenport, January 31, 1945, both in File CPA—III, 1940–45, Box 5, McRP). Maybe McReynolds had expressed himself im-

precisely during his oral history interview. His meeting before the election had been with Kerr and Hannegan, but perhaps this post-election letter to FDR was solely from Kerr and without an explicit request to fire McReynolds.

23. McKim lasted only a month and a half after firing McReynolds. Truman removed him from the White House in mid-June (AP, "Truman Shifts McKin [*sic*] to Post in Loan Agency," *WP*, June 13, 1945, 5). The gossipy Merry-Go-Round column claimed it was because "the genial and likeable McKim seemed too engrossed to Mrs. 'Hope Diamond' McLean's dinner parties and the social whirl of Washington" (Drew Pearson, "Washington Merry-Go-Round," *WP*, June 19, 1945, 9).

24. Kluttz, "Senate Committee Approves 15.8% Basic U.S. Pay Boost," *WP*, May 10, 1945, 3.

25. Kluttz, "Labor Reorganization Survey is Ordered," *WP*, May 15, 1945, 3.

26. "W. H. McReynolds, Roosevelt Aide, Dies," *WP*, January 18, 1951, B2.

27. Kluttz, "Food Prices, Wages to be Increased in Federal Cafeterias," *WP*, January 19, 1951, B1.

28. AP, "Schoeneman Appointed by Truman as Assistant: Rhode Island Man Succeeds McReynolds in Liaison Post," *NYHT*, May 10, 1945, 21.

29. AP, "Zimmerman is Named as Assistant to Truman: Oklahoma Man Fills Post Held by Schoeneman," *NYHT*, September 22, 1945, 9. For a photo of Zimmerman (and Schoeneman), see "FEPC Honors Truman Aides," *WP*, September 30, 1945, M4.

30. United Press, "4-Day Yule Rest for U.S. Workers," *NYT*, November 28, 1945, 19; "U.S. Workers Get Time Off Good Friday," *WP*, April 10, 1946, 6; memo from Zimmerman to the Heads of Executive Departments and Agencies, July 10 and 12, 1946, n.t., File General—Extra Copies of General Letters, Box 17, McRP.

31. For example, Executive Order 9691, "Directing the Civil Service Commission to Resume Operations Under the Civil Service Rules, and Authorizing the Adoption of Special Regulations During the Transitional Period," February 4, 1946; and Executive Order 9830, "Amending the Civil Service Rules and Providing for Federal Personnel Administration," February 24, 1947. For a brief summary of the contents of the 1947 order, see "New Federal Civil Service Rules Issued," *Civil Service Assembly Newsletter*, 13, 3 (March 1947): 10.

32. "State Held Judge of GI Job Training," *NYT*, October 23, 1946, 49.

33. Genevieve Reynolds, "BPWC [Business and Professional Women's Clubs] Plans to Accelerate Health Project" (Club Notes column), *WP*, October 26, 1945, 16; Bert Pierce, "Truman Champions Fight on Accidents," *NYT*, October 8, 1946, 25.

34. Kluttz, "RFC Reorganization is being Discussed," *WP*, February 14, 1947, 5.

35. Zimmerman, "More Teamwork in Management" address to USDA Organization and Procedure Conference, June 5, 1946, mimeograph, located in the collection of the National Agricultural Library, US Department of Agriculture, Beltsville, MD.

36. "Conference Registration List," *Public Personnel Review* 1, 8 (January 1947): 45.

37. Letter of resignation from Zimmerman to Truman, February 14, 1947, File Zimmerman, Raymond R., Official File 740, Truman Library (hereafter OF 740); "Quits

White House Post: Zimmerman was Truman's Aide on Personnel Matters," *NYT*, March 4, 1947, 3.

38. For Immediate Release, n.t., n.d., Washington Chapter, Society for the Advancement of Management, OF 740.

39. Truman to Zimmerman, March 1, 1947, ibid. It is possible Zimmerman resigned due to health issues. A year later, he became a VP for governmental relations at the Washington office of a Cleveland-based engineering company (probably trying to help it get federal construction and engineering contracts). Given Kerr's interests in federal contracts (and pork barrel projects), it is possible he helped Zimmerman get that position. In the early 1950s, Zimmerman returned to federal service to work at several of the (frequently reorganized and renamed) foreign aid agencies. He retired from the federal government in about 1956 and died in 1986.

40. "Truman Appoints Aide," *NYT*, August 6, 1947, 15. For a photo of Dawson, see "Newest Aide at White House," *WP*, August 7, 1947, 3.

41. Another political role, which was his later claim to fame, was serving in the 1948 campaign as advance man for Truman's whistle-stop train tour through the central part of the country when he was denouncing the "do-nothing 80th Congress." Whether fairly or not, that tour was credited as playing a major role in Truman's come-from-behind victory (Wolfgang Saxon, "Donald Dawson: 97, Dies; Master of Truman Whistle-Stop," *NYT*, December 29, 2005, A25).

42. AP, "Truman Greetings to AFGE [American Federation of Government Employees] Praises Government Workers," *WP*, April 29, 1950, 2; Richard L. Lyons, "Robinson Confers with Dawson on Details; Truman's Order Awaited," *WP*, May 1, 1952, B1; Kluttz, "Congressman Named to House Committee on Civil Service," *WP*, January 17, 1953, 13; Kluttz, "Many New Faces Appear in Important Government Jobs," *WP*, January 24, 1953, 11.

43. It is unclear why he resisted. Between 1946 and 1949, he rapidly moved through several increasingly senior federal management positions: director of the Bureau of Demobilization in the Civilian Production Administration, director of Organization and Personnel of the Atomic Energy Commission, assistant general manager of the Atomic Energy Commission, secretary of the National Security Resources Board, and commissioner of special services at the Federal Security Agency (where he oversaw the FDA and the Office of Vocational Rehabilitation). Belsley retired from federal service in 1966 and died in 1993 ("G. Lyle Belsley Dies at 88; Federal Official," *WP*, April 17, 1993, D7).

44. Arnold misspelled his name as Bressor (Arnold 1998, 130), but spelled it correctly later in the text (177). The index followed the incorrect initial spelling (437).

45. Kluttz, "Civil Service Head May Become No. 1 Man on Personnel Problems," *WP*, December 28, 1948, B1. Presumably the leak came from one of the members of the minority on the Hoover Commission.

46. Kluttz, "Hoover Group to Urge DP Commission Switch to State Department," *WP*, March 10, 1949, B1. Presumably, Dawson was the source of the leak, but, based on Truman's behavior through the end of his presidency in January 1953, it was accurate.

47. In mid-1949, Congress passed the Reorganization Act of 1949 (63 Stat. 203–07) giving Truman comparable reorganization powers to those it had delegated to FDR in 1939. The new Act did not explicitly prohibit any change in the CSC, as the 1939 Act had. But its general limitations on what could and could not be reorganized, such as precluding changes affecting any statutes governing an agency's existence and authority, had the indirect effect of protecting the CSC, along with many other agencies and departments (63 Stat. 203–04).

48. 63 Stat. 1067.

49. For the order's complete text, see http://en.wikisource.org/wiki/Executive_Order_10452 (accessed July 8, 2015).

50. Philip Young had been the dean of Columbia's Business School when Eisenhower appointed him to the CSC chairmanship and White House role in 1953. Based on news coverage at the time, there were political attacks on Young because he had grossly exaggerated the number of federal employees who were purged when Eisenhower came into office with the campaign promise to clean house in the wake of Democratic administrations that were supposedly soft on communists and subversives in the federal workforce. Young falsely claimed that about 2,200 civil servants had been fired by the administration due to disloyalty, internal security investigations (including the claim that homosexuals were susceptible to Communist blackmail threats), and un-American activities. As a result of the controversy, the beginning of Eisenhower's second term was likely an opportune political moment to ease Young out without the appearance of yielding to Democratic and media criticism. Young was appointed ambassador to Holland.

51. Arnold refers to the name of the proposed entity as the "bureau of personnel management." Given that he used lower case, it could be he meant this as a generic term of what the new entity would do, rather than what its formal title was proposed to be.

52. Stans returned to federal service under President Nixon. Hoping to be appointed Treasury secretary, he instead was offered the Commerce secretaryship. When the Committee to Re-Elect the President was formed, Stans resigned to be its finance director. The Watergate investigation led to questions about his fundraising, specifically how the checks from some contributors ended up as payments to the Cubans involved in the Watergate break-in. Stans maintained his innocence and was acquitted of perjury and obstruction of justice charges. Later, he pled guilty to violating the reporting sections of the Federal Election Campaign Act and two counts of accepting illegal campaign contributions. He was fined $5,000.

53. Kluttz, "Health Bill Gets Limited Approval of Senate Group," *WP*, June 23, 1959, B1.

54. For a lay summary of the contents of the bill as reintroduced by Clark in the 86th Congress (1959–60), see *CR*, April 10, 1959, 5591–93.

55. It is unclear why the bill never came to the Senate floor for debate, but it was explicitly postponed several times in mid-1960 (*CR*, June 18, 13201; June 28, 14666–14667). There is no archival record on the fate of the bill in the Lyndon B. Johnson Presidential Library (Barbara Cline, Archivist, LBJ Library, e-mail message to author, July 18, 2014). While speculative, a few scenarios seem likely. Given the Eisenhower administration's

opposition, Senate Republicans would probably have been unanimous and forceful in opposing the bill, as articulated by their three members in the committee's minority report (US Senate, 1960, 15–17). They might even have threatened dilatory parliamentary procedures to kill it. Allied with them would have been conservative Democrats carrying on the traditional stance of their political forebears who had opposed tinkering with autonomous CSC in the late 1930s (chap. 2). Some even had *participated* in that earlier fight, including Harry Byrd Sr. (D-VA), who was still in the Senate in 1960. Some mainstream Democratic senators (i.e., non-southern and non-conservative) may have opposed Clark's bill on generic partisan grounds, namely that they hoped a Democrat would win the November presidential election and that the new president would have a chance to make his own recommendation on any changes in the structure of federal personnel management. Personal political ambitions may also have played a part. In June 1960, three Democratic senators were running for president: Kennedy, LBJ, and Symington. None of them was a member of the Post Office and Civil Service Committee, so they would not have detailed familiarity with the bill nor have already voted on it. They, too, may have wanted to have a free hand if they became president. The Democratic nominating convention in Los Angeles occurred in mid-July. After that, with Johnson running on the ticket with Kennedy, there likely was no strong partisan reason to bring up the bill. Before losing the nomination to Kennedy, Johnson had committed the Senate to a post-convention floor session as a way of highlighting his importance to Democrats. During that lame-duck session, in mid-August, he made the third motion on the floor *not* to bring up the bill for debate (*CR*, August 19, 1960, 16745). That can be interpreted as an affirmative political decision to avoid the controversy of the bill. Finally, Senator Ralph Yarborough (D-TX) was a member of the Post Office and Civil Service Committee and so would have been for the bill when it passed the committee on a party-line vote. But Johnson and Yarborough were political and ideological rivals and not on good terms. Therefore, Johnson would likely not have wanted to let Yarborough have a political win, no matter how minor.

56. Campbell was dean of Syracuse University's Maxwell School when I was a doctoral candidate there. In my first year as a grad student in 1970-71, I enrolled in his popular signature course "Introduction to Metropolitan Studies" (SOS 851). Even though as dean he did not have to teach any courses, he insisted on continuing to teach this one. He was a passionate, impressive, and memorable figure, clearly comfortable in dealing with public policy issues from both academic and political perspectives. A few years later, public administration circles were abuzz when Campbell accepted Carter's job offer to head the CSC and lead civil service reform. It happened *ten days* after Campbell had moved from Syracuse to Austin to become dean of the University of Texas's LBJ School.

57. Quoted in Martin Tolchin, "Grappling With the Monster of Bureaucracy: Carter's Reorganization Plan Makes More Ripples than Waves," *NYT* Week in Review Sunday Section, July 23, 1978, 2E.

58. Oddly, Seidman's chapter on reorganization during the Carter presidency omits any discussion of the CSC reorganization (Seidman 1998, chap. 5).

59. The panel preparing the report was co-chaired by Rocco Siciliano, formerly Eisenhower's special assistant for personnel management.

60. In 1970, using his reorganization powers, President Nixon renamed the Bureau of the Budget as the Office of Management and Budget.

61. Rochelle Jones, "The Man Who Abolished His Job," *WP [Sunday] Magazine*, December 3, 1978, 16.

62. Quoted in Larry Kramer, "Carter to Offer Plan to Reform Civil Service," *WP*, February 26, 1978, K2.

63. The other three were OMB, GSA, and GAO. There is a significant literature on the substance of the Civil Service Reform Act of 1978, as well as on the subsequent developments in public sector HR policies. Given that the focus of this inquiry has been the organizational and political history of federal personnel management, those aspects of the topic are beyond the scope of the book. For readers interested in more information on those parts of the story, see Linda J. Bilmes and W. Scott Gould, *The People Factor: Strengthening America by Investing in Public Service* (Washington, DC: Brookings Institution Press, 2009); James S. Bowman and Jonathan P. West, eds., *American Public Service: Radical Reform and the Merit System* (Boca Raton, FL: CRC Press/Taylor & Francis, 2007); James P. Pfiffner and Douglas A. Brook, eds., *The Future of Merit: Twenty Years after the Civil Service Reform Act* (Washington, DC, and Baltimore: Woodrow Wilson Center Press and Johns Hopkins University Press, 2000); Donald F. Kettl, Patricia W. Ingraham, Ronald P. Sanders, and Constance Horner, *Civil Service Reform: Building a Government That Works* (Washington, DC: Brookings Institution Press, 1996); Patricia Wallace Ingraham, *The Foundation of Merit: Public Service in American Democracy* (Baltimore: Johns Hopkins University Press, 1995); Ingraham and David H. Rosenbloom, eds., *The Promise and Paradox of Civil Service Reform* (Pittsburgh, PA: University of Pittsburgh Press, 1992); and Ingraham and Carolyn Ban, eds., *Legislating Bureaucratic Change: The Civil Service Reform Act of 1978* (Albany: State University of New York Press, 1984).

Conclusion

1. Floyd W. Reeves, "Tentative Plan for a Study of Personnel Management and Its Relation to Other Aspects of Administrative Management in the Executive Branch of the Federal Government, May 8, 1936," pp. 13–15, File A-II-21: Outline for the New York Conference, May 9–10, 1936, Box 1, PCAM.

2. I applied these same criteria from Somers to evaluate Nixon's 1973 initiative of appointing super-secretaries as non-statutory presidential coordinators (Lee 2010, 202-06).

3. Letter of greeting from FDR to annual conference of the Civil Service Assembly of the United States and Canada, October 13, 1939, File PPF 4080. The letter was drafted by McReynolds, so one could discount its contents as McReynolds writing his own report card. But a reminder: before WWII, FDR paid very close attention to details and documents that crossed his desk, including reading submitted drafts closely before deciding if he would sign, revise, or reject them.

4. McReynolds, "Relation of Personnel Management to Over-All Management," text of speech delivered to Federal Personnel Management Conference, Cleveland, June 10, 1943, File Federal Personnel Management Conference, Box 17, McRP.

5. Emphasis added. This policy office within EOP was created by Congress in 1976 (90 Stat. 459). About OSTP, see http://www.whitehouse.gov/administration/eop/ostp/about (accessed July 8, 2015).

6. Emphasis added. About ONAP, see http://www.whitehouse.gov/administration/eop/onap/about (accessed July 8, 2015).

7. Sungjoo Choi and Andrew B. Whitford, *Merit-based Pay and Employee Motivation in Federal Agencies*, Issues in Governance Studies No. 63, November 2013, accessed July 8, 2015, http://www.brookings.edu/~/media/research/files/papers/2013/11/26%20merit%20based%20pay%20choi%20whitford/choi%20and%20whitford_merit%20based%20pay_v11.pdf.

8. About Us, Partnership for Public Service, see http://ourpublicservice.org/about-us/index.php (accessed July 9, 2015).

9. Emphasis added. Accessed July 8, 2015, http://ourpublicservice.org/publications/viewcontentdetails.php?id=18. The report was co-sponsored and, apparently, co-authored by Booz Allen Hamilton, a consulting firm with clients in the public sector.

Bibliography

Primary Sources

Archival Collections

Note: All archival documents listed below were located at Franklin D. Roosevelt Presidential Library, Hyde Park, NY, unless otherwise specified.

Brookings Institution Board of Trustees. Minutes. Archives of the Brookings Institution, Washington, DC.

Brownlow, Louis, Diaries (1933–36). Special Collections Research Center, University of Chicago Library.

Civil Service Assembly of the United States and Canada, President's Personal File (PPF) 4080.

Civil Service Commission, Official File (OF) 2.

Government & Municipal Civil Service Employees, President's Personal File (PPF) 807.

Liaison Office for Personnel Management, Official File (OF) 3780.

McReynolds, William H., Official File (OF) 3745.

McReynolds, William H., Papers.

McReynolds, William H., President's Personal File (PPF) 7367.

Meriam, Lewis, Office Files 1928–39. Archives of the Brookings Institution, Washington, DC.

Morgenthau, Henry, Jr., Papers.

President's Committee on Administrative Management. Records.

Recorder of Deeds [of the District of Columbia], Official File (OF) 51-C.

Resignations (1945–52), Official File (OF) 1210, Box 1752. Harry S Truman Presidential Library, Independence, MO.

Roosevelt, Franklin D., Papers. Albert and Shirley Small Special Collections Library, University of Virginia, Charlottesville, VA.

Roosevelt Memorial Foundation. Records.

Smith, Harold, Papers.

Zimmerman, Raymond R., Official File (OF) 740, Box 1697. Truman Library.

Memoirs and Related Writings by Participants

Brownlow, Louis. 1958. *A Passion for Anonymity: The Autobiography of Louis Brownlow; Second Half.* Chicago: University of Chicago Press.

Davenport, Frederick M. 1944. "Let's Look at the Record." *Personnel Administration* 6 (5): 5–11.

———. 1952. *The Reminiscences of Frederick M. Davenport* (microfilm). New York: Oral History Research Office, Columbia University.

Dawson, Donald S. 1980. "Donald Dawson" (transcript of comments at a conference). In *The Truman White House: The Administration of the Presidency, 1945–1953*, edited by Francis H. Heller, 49–51, 62. Lawrence: Regents Press of Kansas.

Emmerich, Herbert. 1950. *Essays on Federal Reorganization.* University [Tuscaloosa]: University of Alabama Press.

———. 1971. "Meeting of the President and His Committee on Administrative Management with the Majority Leaders of the House and Senate." In *Federal Organization and Administrative Management*, 205–14. University [Tuscaloosa]: University of Alabama Press.

Fesler, James W. 1987. "The Brownlow Committee Fifty Years Later." *Public Administration Review* 47 (4): 291–96.

Flemming, Arthur S. 1940. "Emergency Aspects of Civil Service." *Public Administration Review* 1 (1): 25–31.

———. 1942. "The Government's Manpower Problem." In *Industrial Manpower Controls*, proceedings of a conference on Manpower and War Labor Problems, September 29–30, 1942. Personnel Series No. 60, 15–23. New York: American Management Association.

———. 1949. "The Challenge of Governmental Inefficiency." *Annals of the American Academy of Political and Social Science* 266: 24–31.

Flemming, Bernice. 1991. *Arthur Flemming: Crusader at Large; A Memoir.* Revised ed., Washington, DC: Caring. (Note: The author was Arthur Flemming's widow.)

Gulick, Luther. 1937. "The Recent Movement for Better Government Personnel." *American Political Science Review* 31 (2): 292–301.

Harris, Joseph P. 1937. "The Progress of Administrative Reorganization in the Seventy-Fifth Congress." *American Political Science Review* 31 (5): 862–70.

———. 1964. *Congressional Control of Administration.* Washington, DC: Brookings Institution.

———. (1953) 1968. *The Advice and Consent of the Senate: A Study of the Confirmation of Appointments by the United States Senate.* New York: Greenwood.

———. 1983. *Joseph P. Harris: Professor and Practitioner: Government, Election Reform, and the Votomatic.* Oral History interview conducted in 1980 by Harriet Nathan. University History Series. Berkeley, CA: Bancroft Library, University of California-Berkeley.

Hassett, William D. (1958) 1980. *Off the Record with F.D.R., 1942–1945.* Westport, CT: Greenwood.

McReynolds, William H. 1941. "The Liaison Office for Personnel Management." *Public Administration Review* 1 (2): 121–26.

———. 1949. Memorandum of Conversation between William H. McReynolds, Grace Tully, and Sidney Hyman. File IV.A.4. McReynolds, William H., Box 23, Records of the Roosevelt Memorial Foundation, FDRL.

Mitchell, Harry B. 1985. *Memoirs of Harry Brown Mitchell: President, U.S. Civil Service Commission (1933–51)*, typescript. Glasgow, MT: A. & T. Annan & Sons.

Mitchell, James M. 1950. "Recent Progress in Federal Personnel Administration." *Public Personnel Review* 11 (4): 181–89.

Moffett, Guy. 1943. "The Relation of Personnel Management to an Evolving Society." *Personnel Administration* 5 (10): 2–6.

Reeves, Floyd W. 1937. "Essentials of a Modern Personnel System." *Annals of the American Academy of Political and Social Science* 189: 134–41.

———. 1944. "Civil Service as Usual." *Public Administration Review* 4 (4): 327–40.

Roosevelt, Franklin D. (1938–1950) 1969. *Public Papers and Addresses of Franklin D. Roosevelt*, 13 vols. New York: Russell and Russell. (Note: In the volumes published before his death, the commentary and explanatory notes were in FDR's voice ["I"]. In the volumes published after his death, the commentary was written by Samuel Rosenman.)

———. 1972. *Complete Presidential Press Conferences of Franklin D. Roosevelt* (transcripts). New York: Da Capo Press. (Note: This is not a memoir per se, but as it was not published by the federal government, I am listing it here.)

Siciliano, Rocco C. 2004. *Walking on Sand: The Story of an Immigrant Son and the Forgotten Art of Public Service*. Salt Lake City: University of Utah Press.

Stone, Donald C. 1983. Oral history interview. File PAS IV, Box 40, Donald C. Stone Papers, Special Collections Research Center, Syracuse University Libraries, Syracuse, NY.

———.1990. "Administrative Management: Reflections on Origins and Accomplishments." *Public Administration Review* 50 (1): 3–20.

Truman, Harry S. (1955) 1998. *Memoirs: 1945, Year of Decisions*. New York: Konecky & Konecky.

Zimmerman, R. R. 1947. "Better Personnel Management in the Federal Government." *Modern Management* 7 (5): 26–28.

Federal Publications

Advisory Commission to the Council of National Defense. 1946. *Minutes of the Advisory Commission to the Council of National Defense: June 12, 1940, to October 22, 1941*. Historical Reports on War Administration, War Production Board, Documentary Publication No. 1. Washington, DC: US Civilian Production Administration.

Bureau of the Budget. 1943. Division of Administrative Management. "Organization and Responsibility for Personnel Administration." Reprinted in *Personnel Administration* 5, (9): 3–5.

Campbell, Alan K. 1980 (January). *Civil Service Reform: A Report on the First Year*. Washington, DC: Office of Personnel Management.

Carter, Jimmy. 1979. *Public Papers of the Presidents of the United States: Jimmy Carter, 1978; Book I—January 1 to June 30, 1978*. Washington, DC: Government Printing Office.

Commission on the Organization of the Executive Branch of the Government (a.k.a. the

First Hoover Commission). 1948. Personnel Policy Committee. *Programs for Strengthening Federal Personnel Management: A Report with Recommendations*. Washington, DC: Government Printing Office.

———. 1949. *The Hoover Commission Report on Organization of the Executive Branch of the Government*. New York: McGraw-Hill. (Note: While the report was published as an official federal document, I am citing here its publication by a commercial publishing house because that version is more widely accessible.)

Commission on Organization of the Executive Branch of the Government (a.k.a. the Second Hoover Commission). 1955 (February). Task Force on Personnel and Civil Service. *Report on Personnel and Civil Service*. Washington, DC: Government Printing Office.

Eisenhower, Dwight D. 1958. *Public Papers of the Presidents of the United States: Dwight D. Eisenhower, 1956*. Washington, DC: Government Printing Office.

National Archives. 1955. *Numbered Document File of the Advisory Commission to the Council of National Defense, 1940–41*, Microcopy No. 187 (microfilm). Washington, DC: National Archives.

President's Committee on Administrative Management. 1937. *Report of the Committee with Studies of Administrative Management in the Federal Government*. Washington, DC: Government Printing Office.

Roop, Joseph E. 1969 (April). *Foreign Broadcast Information Service: History, Part I: 1941–1947* (mimeograph). Langley, VA [?]: Central Intelligence Agency.

Rosen, Bernard (US Civil Service Commission). 1975. *The Merit System of the United States Civil Service: A Monograph*. Washington, DC: Government Printing Office.

Treasury Department. 1946. Fiscal Service, Bureau of Accounts, Division of Bookkeeping and Warrants. *Digest of Appropriations for the Support of the Government of the United States for the Service of the Fiscal Year Ending June 30, 1946*. Washington, DC: Government Printing Office.

Truman, Harry S. 1961. *Public Papers of the Presidents of the United States: Harry S. Truman, 1945*. Washington, DC: Government Printing Office.

———. 1964. *Public Papers of the Presidents of the United States: Harry S. Truman, 1949*. Washington, DC: Government Printing Office.

US Congress. 1937. Joint Committee on Government Organization. *Reorganization of the Executive Departments*, public hearings. 75th Cong., 1st sess.

US House. 1913. Committee on Appropriations. *President's Commission on Economy and Efficiency*, public hearings. 62nd Cong., 3rd sess.

———. 1931. Committee on the Civil Service. *A Personnel Program for the Federal Civil Service by Herman Feldman; A Report Transmitted by the Director of the Personnel Classification Board*. 71st Cong., 3rd sess., H. Doc. 773.

———. 1932a. *Consolidation of Departments of the Government: Message from the President of the United States*. 72nd Cong., 1st sess., H. Doc. 254.

———. 1932b. *Consolidation of Personnel Agencies*, public hearing. 72nd Cong., 1st sess.

———. 1932c. *Message of the President of the United States Transmitting a Message to Group, Coordinate, and Consolidate Executive and Administrative Agencies of the Gov-*

ernment, as Nearly as Maybe [sic], According to Major Purposes. 72nd Cong., 2nd sess., H. Doc. 493.

———. 1932d. Committee on Expenditures in the Executive Departments. *President's Message on Consolidation of Government Agencies,* public hearing. 72nd Cong., 2nd sess.

———. 1937. Select Committee on Government Organization. *Establishment of Civil Service Administration and Extension of Merit System and Classification Act.* 75th Cong., 1st sess., H. Rep. 1587.

———. 1938. Select Committee on Government Organization. *Government Organization.* 75th Cong., 3rd sess., H. Rep. 2033.

———. 1939a. Select Committee on Government Organization. *Reorganization Bill of 1939.* 76th Cong., 1st sess., H. Rep. 120.

———. 1939b. Committee on Appropriations. *Third Deficiency Appropriation Bill for 1939,* public hearings. 76th Cong., 1st sess.

———. 1940a. Committee on Appropriations. *Independent Offices Appropriation Bill for 1941,* public hearings, Part 1. 76th Cong., 3rd sess.

———. 1940b. Committee on Appropriations. *Independent Offices Appropriation Bill, 1941.* 76th Cong., 3rd sess., H. Rep. 1515.

———. 1941. Committee on Appropriations. *Independent Offices Appropriation Bill for 1943,* public hearings, Part 1. 77th Cong., 2nd sess.

———. 1942. Committee on the Civil Service. *Temporary Additional Compensation for Civilian Employees for the Duration of the War,* public hearings. 77th Cong., 2nd sess.

———. 1943. Committee on Appropriations. *First Supplemental National Defense Appropriation Bill for 1944,* public hearings. 78th Cong., 1st sess.

———. 1944a. *Budget of the United States Government for the Fiscal Year Ending June 30, 1945.* 78th Cong., 2nd sess., H. Doc. 426.

———. 1944b. Committee on Appropriations. *Second Deficiency Appropriation Bill for 1944,* public hearings. 78th Cong., 2nd sess.

———. 1945. *Budget of the United States Government for the Fiscal Year Ending June 30, 1946.* 79th Cong., 1st sess., H. Doc. 27.

———. 1946. *Budget of the United States Government for the Fiscal Year Ending June 30, 1947.* 79th Cong., 2nd sess., H. Doc. 411.

———. 1956. Committee on Post Office and Civil Service. *United States Civil Service Commission: Report.* 84th Cong., 2nd sess., H. Rep. 1844.

———. 1976. Committee on Post Office and Civil Service. *History of Civil Service Merit Systems of the United States and Foreign Countries; Together with Executive Reorganization Studies and Personnel Recommendations.* 94th Cong., 2nd sess., Committee Print 94–29.

US Senate. 1913. *Message of the President of the United States Submitting for the Consideration of the Congress a Budget with Supporting Memoranda and Reports.* 62nd Cong., 3rd sess., S. Doc. 1113.

———. 1937a. *Message from the President of the United States Transmitting a Report on Reorganization of the Executive Departments of the Government.* 75th Cong., 1st sess., S. Doc. 8.

———. 1937b. Select Committee to Investigate the Executive Agencies of the Government. *Investigation of Executive Agencies of the Government, Preliminary Report*. 75th Cong., 1st sess., S. Rep. 1275.

———. 1937c. Select Committee on Government Organization. *Reorganization of the Government Agencies*, public hearings. 75th Cong., 1st sess.

———. 1938. Select Committee on Government Organization. *Government Organization*. 75th Cong., 3rd sess., S. Rep. 1236 (Part 2).

———. 1939a. Committee on Appropriations. *Second Deficiency Appropriation Bill for 1939*, public hearings. 76th Cong., 1st sess.

———. 1939b. *Communication from the President of the United States: Council of Personnel Administration*. 76th Cong., 1st sess., S. Doc. 57.

———. 1940. Committee on Appropriations. *Independent Offices Appropriation Bill for 1941*, public hearings. 76th Cong., 3rd sess.

———. 1943. Committee on Civil Service. *Overtime Compensation to Government Employees*, public hearings. 78th Cong., 1st sess.

———. 1945. Committee on Civil Service. *Salary and Wage Administration in the Federal Service*, public hearings. 79th Cong., 1st sess.

———. 1949. Committee on Expenditures in the Executive Departments. *Progress on Hoover Commission Recommendations*. 81st Cong., 1st sess., S. Rep. 1158.

———. 1958a. Committee on Post Office and Civil Service, Special Subcommittee on S. 3888. *To Provide an Effective System of Personnel Administration*, public hearings. 85th Cong., 2nd sess.

———. 1958b. Committee on Post Office and Civil Service, Special Subcommittee on S. 3888. *To Provide an Effective System of Personnel Administration: Report*. 85th Cong., 2nd sess., Committee Print.

———. 1959. Committee on Post Office and Civil Service, Subcommittee on Civil Service. *To Provide for an Effective System of Personnel Administration*, public hearings. 86th Cong., 1st sess.

———. 1960. Committee on Post Office and Civil Service. *Federal Personnel Administration*. 86th Cong., 2nd sess., S. Rep. 1545.

Reports of Nonprofit Organizations

Beyer, William C. 1935. "Municipal Civil Service in the United States." Monograph 8 of the Commission of Inquiry on Public Service Personnel. In *Problems of the American Public Service: Five Monographs on Specific Aspects of Personnel Administration*, edited by Carl J. Friedrich et al., 75–168. New York: McGraw-Hill.

Commission of Inquiry on Public Service Personnel. 1935a. *Minutes of Evidence Taken Before the Commission of Inquiry on Public Service Personnel at Hearings Held in Washington, New York, Chicago, Minneapolis, St. Paul, Seattle, San Francisco, Berkeley, Palo Alto, Los Angeles, [and] Richmond; 1934*. New York: McGraw-Hill.

———. 1935b. *Better Government Personnel: Report of the Commission of Inquiry on Public Service Personnel*. New York: Whittlesey House, McGraw-Hill.

Governmental Research Conference of the United States and Canada. 1922. Committee on Civil Service. *The Character and Functioning of Municipal Civil Service Commissions in the United States.* Ann Arbor, MI [?]: Governmental Research Conference of the United States and Canada.

Meriam, Lewis. 1928. *The Problem of Indian Administration: Report of a Survey made at the request of Honorable Hubert Work, Secretary of the Interior, and submitted to him, February 21, 1928.* Baltimore: Johns Hopkins Press.

———. 1937. *Personnel Administration in the Federal Government: An Examination of Some Pending Proposals.* Pamphlet Series No. 19. Washington, DC: Brookings Institution.

———. 1938. *Public Personnel Problems: From the Standpoint of the Operating Officer.* Washington, DC: Brookings Institution.

Miller, John F. 1935. "Veteran Preference in the Public Service." Monograph 10 of the Commission of Inquiry on Public Service Personnel. In *Problems of the American Public Service: Five Monographs on Specific Aspects of Personnel Administration,* edited by Carl J. Friedrich et al., 241–334. New York: McGraw-Hill.

National Academy of Public Administration. 1980 (November). *A Presidency for the 1980s: A Report on Presidential Management by a Panel of the National Academy of Public Administration.* Washington, DC: National Academy of Public Administration.

National Assembly of Civil Service Commissions. 1915. *Draft of a Model Civil Service Law.* Washington, DC [?]: National Assembly of Civil Service Commissions.

National Civil Service League. 1970. *A Model Public Personnel Administration Law.* Washington, DC: National Civil Service League.

———, and National Municipal League. 1953. *A Model State Civil Service Law; A Model State Merit System Constitutional Provision.* New York: National Civil Service League and National Municipal League.

National Civil Service Reform League. 1931a. *Draft of a City Civil Service Law.* New York: National Civil Service Reform League.

———. 1931b. *Draft of a State Civil Service Law.* New York: National Civil Service Reform League.

———, and National Municipal League. 1939. *Draft of a State Civil Service Law.* New York: National Civil Service Reform League and National Municipal League.

National Municipal League. 1923. Special Committee on Civil Service. "Letter of Transmittal." *National Municipal Review* 12 (8): 442–71.

Wilmerding, Lucius, Jr. 1935. *Government By Merit: An Analysis of the Problem of Government Personnel.* Monograph 12 of the Commission of Inquiry on Public Service Personnel. New York: McGraw-Hill.

Secondary Sources: Books and Articles

Allen, Robert S., and William V. Shannon. 1950. *The Truman Merry-Go-Round.* New York: Vanguard.

Arnold, Peri E. 1997. "Executive Reorganization and the Executive Office of the President." In *The Executive Office of the President: A Historical, Biographical, and Bibliographical Guide,* edited by Harold C. Relyea, 407–43. Westport, CT: Greenwood.

———. 1998. *Making the Managerial Presidency: Comprehensive Reorganization Planning, 1905–1996*, 2nd ed. Lawrence: University Press of Kansas.

Beard, Charles A. 1935. Review of *Better Government Personnel* by the Commission of Inquiry on Public Service Personnel. *American Political Science Review* 29 (2): 296–97.

Beaumont, Enid F. 1974. "A Pivotal Point for the Merit Concept." *Public Administration Review* 34 (5): 426–30.

Bertelli, Anthony M., and Laurence E. Lynn Jr. 2006. *Madison's Managers: Public Administration and the Constitution*. Baltimore: Johns Hopkins University Press.

Betters, Paul V. (1931) 1974. *The Personnel Classification Board: Its History, Activities and Organization*. No. 64, Service Monographs of the United States Government, Institute for Government Research, Brookings Institution. New York: AMS Press.

Bilmes, Linda J., and W. Scott Gould. 2009. *The People Factor: Strengthening America by Investing in Public Service*. Washington, DC: Brookings Institution Press.

Binkley, Wilfred E., and Malcolm C. Moos. 1949. *A Grammar of American Politics: The National Government*. New York: Alfred A. Knopf.

Blacklow, Robert S. 2007. "Actuarially Speaking: An Overview of Life Expectancy; What Can We Anticipate?" *American Journal of Clinical Nutrition* 86 (5): 1560S–62S.

Blum, John Morton. 1959. *From the Morgenthau Diaries: Years of Crisis, 1928–1938*. Boston: Houghton Mifflin.

Bowman, James S., and Jonathan P. West, eds. 2007. *American Public Service: Radical Reform and the Merit System*. Boca Raton, FL: CRC Press/Taylor & Francis.

Chandler, Alfred D. (1977) 1999. *The Visible Hand: The Managerial Revolution in American Business*. Cambridge, MA: Belknap Press of Harvard University Press.

Clawson, Marion. 1981. *New Deal Planning: The National Resources Planning Board*. Baltimore: Johns Hopkins University Press for Resources for the Future.

Colegrove, Kenneth. 1941. "Thirty-sixth Annual Meeting of the American Political Science Association." *American Political Science Review* 35 (1): 114–41.

Critchlow, Donald T. 1981. "Lewis Meriam, Expertise, and Indian Reform." *The Historian* 43 (4): 325–44.

Dresang, Dennis L. 2009. *Personnel Management in Government Agencies and Nonprofit Organizations*, 5th ed. New York: Pearson/Longman.

Dunn, Susan. 2010. *Roosevelt's Purge: How FDR Fought to Change the Democratic Party*. Cambridge, MA: Belknap Press of Harvard University Press.

Durant, Robert F. 2014. "Taking Time Seriously: Progressivism, the Business–Social Science Nexus, and the Paradox of American Administrative Reform." *PS: Political Science & Politics* 47 (1): 8–18.

Ferrell, Robert H. 1994. *Choosing Truman: The Democratic Convention of 1944*. Columbia: University of Missouri Press.

Filer, Herbert A. 1924. "The Need for Correlation of Personnel Activities in the Federal Service." *Annals of the American Academy of Political and Social Science* 113: 220–26.

Fischer, John. 1945. "Let's Go Back to the Spoils System." *Harper's Magazine* 191 (1145): 362–68.

Fisher, Louis. 1998. *The Politics of Shared Power: Congress and the Executive*, 4th ed. College Station: Texas A&M University Press.

Foulke, William Dudley. 1923. "Spoils System Still an Active Factor." *National Municipal Review* 12 (8): 507–13.

Frug, Gerald E. 1976. "Does the Constitution Prevent the Discharge of Civil Service Employees?" *University of Pennsylvania Law Review* 124 (4): 942–1012.

Gailmard, Sean, and John W. Patty. 2013. *Learning While Governing: Expertise and Accountability in the Executive Branch*. Chicago: University of Chicago Press.

Gaus, John M. 1922. "Personnel and the Civil Service." *North American Review* 215 (799): 767–74.

———, and Leonard D. White. 1934. "Public Administration in the United States in 1933." *American Political Science Review* 28 (3): 443–56.

———, and Leonard D. White. 1935. "Public Administration in the United States in 1934." *American Political Science Review* 29 (3): 442–51.

Golway, Terry. 2014. *Machine Made: Tammany Hall and the Creation of Modern American Politics*. New York: Liveright/W. W. Norton.

Goodnow, Frank J. (1900) 1967. *Politics and Administration: A Study in Government*. New York: Russell & Russell.

Goodwin, Doris Kearns. 2013. *The Bully Pulpit: Theodore Roosevelt, William Howard Taft, and the Golden Age of Journalism*. New York: Simon & Schuster.

Graves, W. Brooke. (1950) 1972. *Public Administration in a Democratic Society*. Westport, CT: Greenwood.

Hays, Steven W., Richard C. Kearney, and Jerrell D. Coggburn, eds. 2009. *Public Human Resource Management: Problems and Prospects*, 5th ed. New York: Longman/Pearson.

Heady, Ferrel. 1947. "American Government and Politics: The Hatch Act Decisions." *American Political Science Review* 41 (4): 687–99.

Henry, Nicholas. 2006. "Good Government: An Unstylish Idea That Warrants a Worldwide Welcome." *Research in Public Policy Analysis and Management* 15: 905–15.

Hess, Stephen. 2002. *Organizing the Presidency*, 3rd ed. Washington, DC: Brookings Institution Press.

Hobbs, Edward H. 1954. *Behind the President: A Study of Executive Office Agencies*. Washington, DC: Public Affairs.

Ingraham, Patricia Wallace. 1995. *The Foundation of Merit: Public Service in American Democracy*. Baltimore: Johns Hopkins University Press.

———, and Carolyn Ban, eds. 1984. *Legislating Bureaucratic Change: The Civil Service Reform Act of 1978*. Albany: State University of New York Press.

———, and David H. Rosenbloom, eds. 1992. *The Promise and Paradox of Civil Service Reform*. Pittsburgh, PA: University of Pittsburgh Press.

Jordan, David M. 2011. *FDR, Dewey, and the Election of 1944*. Bloomington: Indiana University Press.

Kahn, Jonathan. 1997. *Budgeting Democracy: State Building and Citizenship in America, 1890–1928*. Ithaca, NY: Cornell University Press.

Kaiser, David. 2014. *No End Save Victory: How FDR Led the Nation into War*. New York: Basic/Perseus.

Kammerer, Gladys M. 1951. *Impact of War on Federal Personnel Administration, 1939–1945*. Lexington: University of Kentucky Press.

Karl, Barry Dean. (1963) 1979. *Executive Reorganization and Reform in the New Deal: The Genesis of Administrative Management, 1900–1939*. Chicago: University of Chicago Press.

Katznelson, Ira. 2013. *Fear Itself: The New Deal and the Origins of Our Time*. New York: Liveright/W. W. Norton.

Kaufman, Herbert. 1956. "Emerging Conflicts in the Doctrines of Public Administration." *American Political Science Review* 50 (4): 1057–73.

Kennedy, David M. (1999) 2005. *Freedom from Fear: The American People in Depression and War, 1929–1945*. New York: Oxford University Press.

Kettl, Donald F. 2009. *The Next Government of the United States: Why Our Institutions Fail Us and How to Fix Them*. New York: W. W. Norton.

———. 2015. "Ten Secret Truths about Government Incompetence." *Washington Monthly* 47 (1–2): 17–23.

———, Patricia W. Ingraham, Ronald P. Sanders, and Constance Horner. 1996. *Civil Service Reform: Building a Government That Works*. Washington, DC: Brookings Institution Press.

Klingner, Donald E. 2009. "Competing Perspectives on Public Personnel Administration: Civil Service, Patronage, and Privatization." In *Public Human Resource Management: Problems and Prospects*, 5th ed., edited by Steven W. Hays, Richard C. Kearney, and Jerrell D. Coggburn, 3–16. New York: Longman/Pearson.

Lee, Mordecai. 1979. "Personnel Management in Wisconsin." In *Proposition 13 and Its Consequences for Public Management*, edited by Selma J. Mushkin, 101–05. Cambridge, MA: Abt Books for the Council for Applied Social Research.

———. 2005a. *The First Presidential Communications Agency: FDR's Office of Government Reports*. Albany: State University of New York Press.

———. 2005b. "The US Bureau of Efficiency: Not RIP in 1933?" *Public Voices* 8 (1): 44–60.

———. 2006. *Institutionalizing Congress and the Presidency: The U.S. Bureau of Efficiency, 1916–1933*. College Station: Texas A&M University Press.

———. 2007. "When Politics Overwhelms Administration: Historical Proofs for Fesler's Maxim Against State-based Federal Regions, 1934–1943." *Public Voices* 9 (2): 25–45.

———. 2010. *Nixon's Super-Secretaries: The Last Grand Presidential Reorganization Effort*. College Station: Texas A&M University Press.

———. 2011. "History of US Public Administration in the Progressive Era: Efficient Government by and for Whom?" *Journal of Management History* 17 (1): 88–101.

———. 2012a. *Promoting the War Effort: Robert Horton and Federal Propaganda, 1938–1946*. Baton Rouge: Louisiana State University Press.

———. 2012b. "US Administrative History: Golem Government." In *SAGE Handbook of Public Administration*, 2nd ed., edited by B. Guy Peters and Jon Pierre, 215–27. London: Sage.

———. 2013a. "A Progressive Era Idea for Reforming Government that Didn't Make It: Recall of Judicial Decisions." *Public Voices* 13 (1): 58–78.

———. 2013b. "Glimpsing an Alternate Construction of American Public Administration: The Later Life of William Allen, Co-Founder of the New York Bureau of Municipal Research." *Administration & Society* 45 (5): 522–62.

———. 2014. "Colluding to Create the American Society for Public Administration and the Consequent Collateral Damage." *Public Voices* 14 (1): 2–27.

Levy, Herbert. 2010. *Henry Morgenthau, Jr.: The Remarkable Life of FDR's Secretary of the Treasury*. New York: Skyhorse.

Light, Paul C. 2008. *A Government Ill Executed: The Decline of the Federal Service and How to Reverse It*. Cambridge, MA: Harvard University Press.

Llorens, Jared J. 2013. "Public Sector Human Resource Management Education in the United States: Contemporary Challenges and Opportunities for Performance Improvement." In *Human Resource Management in the Public Sector*, edited by Ronald J. Burke, Andrew J. Noblet, and Cary L. Cooper, 303–19. Cheltenham, UK: Edward Elgar.

Loverd, Richard A., and Thomas J. Pavlak. 1995. "Analyzing the Historical Development of the American Civil Service." In *Handbook of Public Personnel Administration*, edited by Jack Rabin, Thomas Vocino, W. Bartley Hildreth, and Gerald J. Miller, 1–19. New York: Marcel Dekker.

Macmahon, Arthur W., and John D. Millett. (1939) 1967. *Federal Administrators: A Biographical Approach to the Problem of Departmental Management*. New York: AMS Press.

The Man At the Microphone [pseud. Wythe Williams and Frank L. Baer]. 1944. *Washington Broadcast*. Garden City, NY: Doubleday, Doran.

Mangan, Robert M. 1944. "The Legal Framework of Federal Personnel Administration." *Personnel Administration* 7 (2): 7–14.

Mashaw, Jerry L. 2012. *Creating the Administrative Constitution: The Lost One Hundred Years of American Administrative Law*. New Haven, CT: Yale University Press.

Mayers, Lewis. 1922. *The Federal Service: A Study of the System of Personnel Administration of the United States Government*. New York: D. Appleton.

McDiarmid, John. 1946. "The Changing Rôle of the U.S. Civil Service Commission." *American Political Science Review* 40 (6): 1067–96.

McCraw, Thomas K. 2012. *The Founders and Finance: How Hamilton, Gallatin, and Other Immigrants Forged a New Economy*. Cambridge, MA: Belknap Press of Harvard University Press.

Millett, John D. 1959. *Government and Public Administration: The Quest for Responsible Performance*. New York: McGraw-Hill.

Moe, Ronald C. 2003. *Administrative Renewal: Reorganization Commissions in the 20th Century*. Lanham, MD: University Press of America.

Morris, Edmund. 2010. *The Rise of Theodore Roosevelt*. New York: Random House.

Morstein Marx, Fritz. 1947. *The President and His Staff Services*. Publication No. 98. Chicago: Public Administration Service.

Moses, Robert. 1923. "Committee's Proposals Unworkable." *National Municipal Review* 12 (8): 477–79.

Mosher, Frederick C. 1982. *Democracy and the Public Service*, 2nd ed. New York: Oxford University Press.

Mosher, William E. 1921. "The Next Step in Civil Service Reform." *National Municipal Review* 10 (7): 386–91.

Naff, Katherine C., Norma M. Riccucci, and Siegrun Fox Freyss. 2014. *Personnel Management in Government: Politics and Process*, 7th ed. Boca Raton, FL: CRC/Taylor & Francis.

Newbold, Stephanie P., and Larry D. Terry. 2006. "The President's Committee on Administrative Management: The Untold Story and the Federalist Connection." *Administration & Society* 38 (5): 523–55.

Newland, Chester A. 2015. "From Trust to Doubt: The Federal Government's Tough Challenges." In *Public Administration Evolving: From Foundations to the Future*, edited by Mary E. Guy and Marilyn M. Rubin, 39–63. New York: Routledge.

Nicol, Eric A. 1940 (October 1). "The Role of the Personnel Director in Management," address to the annual conference of the Civil Service Assembly of the United States and Canada, Cleveland (mimeograph). Located in the collection of the National Agricultural Library, US Department of Agriculture, Beltsville, MD.

———. 1941. "Management Is Training." *Journal of Educational Sociology* 14 (1): 298–308.

Niehoff, Richard O. 1991. *Floyd W. Reeves: Innovative Educator and Distinguished Practitioner of Public Administration*. Lanham, MD: University Press of America and Michigan State University.

Ogg, Frederic A. 1934. "Personnel Questions of Interest to the Political Scientist." *American Political Science Review* 28 (6): 1105–09.

Patterson, Bradley H., Jr. 1994. "Teams and Staff: Dwight Eisenhower's Innovations in the Structure and Operations of the Modern White House." *Presidential Studies Quarterly* 24 (2): 277–98.

Patterson, C. Perry, and Harvey Walker. 1949. *American National Government*. Boston: D. C. Heath.

Pfiffner, James P., ed. 1999. *The Managerial Presidency*, 2nd ed. College Station: Texas A&M University Press.

———. 2011. *The Modern Presidency*, 6th ed. Boston: Wadsworth Centage.

———, and Douglas A. Brook, eds. 2000. *The Future of Merit: Twenty Years after the Civil Service Reform Act*. Washington, DC, and Baltimore: Woodrow Wilson Center Press and Johns Hopkins University Press.

Pfiffner, John M. 1932. "Trends in Public Personnel Administration." *American Political Science Review* 26 (2): 324–32.

———. 1946. *Public Administration*, revised ed. New York: Ronald.

Polenberg, Richard. 1966. *Reorganizing Roosevelt's Government: The Controversy Over Executive Reorganization, 1936–1939*. Cambridge, MA: Harvard University Press.

Raadschelders, Jos C. N. 2010. "Is American Public Administration Detached from Historical Context? On the Nature of Time and the Need to Understand it in Government and its Study." *American Review of Public Administration* 40 (3): 235–60.

Reeves, William D. 1973. "PWA and Competitive Administration in the New Deal." *Journal of American History* 60 (2): 357–72.

Reining, Henry, Jr. 1944. "The First Federal In-Service Internship Program." *Personnel Administration* 7 (4): 8–20.

———, and Karl E. Stromsem. 1942. "An Approach to Public Service Training: Government Internships." *Public Personnel Review* 3 (3): 190–99.

Roberts, Alasdair. 1994. "Demonstrating Neutrality: The Rockefeller Philanthropies and the Evolution of Public Administration, 1927–1936." *Public Administration Review* 54 (3): 221–28.

———. 1995. "The Brownlow-Brookings Feud: The Politics of Dissent within the Academic Community." *Journal of Policy History* 7 (3): 311–40.

———. 1996a. *So-Called Experts: How American Consultants Remade the Canadian Civil Service, 1918–1921*. Monograph 18. Toronto, ON: Institute of Public Administration of Canada.

———. 1996b. "Why the Brownlow Committee Failed: Neutrality and Partisanship in the Early Years of Public Administration." *Administration & Society* 28 (1): 3–38.

Rosenbloom, David H. 1971. *Federal Service and the Constitution: The Development of the Public Employment Relationship*. Ithaca, NY: Cornell University Press.

———. 2000. *Building a Legislative-Centered Public Administration: Congress and the Administrative State, 1946–1999*. Tuscaloosa: University of Alabama Press.

Rosenthal, Albert J. 1987. "Conditional Federal Spending and the Constitution." *Stanford Law Review* 39 (5): 1103–64.

Sayre, Wallace S., ed. 1965. *The Federal Government Service*, 2nd ed. Englewood Cliffs, NJ: Prentice-Hall.

Seidman, Harold. 1998. *Politics, Position, and Power: The Dynamics of Federal Organization*, 5th ed. New York: Oxford University Press.

Shafritz, Jay M. 1975. *Public Personnel Management: The Heritage of Civil Service Reform*. New York: Praeger.

Skowronek, Stephen. 1982. *Building a New American State: The Expansion of National Administrative Capacities, 1877–1920*. Cambridge, UK: Cambridge University Press.

Somers, Herman Miles. 1954. "The Federal Bureaucracy and the Change of Administration." *American Political Science Review* 48 (1): 131–51.

———. (1950) 1969. *Presidential Agency: OWMR, The Office of War Mobilization and Reconversion*. New York: Greenwood.

Spero, Sterling D., ed. 1962. "Symposium on Collective Bargaining in Public Employment: Form and Scope." *Public Administration Review* 22 (1): 1–23.

Stanton, Thomas H., and Benjamin Ginsberg, eds. 2004. *Making Government Manageable: Executive Organization and Management in the Twenty-First Century*. Baltimore: Johns Hopkins University Press.

Steil, Benn. 2013. *The Battle of Bretton Woods: John Maynard Keynes, Harry Dexter White, and the Making of a New World Order*. Princeton, NJ: Princeton University Press for the Council on Foreign Relations.

Stillman, Richard J., II. 1998. *Creating the American State: The Moral Reformers and the Modern Administrative World They Made*. Tuscaloosa: University of Alabama Press.

Stivers, Camilla, and Ralph P. Hummel. 2007. "Personnel Management: Politics, Administration, and a Passion for Anonymity." *Public Administration Review* 67 (6): 1010–17.

Telford, Fred. 1923. "The One-Man Civil Service Commission in Maryland." *National Municipal Review* 12 (7): 358–62.

Teti, Frank M. 1967. "Profile of a Progressive: The Life of Frederick Morgan Davenport." D.S.S. diss., Syracuse University, Syracuse, NY.

Van Riper, Paul P. 1958. *History of the United States Civil Service*. Evanston, IL: Row, Peterson.

Vaughn, Robert G., and Marion Weldon Brewer. 1975. *The Spoiled System: A Call for Civil Service Reform*. New York: Charterhouse.

Vieg, John A. 1946. "The Chief Executive." In *Elements of Public Administration*, edited by Fritz Morstein Marx, 158–83. New York: Prentice-Hall.

White, Leonard D. 1926. *Introduction to the Study of Public Administration*. New York: Macmillan.

———. 1929. "Public Administration, 1928." *American Political Science Review* 23 (2): 427–40.

———. 1937. "Recent Trends in the Public Service of the United States." *Political Quarterly* 8 (4): 542–53.

———. 1942. *Research in Public Personnel Administration: An Outline of Suggested Research Topics*. Washington, DC: Committee on Public Administration of the Social Science Research Council.

———. 1944. "Congress and the Civil Service." *Public Personnel Review* 5 (2): 65–69.

———. 1945. "Franklin Roosevelt and the Public Service." *Public Personnel Review* 6 (3): 139–46.

White, Richard D. 2003. *Roosevelt the Reformer: Theodore Roosevelt as Civil Service Commissioner, 1889–1895*. Tuscaloosa: University of Alabama Press.

Willoughby, W. F. 1927. *Principles of Public Administration: With Special Reference to the National and State Governments of the United States*. Washington, DC: Brookings Institution.

Woodruff, Clinton Rogers. 1923. "One Commissioner or Three." *National Municipal Review* 12 (8): 495–99.

———. 1935. Review of *Better Government Personnel* by the Commission of Inquiry on Public Service Personnel. *Annals of the American Academy of Political and Social Science* 182: 204–5.

Zelizer, Julian E. 2012. *Governing America: The Revival of Political History*. Princeton, NJ: Princeton University Press.

Index